Michael Oakeshott on Hobbes

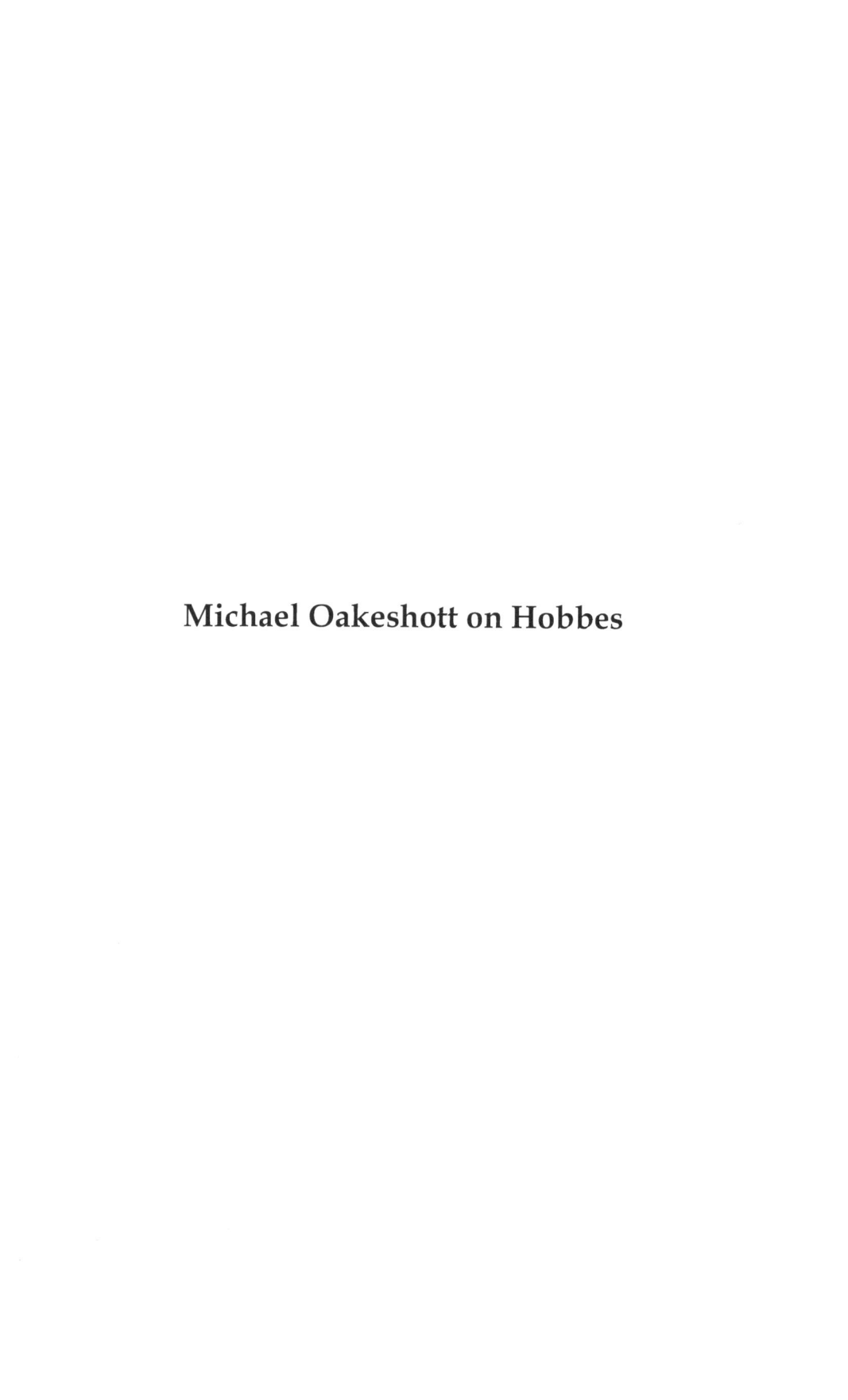

British Idealist Studies Series 1: Oakeshott

Roy Tseng, *The Sceptical Idealist*
Luke O'Sullivan, *Oakeshott on History*
Ian Tregenza, *Michael Oakeshott on Hobbes*
Efraim Podoksik, *In Defence of Modernity*
Glenn Worthington, *Religious and Poetic Experience
in the Thought of Michael Oakeshott*

www.imprint-academic.com/idealists

Michael Oakeshott on Hobbes

A Study in the Renewal of Philosophical Ideas

Ian Tregenza

ia

IMPRINT ACADEMIC

Published in the UK by Imprint Academic
PO Box 200, Exeter EX5 5YX, UK

Published in the USA by Imprint Academic
Philosophy Documentation Center
PO Box 7147, Charlottesville, VA 22906-7147, USA

ISBN 0 907845 592

A CIP catalogue record for this book is available from the
British Library and US Library of Congress

www.imprint-academic.com/idealists

Contents

Acknowledgements vii

Abbreviations ix

Introduction. 1

Chapter 1
Philosophy, History, and the Theory of Politics 17

Chapter 2
Will, Agency, Individuality 53

Chapter 3
Authority, Freedom, and Civil Association 81

Chapter 4
Religion, the World, and Human Conduct. 129

Chapter 5
Science, Myth, and Civilization 161

Conclusion 195

Bibliography 211

Author Index. 225

Subject Index 229

Acknowledgements

This book is a revised version of a PhD thesis commenced at the University of Sydney and completed at the University of New South Wales. My thanks go firstly to Patricia Springborg who supervised the project in its early stages. Though the work took a different form than that originally envisaged, Patricia's enthusiasm for the topic in its early formulations sustained me when I was trying to work out precisely what it was I wanted to say. My special thanks go to Conal Condren who supervised the thesis for the majority of the time I was at work on it. Conal provided a wealth of sound advice not only on Oakeshott and Hobbes, but on the range of interpretative issues a study such as this presents. To the extent that the book still contains deficiencies in this regard it undoubtedly stems from my not pursuing as adequately as I might have Conal's always insightful suggestions.

By a happy coincidence while I was working on the thesis in Sydney, Glenn Worthington and Luke O'Sullivan were also working on Oakeshott at the Australian National University in Canberra. I have benefitted from a number of stimulating conversations with them and am grateful to Luke for providing me with some relatively inaccessible works by Oakeshott which I have used here.

At different stages of the project I have received helpful advice from David Boucher, Robert Orr, and Timothy Fuller. My thanks also go to Keith Sutherland from Imprint Academic who has been very helpful in preparing the manuscript for publication.

Finally, my son Thomas deserves special mention for providing me with the sort of distractions from academic work that only a toddler can, as does my wife, Bronwyn, for her wonderful support, companionship, and a number of shared adventures of which this book is just one.

Abbreviations

Oakeshott

EM   *Experience and Its Modes* (Cambridge: Cambridge University Press. 1933)

RP   *Rationalism in Politics and Other Essays* (Indianapolis: Liberty Press, 1991) ed. Timothy Fuller

OHC   *On Human Conduct* (Oxford: Oxford University Press, 1975)

HCA   *Hobbes on Civil Association* (Oxford: Basil Blackwell, 1975)

OH   *On History and Other Essays* (Oxford: Basil Blackwell, 1983)

Intro   Introduction to Hobbes's *Leviathan* (Oxford: Basil Blackwell, 1960, originally published 1946)

TH   'Thomas Hobbes', Scrutiny, 4 (1935-6), 263-77

RPM   *Religion, Politics and the Moral Life* (New Haven and London: Yale University Press, 1993.) ed. Timothy Fuller

MPME   *Morality and Politics in Modern Europe: The Harvard Lectures* (New Haven and London: Yale University Press, 1993) ed. Shirley Robin Letwin

PFPS   *The Politics of Faith and the Politics of Scepticism* (New Haven and London: Yale University Press, 1996) ed. Timothy Fuller

VLL   *The Voice of Liberal Learning: Michael Oakeshott on Education* (New Haven and London: Yale University Press, 1989) ed. Timothy Fuller

CPJ   'The Concept of a Philosophical Jurisprudence', *Politica*, 3 (1938), 203-22, 345-60

Hobbes

Lev   *Leviathan* (Oxford: Basil Blackwell, 1960) ed. Michael Oakeshott

Introduction

I

Michael Oakeshott is widely recognized as one of the most significant political philosophers of the twentieth century. His contribution to twentieth century Hobbes scholarship is also acknowledged by Hobbes specialists to be of great importance. While most studies of Oakeshott have noted the significance of his reading of Hobbes for understanding his own political theory, few have given it the prominence that it deserves.[1] This study offers a reading of the major developments in Oakeshott's theory in the light of his own changing reading of Hobbes. As Stephen Gerencser[2] has recently shown, despite

[1]   Recent studies that have paid close attention to the Hobbes connection include Stephen Gerencser, *The Skeptic's Oakeshott* (New York: St. Martin's Press, 2000), Ted H. Miller, 'Oakeshott's Hobbes and the Fear of Political Rationalism' *Political Theory* 29, December 2001, 806–83, Bruce Frohnen, 'Oakeshott's Hobbesian myth: pride, character and the limits of reason', *Western Political Quarterly*, December 1990, 43, 789–809. See also my 'The Life of Hobbes in the Writings of Michael Oakeshott', *History of Political Thought*, vol.XVIII. no.3. Autumn 1997, 531–557, and 'Leviathan as Myth: Michael Oakeshott and Carl Schmitt on Hobbes and the Critique of Rationalism', *Contemporary Political Theory*, 1, October 2002, 349–369.

[2]   *The Skeptic's Oakeshott*. This present study has much in common with Gerencser's work, which also pays close attention to the Hobbes material. Gerencser's claim is that in a variety of ways Oakeshott's thought becomes increasingly sceptical as it develops and this is partly attributed to Oakeshott's engagement with Hobbes's philosophy. Though Gerencser probably overstates Oakeshott's 'break' with Idealism I am broadly sympathetic with his reading of the material and chapters 1 and 3 of this present book covers some similar territory to chapters 4 and 5 of Gerencser's work. However, since Gerencser is primarily concerned with tracing Oakeshott's emerging scepticism a number of important issues, it seems to me, are not addressed in his work. These include both methodological and moral issues. By methodological I refer to the way that Oakeshott contextualises Hobbes's thought and its implications for understanding Oakeshott himself and the history of political thought more generally. By moral I'm thinking of what Oakeshott refers to as 'the morality of

Oakeshott's early admiration for, and emulation of, writers such as Hegel, Bradley and Bosanquet, Thomas Hobbes is in fact the crucial figure behind the development of his political theory. Oakeshott's interest in political philosophy seems to have coincided in the mid 1930s with an interest in Hobbes and he wrote substantially more on Hobbes than any other philosopher or political thinker. In all, Oakeshott wrote six essays on Hobbes or Hobbes interpretation.[3] Because they were written at different stages in his career it is possible to mark the changes in his reading and indicate the way they reflect certain changes in his own theory.

Oakeshott was not only one of the most original political thinkers of the twentieth century as well as one of its most astute, if selective, readers of Hobbes, he was also deeply reflective about the nature of interpretation itself. Like his contemporary Gadamer, Oakeshott considered the problem of hermeneutics to be more than an academic concern over the meaning of texts, but to be central to understanding what it means to be human. "Thinking", he claimed, "is not a professional matter; if it were it would be something much less important than I take it to be" (EM 7). The human world, for Oakeshott, is a world of languages or modes of understanding which provide for us the terms of our experience. In order to clarify his philosophy of agency, morality, authority, history and religion, Oakeshott did not simply isolate each of these questions from the rest of human experience but proceeded by examining in a fundamental way the very nature of human understanding. Instead of asking questions of the type, 'what is history?', 'what is science?', 'what is practice?', as if history, science, and practice were all things separate from human participants, Oakeshott asks what it means to be an historian, a scientist, a practitioner.[4] True to the calling of the philosopher Oakeshott returned again and again to these fundamental

---

individuality' which is a crucial aspect of his reading of Hobbes. It also underlies Oakeshott's critique of rationalism and collectivism, on which his reputation as a political thinker still largely rests. These themes will be discussed further shortly.

[3]   Two of which appeared as newspaper articles—"The Collective Dream of Civilization", *Listener*, 37 (1947), 966–7, subsequently reprinted in *Hobbes on Civil Association* (Oxford: Basil Blackwell, 1983) as "*Leviathan*: a myth", and "A Reminder from *Leviathan*", *The Observer*, (29 July, 1951).

[4]   Cf. Coleridge, ch.14, *Biographia Literaria*: 'What is poetry? is nearly the same question with, what is a poet? that the answer to the one is involved in the solution of the other. For it is a distinction resulting from the poetic genius itself, which sustains and modifies the images, thoughts, and emotions of the poet's own mind.' From *Selected Poetry and Prose of Coleridge* (random House, 1951), ed. D. Stauffer.

questions — all the time clarifying, expanding, and reworking what he understood interpretation in its various modes to entail. Similarly, Hobbes emerges repeatedly in Oakeshott's work each time with a slightly altered emphasis or a new line of thought developed. More than any other philosopher that he discussed, with impressive persistence Oakeshott sought to clarify the meaning and significance of Hobbes. Given that Oakeshott understood the thoroughly conditional nature of textual interpretation, the task of grappling with the meaning of Hobbes was never going to be one resulting in a final, definitive picture of the seventeenth century philosopher. I want to suggest that this body of work on Hobbes provides us with not only material which enriches our understanding of Hobbes but a useful perspective for making sense of Oakeshott's own philosophical agenda. One way of clarifying this further is to ask the question what it was — in terms of his own understanding of the modal nature of interpretation — that Oakeshott was doing in interpreting Hobbes. Was it history, philosophy, philosophical history,[5] or myth building?[6] Though the answer to this question will, I hope, be clarified as I develop my argument, for the moment I simply want to suggest that analyzing Oakeshott's *practice* as an intellectual historian, political theorist, polemicist (to miss this aspect of Oakeshott is to miss much), all of which find a fascinating focal point in his readings of Hobbes, helps clarify and points to the limitations of Oakeshott's modal *theory* of human experience. In this work I want to bring these two aspects of Oakeshott's writings together to see how each illuminates the other. I do not want to claim that everything that is distinctive and original in Oakeshott's thought is really just an elaboration of his writings on Hobbes. Indeed, my approach prevents me from discussing in any great depth either Oakeshott's aesthetics or the subtleties of his philosophy of history. Nor would I suggest that when he came to concern himself with Hobbes's work Oakeshott in any simple sense just read his own set of priorities into Hobbes. Nevertheless, the affinities between Oakeshott's Hobbes and Oakeshott himself extend all the way from a common set of philosophical assumptions and arguments concerning both the artificial and modal nature of human knowledge to a fully elaborated moral and legal theory.

---

[5]   Though he originally deemed such an inquiry to be an *ignoratio elenchi* — a misplaced mixture of the modes of experience — later he appears, in practice at least, to have relaxed this view.
[6]   This is a view that I partially endorse towards the end of this book. See chapter 5.

II

Though Oakeshott's reading has been of great interest to many Hobbes scholars, his approach to Hobbes should not be assessed purely in terms of its contribution to contemporary Hobbes studies. Oakeshott's attitude to Hobbes seems to slide between straightforward scholarly interests and his own philosophical project, which itself depends on a certain reading of the philosophical (and non-philosophical) past. In this sense Oakeshott never entirely leaves behind the approach to political philosophy characteristic of earlier Idealist thought in which the history of political philosophy assumes an integral relation to present theoretical activity. Oakeshott himself makes the point that the philosophical enterprise cannot begin *de novo*, but must begin with a recognition that the entire history of (political, legal or any other) philosophy is the appropriate context which the activity itself assumes.

In his first essay on Hobbes Oakeshott spells out in general terms what he takes to be the appropriate interpretative approach to past philosophers. Here it is claimed that "the only healthy attitude towards the writings of a philosopher is a philosophical attitude" (TH 265). This excludes both the sort of approach which attempts to uncover the meaning of a political philosopher's ideas from an account of his political opinions as well as a *merely* historical or antiquarian interest in his works. The first approach is deemed inappropriate because it takes the least important aspect of a philosopher's thought to be the key which illuminates the whole. However, according to Oakeshott, the political philosopher's most valuable contribution to an understanding of political activity arises from his broader, more comprehensive vision of the place of politics on the whole map of human experience. In *Experience and Its Modes* Oakeshott claimed that the philosopher views the world *sub specie aeternitatis*. And in his introduction to Hobbes's *Leviathan* he suggested that the task of the political philosopher is "to establish the connections, in principle and in detail, directly or mediately, between politics and eternity" (RP 225). Oakeshott consistently maintained that a philosopher's opinions are the least important aspect of his thought and so should not be taken to be the central source for understanding the entire philosophical system. In a 1975 review of Shlomo Avineri's *Hegel's Theory of the Modern State*, for instance, we are told that the place to look for Hegel's philosophical theory of the state is not in the myriad of circumstantial issues Hegel chose to comment on but in his account of crucial concepts such as *der Geist, das Subjekt, der Wille, Sittlich, das Recht*, all of which together comprise his understanding of the modern state in philosophical terms, and, according to Oakeshott, "none of which are merely contingent states of affairs to be preferred".[7]

So the philosopher moves within an entirely different world of ideas to the analyst, commentator, or political practitioner. Moreover, Oakeshott's contention that philosophical ideas operate within a world which is *sui generis* by implication rules out the second attitude, the merely historical or antiquarian, as inappropriate since, he argues, "it is the business of philosophy continuously to renew itself. And such new philosophy may arise from the study of what belongs to an earlier time; and the study of what belongs to an earlier time is profitable, in the end, only when it is related to a genuine renaissance" (TH 267). In contrast to the philosopher, the historian works with a past that is dead. The historian's past is neither an "inheritance" nor does it offer "an inspiration for fresh thought" (TH 267). Above all it is marked by its disjunction from the present. The philosopher must therefore approach the philosophical past from a philosophical, not a historical, perspective. The 'pastness' of past philosophy is its least important aspect. Indeed, when the history of philosophy is understood in these terms it is "seen as a living, extemporary whole in which past and present are comparatively insignificant" (CPJ 359). This is clearly Oakeshott's intention in his approach to the history of political philosophy generally, and Hobbes in particular. Oakeshott does not deny the value of historical works which help illuminate past philosophers. Indeed, he suggested that most of the best works on Hobbes in the years immediately prior to his review were of this kind. His point seems to be that a philosopher must be understood on his own terms and any other account, however illuminating in other ways, is less than complete.

Though, as I will show in the first chapter, Oakeshott's understanding of political philosophy, and the past that it draws on, changes considerably as his thought develops, for now it is enough to point out that his explicit approach to Hobbes is a philosophical one. With some scepticism Oakeshott asks the question in this early essay "whether Hobbes's writings, when studied in this way, can ever yield the philosophical inspiration which has come from (for example) either Plato or Spinoza". This is a question, he suggests, which "cannot be answered in advance", though, "the attempt (if it attracts us) is worth making" (TH 267). It is my contention that, on one level, this sort of inspiration underlies Oakeshott's political theory and I have attempted to chart the course of his philosophy of politics while keeping his reading of Hobbes firmly in view. Importantly, I also want to argue that the inspiration Oakeshott found in Hobbes was not exhausted by his philosophical interest, but was the expression of a deep moral and practical commitment to a particular vision of European civilization threatened by forces not dissimilar to those that Hobbes himself confronted. By exploring what I would call Oakeshott's 'moral vision' as it appears both in his writings on Hobbes and elsewhere it is possible to test Oakeshott's modal theory of human understanding. Indeed, I would argue that Oakeshott constructs a version, not only of the philosophical, but also of the practical past in his interpretation and appropriation of Hobbes.

However, as alluded to earlier, Oakeshott seems at times to put aside his effort to appropriate Hobbes to his own philosophical purposes and approaches the latter in the manner of an intellectual historian, engaging other Hobbes scholars — notably Strauss, Warrender and Spragens — in debate on points of detail. It is on this level that Oakeshott's writings on Hobbes have mostly been read and have had considerable influence. Though this is a study of Oakeshott via his reading of Hobbes, not Hobbes himself, in order to assess the distinctiveness of Oakeshott's reading of Hobbes it has been necessary to discuss it in the context of other major twentieth century interpretations. Where I have elaborated Hobbes's thought, it is principally for the purpose of elucidating Oakeshott's understanding of him. This does not mean that I have nothing to say about Hobbes, nor would I suggest that Oakeshott's reading is without its limitations. In the chapter on authority, for instance, I will suggest that the difficulties of conceiving of civil association in purely procedural terms, which many of Oakeshott's critics have made much of, is also a feature of the way he comes to read Hobbes, and his reading contains similar explanatory difficulties and ambiguities. Hobbes's legal theory, I will suggest, can only be assimilated to Oakeshott's procedural theory of civil association by overlooking some of Hobbes's explicit claims. Moreover, I also want to question the distance that Oakeshott opens up between Hobbes's rationalism and the rationalism that Oakeshott takes a hostile attitude towards as well as Oakeshott's reluctance to acknowledge Hobbes's own understanding of the utilitarian nature of his theory. To admit this could carry the implication that Hobbes, contrary to just about everything Oakeshott says about him, is in fact an example of the lowest of intellectual creatures — the theoretician (see OHC, 26,30).

In order to determine the extent to which Oakeshott's reading was one of mere plunder for his own (philosophical or practical) purposes, as opposed to one guided by the disinterested concern of the scholar,[8] requires making judgements about the validity of Oakeshott's Hobbes. So although this is a work principally about Oakeshott, and only derivatively about Hobbes, the nature of the task precludes an attitude of complete agnosticism towards the latter. This does not entail — at least this is my contention — juxtaposing Oakeshott's Hobbes with an idea of what Hobbes 'really meant'. Even if such a task was possible a preliminary acquaintance with the secondary literature, wherein many versions of Hobbes appear, highlights the difficulties of such an endeavour. But it is necessary to take a critical stance towards the way in which Oakeshott treats Hobbes's writings and to ask why it is, for instance, that certain aspects of Hobbes are emphasised and others are ignored or minimised. In other words, the task of determining the extent to which Hobbes is used as a more or less silent interlocutor through which Oakeshott can write his own script, as opposed to a relationship of straightforward influence where Hobbes has his own voice, requires being sensitive to the way that Oakeshott deals with the evidence presented by Hobbes's writings. So even though the principal aim of this study is to provide a new perspective through which Oakeshott's political theory can be read I am also hopeful that it might even throw fresh light on the figure of Hobbes himself. Further, there are issues in Hobbes which Oakeshott only briefly mentions without explicitly drawing out their full implications. This is only to be expected in a series of writings which serve either as introductions or review essays. At times, such as in chapters 4 and 5, I have developed the lines of Oakeshott's interpretation, mostly by drawing on authors who read Hobbes in ways consistent with his, in order to explore more fully the affinities between Oakeshott and Hobbes.

By breaking down the entire body of Oakeshott's work into manageable thematic units the interpreter runs the risk of reducing what is a complex, nuanced philosophical outlook to a series of theoretical excurses on isolated topics. As will become apparent throughout the course of this work the topics discussed in the various chapters not only build on the arguments developed in those preceding it, they

[8] I hesitate to say something along the lines of — "the endeavour to understand Hobbes as he understood himself" — because such an aim is precluded by Oakeshott's understanding of human experience. For Oakeshott, the past *an sich* does not exist. Various pasts — practical, philosophical, historical — exist in the present, and though the historian's concern is with the historical past this is not an inherently privileged form of knowledge of the past. Oakeshott, therefore, denies claims such as Collingwood's, that the past can be re-enacted, as well as Skinner's contention that history is in some sense the primary mode for understanding past ideas. Oakeshott's interpretative system (if I can describe it as such) precludes the privileging of any particular mode of understanding.

also overlap in various ways. In chapter 3, for instance, I discuss not only the idea of civil or legal authority but also the concept of a moral practice on which the former is based. Indeed, civil association, according to Oakeshott, is but one instance of the general class of practices Oakeshott terms moral. So, for example, the essay on "The Civil Condition" in *On Human Conduct*, does not stand on its own but presupposes the account of human agency developed in the first essay of that book, which in turn arises from his theory of human understanding. Since Oakeshott argues that human conduct is invariably conditioned by the requirements of a moral practice or practices, the theory of agency discussed in chapter 2 clearly overlaps with material covered in chapter 3. I have chosen, therefore, to elaborate the meaning of many of these themes as they appear in their various, overlapping contexts. All of Oakeshott's writings are held together by a conception of philosophy which, despite subtle shifts and changes in emphasis, ties the various themes into a more or less coherent whole. It is necessary to qualify the coherence of Oakeshott's system since, as I intend to show, in various works Oakeshott breaks out of the tightly argued theory of modality that he sets out most fully in *Experience and Its Modes*.

By stressing the importance of approaching Oakeshott in terms of his philosophical system I am, of course, reiterating the point that Oakeshott made in his reading of Hobbes. In the introduction to *Leviathan* Oakeshott suggested that Hobbes had suffered at the hands of those interpreters who had largely failed to appreciate what a philosophical system entails. Moreover, this interpretative sloppiness resulted in a misidentification of Hobbes with writers whom he had little if anything in common — a case in point being Erastus. Though both Hobbes and Erastus agree that civil and ecclesiastical power should converge, as thinkers they are worlds apart. Where Erastus's argument is based on political expediency, Hobbes derives his conclusion from a thorough chain of reasoning based on the fundamental limitations of human understanding. According to Oakeshott, Hobbes's theory, deduced as it was from man's existential predicament, and not from mere expediency or the contingencies of the moment, marks him as a genuine philosopher (see TH 277). Equally, I would argue that Oakeshott's misidentification with a writer like Burke arises from a similar misunderstanding of Oakeshott's philosophical system. Some of the early interpretations of Oakeshott's critique of Rationalism, for instance, which failed to see the argument in terms of the concrete, Hegelian conception of rationality outlined in *Experience and Its Modes*, concomitantly failed to appreciate that the polemical style of these post-war essays contained a deeper philosophical point.[9]

Though Oakeshott's account of the philosophical enterprise undergoes various significant alterations he never severed his substantive connection with the general Idealist position given full expression in *Experience and Its Modes*. Ostensibly, Oakeshott's philosophical Idealism is the complete antithesis of Hobbes's supposed materialism. As will be subsequently shown, however, there are important affinities between the Idealist notion that mind is constitutive of reality and (at least on Oakeshott's reading) Hobbes's scepticism regarding the possibility of harmony between knowledge which is created by the mind and the world itself. This anti-positivist reading of Hobbes, where knowledge is propositional and discursive, is one that holds obvious attractions for the philosophical Idealist. In chapter 1 I will explore in some depth Oakeshott's modal understanding of the whole of experience in the light of his reading of Hobbes's similarly categorial or modal account of human knowledge.

Oakeshott consistently resists the sort of identification of Hobbes's epistemology with Baconian empiricism common in earlier readings and this account of Hobbes's epistemological project also underlines his own attack on Rationalism. Hobbes has traditionally been read as an archetypal rationalist philosopher. As Oakeshott put it, "his place in the Saint's Calender of Rationalism was never disputed" (TH 263). Hobbes was seen as a defender of the very intellectual project that Oakeshott persistently criticized and on which his academic reputation still largely rests. A closer examination of the way Oakeshott reads Hobbes's philosophical system, particularly in the light of the former's account of other seventeenth century rationalists such as Bacon and Descartes, shows the distance there is between Oakeshott's Rationalist and Oakeshott's Hobbes. This will be developed especially in chapter 5.

On questions with a direct bearing on political philosophy, such as will, agency, freedom and authority, the alterations Oakeshott makes demonstrate a shift away from the manner in which these issues were treated by his Idealist predecessors such as Green and

---

[9] Fortunately this view and the identification of Oakeshott with Burke that tended to go with it is now being corrected, most recently by Roy Tseng's *The Sceptical Idealist: Michael Oakeshott as a Critic of the Enlightenment* (Thorverton: Imprint Academic, 2003). See also Paul Franco in *The Political Philosophy of Michael Oakeshott*, (New Haven and London: Yale University Press, 1990) and Jeremy Rayner, "The legend of Oakeshott's conservatism: Sceptical philosophy and limited politics", *Canadian Journal of Political Science*, 18 (1985), pp. 90–112. Needless to say, this study is a further contribution to this project of reassessment.

Bosanquet to a position more recognizably Hobbesian, albeit a Hobbes seen through Oakeshott's distinctive interpretative glasses. Chapters 2 and 3 will chart the course of these changes. These chapters are arranged in roughly chronological order in order to illustrate the way in which Oakeshott's theory comes to converge with his reading of Hobbes.

In chapters 4 and 5 I take a different tack. The fourth chapter takes up the question of religion, which was of immense interest to Oakeshott. Indeed, I would argue that many interpretations of Oakeshott's political philosophy have suffered by not fully appreciating the essentially religious nature of his entire project. Though he does not say a great deal about Hobbes's theology it is significant that Oakeshott recognized it to be by no means peripheral to the coherence of the argument of *Leviathan*. In this chapter I have drawn out the affinities between Oakeshott's and Hobbes's understanding of religious experience and the way in which each arises from an attempt to accommodate religion in the light of the contemporary intellectual preoccupations that they respectively sought to address. For Hobbes this involved grappling with the emergent mechanistic science, for Oakeshott it centered on the claims of historical understanding. At a more fundamental level, both were concerned with the vexed issue of hermeneutics arising from the limitations of human understanding and of the threats that substantive beliefs about the world — whether they be in a 'religious' or 'secular' form — potentially pose to civil authority.

In chapter 5 I will assess Oakeshott's estimation of those forces which threaten civil association and the ideal of civilization which it reflects. Along with Hobbes and Augustine, Oakeshott understood civilization to be imperiled by recurrent manifestations of pelagianism. Here Oakeshott's debt to Hobbes, especially in his essay "*Leviathan*: a myth", clearly transcends that of the specialist philosopher. I will show that Oakeshott's return to Hobbes went beyond academic interest and was guided by a deep moral concern with the fate of civilization. In the final chapter, as well as in the conclusion, I will question the extent to which Oakeshott's political theory remains faithful to the highly circumscribed theory of knowledge that he first outlined in *Experience and Its Modes* and developed and modified throughout his career.

Though this is a study about the relationship between two philosophers, it raises issues of wider relevance in the field of intellectual history concerning textual interpretation and the transmission and understanding of ideas. Consequently I have used the conclusion as an opportunity to explore such themes and have attempted to place Oakeshott's reading of Hobbes in the context of recent debates in the history of ideas.

III

Before concluding this introduction, it is necessary to examine some important preliminary issues concerning the way in which Oakeshott proceeds to 'contextualise' Hobbes's political theory. As will subsequently become apparent, these questions of interpretation not only affect the way Oakeshott reads Hobbes, they also carry implications for Oakeshott's entire philosophical project.

At the outset of his two most substantial works on Hobbes (the introduction to *Leviathan* and "The Moral Life in the Writings of Thomas Hobbes") Oakeshott invokes two distinct frameworks in order to instill intelligibility into past political thought in general and Hobbes in particular. It is notable that these frameworks or contexts are deployed at the outset of these works on Hobbes as this indicates that his engagement with Hobbes was central to the working out of his methodological or hermeneutical concerns.

In the introduction to *Leviathan* Oakeshott makes his famous claim that the appropriate context for considering a masterpiece such as *Leviathan* ("the greatest, perhaps the sole, masterpiece of political philosophy written in the English language" — RP 223) is nothing short of the entire history of political philosophy. This history can be analytically broken into three distinct sub-traditions. They are, Reason and Nature, Will and Artifice, and Rational Will. Plato, Hobbes and Hegel are recognized as the masters of these respective traditions. Of the tradition of Rational Will Oakeshott observes that "its followers may be excused the belief that in it the truths of the first two traditions are fulfilled and their errors find a happy release" (RP 227). Here Oakeshott is clearly employing the sort of triadic framework common to other post Hegelian philosophical Idealists. Though not always so explicitly presented, the British Idealists developed their own philosophical concerns in the light of a dialectical reading of the history of political thought. The British Idealists, as David Boucher puts it, "had a conception of the subject matter, an intellectual framework if you like, in terms of which they appraised past systems of thought in order to advance their own".[10] Like Hegel they sought to overcome the deficiencies in past political thought, not by rejecting it *in toto*, but by incorporating the important insights of each tradition and superseding the defects.

---

[10] "W.H. Greenleaf, Idealism and the Triadic Conception of the History of Political Thought", *Idealistic Studies*, 16 (1986), pp. 237–52, at p. 243.

Though Oakeshott never endorses their teleological reading of histori-cal development he shares their conviction that the history of philoso-phy is central to its current practice.

This attitude is exemplified in R.G. Collingwood's *The New Levia-than*, which, the author claims, "is best understood as an attempt to bring the *Leviathan* up to date, in the light of the advances made since it was written, in history, psychology, and anthropology".[11] Like Oakeshott, Collingwood attempts to renew the philosophy of the past to make it speak to the present.[12]

As Boucher has recently shown, Collingwood's project of bring-ing Hobbes up to date needs to be understood in terms of the triadic conception of the history of political thought that Collingwood con-structs in order to address issues of present philosophic concern.[13] The three traditions that Collingwood invokes, Boucher terms the objective, subjective, and immanent. Since, according to Collingwood, the last tradition overcomes the deficiencies in the for-mer two and Hobbes is associated with the second, Collingwood's task of renewing Hobbes involved superseding those aspects of Hobbes's thought that the tradition of immanent reason has made redundant.

Whatever the explanatory merit these traditions have for coming to terms with past political philosophy (which at this stage can only be crudely hinted at) they need to be kept in mind when approach-ing the Idealists themselves, as they each employed them in more or less self-conscious ways. For instance, in his study of Oakeshott, Greenleaf, who of recent theorists has done most to turn these tradi-tions of political philosophy into something approaching a system-atic methodological program,[14] has described these traditions respectively as 'transcendental realism', 'empirical nominalism', and 'Idealism', and explained Oakeshott's thought in terms of the last of

---

[11] *New Leviathan: Or Man, Society, Civilization, and Barbarism* (Oxford: Clarendon Press, 1942), p. iv.

[12] It should be stressed however that Collingwood set himself the task of bringing about a *rapprochement* between both history and philosophy as well as theory and practice and so his task of updating Hobbes involved what Oakeshott would term an *ignoratio elenchi* — a confusion of the modes of experience. Oakeshott's renewal of Hobbes, at least according to his explicit pronouncements, is purely philosophical and so leaves enquiries such as "history, psychology and anthropology" untouched. In this respect, ie. in the deployment of a linked hierarchy of forms, Collingwood is closer to Hegel than is Oakeshott.

[13] See Boucher, *The Social and Political Thought of R.G. Collingwood* (Cambridge: Cambridge University Press, 1989), pp. 71–80.

[14] For a full account see Boucher "W.H. Greenleaf " and *Texts in Context: Revisionist methods for studying the history of ideas* (Dordrecht: Martinus Nijhof, 1985), ch. 3.

these.[15] At least for this limited project the invocation of these traditions serves a useful heuristic role.

It should be stressed that the only place Oakeshott mentions this tripartite account of the history of political philosophy is in the introduction to *Leviathan*.[16] He never fills in the detail of this history in the way Hegel, or indeed, Collingwood does. Moreover, he never employed it as a means to draw the sort of concrete historical accounts of political thought that Greenleaf has. Indeed, I will contend that Oakeshott's changing reading of Hobbes, which demonstrates a substantial convergence with his own thought, points to a modification in his understanding of the adequacy of these Idealist traditions in interpreting the history of political philosophy. Moreover, these traditions cannot be separated from the way in which he conceives philosophical activity to proceed, and they do not readily transfer to purposes independent of this.

On this point, Paul Franco notes Oakeshott's remark that the inadequacy of Hobbes's theory of volition was only overcome in the Hegelian theory of rational will, which, according to Oakeshott, was yet to receive a fully convincing rendition. Franco takes this judgement to be a key factor in understanding Oakeshott's project of developing a more complete theory of the will than that bequeathed by Bosanquet. Thus Oakeshott is said to present a Hegelian theory of the will chastened by a form of Hobbesian anti-teleology. The traditions of 'Will and Artifice' and 'Rational Will' are said to converge in Oakeshott's account.[17] With some qualifications I endorse this reading. Oakeshott does not simply take over from Hobbes everything he finds there and he clearly grafts on to his understanding of Hobbes's theory of agency, for instance, insights gleaned from his Idealist predecessors. However, it is clear that Oakeshott's reading of Hobbes, on the question of volition (amongst other things) changes, in line with his own theory. This convergence seems to suggest that these traditions are open and porous and their importance appears to fade as his thought develops. Indeed, he seems to retreat from his early judgment that Hobbes's theory of volition contains inadequacies that need to be superseded.

As I mentioned earlier, there is also another framework Oakeshott employs in order to instill intelligibility into past political thought.

[15] *Oakeshott's Philosophical Politics*, (London: Longmans, 1966), pp. 6–16.
[16] Though according to Ken Minogue he also used it in his lectures on the history of political thought at the LSE. See his introduction to *Morality and Politics in Modern Europe: The Harvard Lectures*, (New Haven and London: Yale University Press, 1993), Shirley Letwin ed. p. vii–viii.
[17] *The Political Philosophy of Michael Oakeshott*, pp. 102,178.

This was developed in "The Moral Life in the Writings of Thomas Hobbes" and it tends to assume a preponderant place in the philosophical history he constructs later in his career, cutting across and in some sense surpassing the earlier tripartite account set out in the introduction to *Leviathan*. This second context adds another layer of complexity to Oakeshott's reading of Hobbes, adding richness, yet making the relationship between the two philosophers less straightforward. In this case he also employs a triadic framework, this time in an attempt to make intelligible the moral experience of post-medieval Europe, and its reflection in the moral and political thought of the period.

The three specific moral idioms (as he refers to them here) are the morality of communal ties, the morality of individuality, and the morality of the common good. Since the first of these fell into desuetude with the break up of the medieval order, the second and third are the crucial ones for understanding the thought and experience of morality and its reflection in politics in modern times. As a philosopher of the morality of individuality, Hobbes is recognized to be a master. A similar framework is also employed in his essay "The Masses in Representative Democracy" as well as the recently published *Morality and Politics in Modern Europe* and *The Politics of Faith and the Politics of Scepticism*.[18]

All of these works touch on themes which were given expression in the last essay of *On Human Conduct* where the history of modern understandings of the state in terms of the opposition between the ideal characters civil and enterprise association (or *societas* and *universitas*) was fully developed. What I want to suggest here is that this triadic framework was different from the former in that it was deployed for a different purpose and dealt with different subject matter. Where the former dealt with the whole history of political philosophy — a history conceived philosophically, not historically — the focus in the latter is primarily on the *history* of modern political *thought*. For Oakeshott, reflection on politics occurs on one of three, not always readily distinct, levels and political thinkers rarely attain that level of abstraction whereby the link between politics and the whole of human experience is made. Plato, Augustine, Spinoza, Hobbes and Hegel undoubtedly qualify here, but the status of others such as Locke, Burke and Mill is less clear.

Oakeshott, of course, despite what he says about the importance of studying the classic texts of political or legal philosophy, has no intention of compiling a list of 'Greats'. Rather, his account of the

---

[18]   (New Haven and London: Yale University Press, 1996), ed. Timothy Fuller.

modern history of political reflection in terms of the opposition between individualism and collectivism enables him to cover a broader category of thought than the purely philosophical. As he pointed out in his first essay on Hobbes, the interpreter who approaches a past philosopher from a philosophical perspective must leave to one side everything he said of a non-philosophical nature.

There seems to me to be two ways of understanding these later writings. It is possible to argue, as Boucher has done, for the basic consistency of these works with the modal conception of experience laid out in *Experience and its Modes*.[19] On this reading the past invoked in his account of the respective moral idioms or ideal characters is a philosophical past with no connection with the determinate mode of experience Oakeshott terms history. The other approach, which seems to me the more likely explanation, is to leave the ambiguity and suggest that Oakeshott's later attempt to give an historical account of the modern state in order to buttress his philosophical account of civil association actually breaks out of the rather rigidly defined map of experience set out in *Experience and Its Modes* and which informs much of what he wrote elsewhere. This suggests that his modal account of experience was simply inadequate to deal with the range of concerns he wanted to cover in his later writings. In these later works, especially *Morality and Politics in Modern Europe* and the last essay of *On Human Conduct*, Oakeshott makes it quite clear that he is offering a form of historical explanation, even if it is not quite consistent with his other writings on the nature of history.

These questions will be discussed further in the first chapter as well as the conclusion. For now it is enough to stress that a theorist who has laid his cards on the table and insistently urged the independence of philosophical and historical modes of understanding, is liable to drift into ambiguity when attempting to make the past intelligible without any reference to a form of historical explanation. For someone like Oakeshott who throughout his long career consistently returned in a fundamental way to the nature of understanding it would be unusual to expect complete consistency on all issues. Moreover, the temptation for a historically aware philosopher (as indeed, for a philosophically inclined historian — Quentin Skinner, for instance) to combine the role of the philosopher with that of the

---

[19] "Politics in a Different Mode: an Appreciation of Michael Oakeshott 1901–1990", *History of Political Thought*, vol. xii. no.4, Winter 1991, pp. 717–728, at p. 723.

historian, however the relationship between these modes is conceived, is always great.

In this study I will explore the tensions in Oakeshott's account of modality through his substantial philosophical teaching. As will be seen as the study develops, his reading of Hobbes is never far from the center of this project. Hobbes continually surfaces in his work as a figure from the philosophical past who has something important to add to our conversation. But the voice of Hobbes as it is relayed through Oakeshott is a distinctive one which closely mirrors the preoccupations of its creator. As Ken Minogue has aptly put it, "Oakeshott's engagement with Hobbes has been a central feature of his own philosophy, and is a model of what one philosopher can do with another."[20]

---

[20]   "Hobbes and his critics", in *Leviathan* (London: Everyman, 1994), ed. K. Minogue, p. 448.

Chapter 1

Philosophy, History, and the Theory of Politics

If you will be a philosopher in good earnest, let your reason move upon the deep of your own cogitations and experience. Those things that lie in confusion must be set asunder, distinguished, and every one stamped with its own name set in order; that is to say, your method must resemble that of creation.

Thomas Hobbes, Epistle to the Reader, *De Corpore*

I

In his seminal introduction to *Leviathan* Oakeshott suggested that much previous commentary on Hobbes had mistakenly conceived the civil philosophy to be the apex of a thoroughly scientific–mechanistic super-structure which, for many, was finally unsuccessful because the parts were ill-fitting. The conclusions of *Leviathan* (the apex) were said to follow from the doctrine of materialism worked out in *De Corpore*, *De Homine*, and *De Cive* (the foundation). According to Oakeshott, this reading of Hobbes stems from a broader misunderstanding of what is entailed in the idea of a philosophical system. At least for the purpose of understanding Hobbes, the architectural analogy is inadequate. For Oakeshott, Hobbes's system is coherent because it is united by a 'single passionate thought', which, like the thread of Ariadne, ties together all the seemingly multifarious aspects into a single whole. This thought, or 'guiding clue', "is the continuous application of a doctrine about the nature of philosophy". And Hobbes's philosophy is like a mirror held up to the world so that what is seen by the philosophic eye is determined by the nature of the mirror itself. The philosophic mirror is the mirror of reason; that is, a world governed by cause and effect. These, according to Oakeshott's reading of Hobbes, are the categories of philosophy (RP 235-6).

From his first published essay on Hobbes (TH) Oakeshott insisted on the importance of following Hobbes's thought through from its presuppositions in a theory of knowledge. Hobbes's civil philosophy can only be properly appreciated when it is seen in the light of this epistemology. As mentioned in the introduction I think the same could be said about interpretations of Oakeshott. Though the style and mood of Oakeshott's writings vary considerably — from the dense and closely argued pages of *Experience and Its Modes, On History* and *On Human Conduct* to the polemical but polished essays collected in the *Rationalism in Politics* volume and elsewhere[1] — there is in Oakeshott a search, if not for system, at least for the sort of coherence that comes from taking seriously the idea of philosophy as a sustained exercise in the questioning of presuppositions. As Oakeshott suggested in relation to Hobbes, "the impulse to think systematically is, at bottom, nothing more than the conscientious pursuit of what is for every philosopher the end to be achieved". Further, "the principle in system is not the simple exclusion of all that does not fit, but the perpetual re-establishment of coherence". But at the same time as he built a system, Oakeshott claimed that Hobbes knew how to escape its constraints, to avoid becoming its slave. "To become the slave of a system in life is not to know when to 'hang up philosophy', not to recognize the final triumph of inconsequence; in philosophy, it is not to know when the claims of comprehension outweigh those of coherence" (RP231). As with so much that Oakeshott says about Hobbes the same could be said of Oakeshott himself. As I intend to show in this chapter and subsequently there is a tension in Oakeshott between the search for philosophical coherence or consistency and the temptation (often yielded to) to free himself from such strictures in the pursuit of non-philosophic concerns.

This chapter has several closely related purposes. The first is to give something of an overview of what might loosely be termed Oakeshott's philosophical system, focusing on certain lines of development within that system.[2] In particular I will look at the way Oakeshott develops his understanding of political philosophy espe-

---

[1]   This variety no doubt has something to do with Oakeshott's taste for both philosophy and provocation — again, something that aligns him with Hobbes.

[2]   Oakeshott suggested in *Experience and its Modes* that he sought "to achieve a general point of view, neither complete nor final, but systematic as far as it goes and presented as a reasoned whole" (EM 8).

cially in the middle period of his career. This conception of political philosophy is subsequently modified in Oakeshott's later intellectual
career by a turn to a type of historical understanding. Both Oakeshott's
substantive political (or civil) theory — the theory of civil association —
as well his later writings on the activity of theorizing itself is a reflection
of what we might with some license call Oakeshott's 'historical turn'. In
the following chapter and in chapter 5 I will say more about the detail of
Oakeshott's reading of the past. In the present chapter I am simply
interested in exploring the implications that this historical turn has for
Oakeshott's conception of the theoretical understanding of politics.

In conjunction with this I will look closely at Oakeshott's writings
on Hobbes to see how they shape and are shaped by Oakeshott's
own theoretical concerns, since I am interested in both the significance of Hobbes for Oakeshott as well as exploring some of the
implications of this reading for intellectual history more generally.
Commencing with a very brief discussion of the argument of *Experience and Its Modes* I will try to give an indication of the distinctive nature
of Oakeshott's philosophical Idealism and what it was about Hobbes's
thought — specifically the sceptical and modal theory of knowledge —
that Oakeshott found so conducive to his own philosophical reflections. Though it is undoubtedly the case that Oakeshott makes a great
deal of those aspects of Hobbes's thought in sympathy with his own
ideas, this is not to say that Oakeshott simply attributes to Hobbes ideas
that are not there. Indeed, Oakeshott opened lines of interpretation that
are still being pursued by Hobbes scholars. But there are also by no
means peripheral aspects of Hobbes that Oakeshott leaves out — in
particular the consistent claims that Hobbes makes about the practical
utility of his philosophy. This contrasts starkly with Oakeshott's
equally insistent claim regarding the irrelevance of philosophy (including political philosophy) to the world of practice. I will say a few things
about this discrepancy at the end of the chapter.

Stephen Gerencser has recently argued that Oakeshott's thought
became increasingly sceptical as it developed and that this can be
partly attributed to an engagement with Hobbes's ideas. Indeed
Oakeshott's scepticism becomes directed to philosophy itself.
Where in *Experience and Its Modes* philosophy was described in teleological overtones as the pursuit of an unmodified form of experience,
subsequently Oakeshott would describe philosophy as just one voice
among many voices, and indeed, as parasitic on other voices in the conversation of mankind. I largely endorse Gerencser's suggestion that the
sceptical themes in Oakeshott come to the fore as his thought develops
and that the modes of experience become increasingly permeable to

each other.[3] Indeed much of what I say in this chapter supports Gerencser's argument, but takes it in a slightly different direction. This increased scepticism about philosophy and about the strict demarcation between the modes themselves is reflected, not only in Oakeshott's appropriation of Hobbes's substantive political theory, but also in the changing contexts that Oakeshott uses to illicit the meaning of Hobbes — the shift from a philosophical to a type of historical interpretation. In the introduction to *Leviathan* (1946) Oakeshott suggested that nothing short of the entire history of political philosophy was the appropriate context for considering a work such as *Leviathan* which, as a masterpiece of philosophical reflection, aims to "establish the connections, in principle and in detail, directly or mediately, between politics and eternity" (RP 225). In a much more modest vein, Oakeshott subsequently made the claim in "The Moral Life in the writings of Thomas Hobbes" (1960) that Hobbes sought to systematize the historical experience of modern individuality. As I suggested in the introduction it is this account of modern European history that comes to assume an increasingly important place in Oakeshott's later writings. Indeed, civil association is an ideal character distilled from the political experience of modern Europe. This shift towards a type of historical understanding seems to reinforce the more modest conception of philosophy that characterizes Oakeshott's later work. In *On Human Conduct* Oakeshott describes the enterprise of theory rather than philosophy and suggests that the theorist of human conduct surveys his subject from a conditional platform of understanding which excludes metaphysical speculation. In other words, he is to avoid the temptation to try to bridge the gap between politics and eternity. What seems to have occurred is that as Oakeshott comes to work out the content of his political/civil philosophy he simultaneously articulates a more qualified conception of theory itself. In the following pages I will outline these developments with an eye on the place of Hobbes in Oakeshott's thinking about the philosophical or theoretical endeavour.

II

Shortly I will discuss the general argument of *Experience and Its Modes* and why Oakeshott claimed that philosophical experience is finally the most satisfactory form of experience before considering why political philosophy is a form of 'pseudo philosophy'. In order to set the context

[3] Though, as suggested earlier, Gerencser probably overstates his case when he suggests that Oakeshott 'abandons' Hegel and idealism in favour of scepticism. *The Skeptic's Oakeshott*, p. 8. For a critique see D. Boucher, 'The Idealism of Michael Oakeshott', *Collingwood and British Idealism Studies*, vol.8, 2001, pp. 73-98.

for this discussion I should say a few things about the place of *Experience and Its Modes* in the context of British Idealism generally, not only to help elucidate the character of this work itself, but also to help explain Oakeshott's attraction to a thinker like Hobbes.

Experience and Its Modes appeared at the time (1933) when philosophical Idealism in Britain was in rapid decline. It was thirty years since the one time Idealists Bertrand Russell and G.E.Moore had published works[4] often credited with augmenting the decline of Idealism in the name of a 'realist' philosophy which took up with renewed vigour the attempt to assimilate all knowledge to that which could be scientifically verified. In the wake of this seeming triumph of positivism, Oakeshott and his slightly older contemporary, Collingwood, were the remaining significant voices of a philosophical outlook that, despite its profound impact on intellectual life from the 1870s to shortly after the First World War, was no longer fashionable. Oakeshott was not perturbed about this fall from favour, claiming that it offered a chance to think through some of the basic principles of the Idealist philosophical approach unhindered by 'authorities'. This situation, he thought, was conducive to serious philosophy because a "received philosophy is already a dead one" (EM 6). Though acknowledging a debt to Hegel's *Phänomenologie des Geistes* and Bradley's *Appearance and Reality*, Oakeshott develops his argument with the sort of independence and self confidence reminiscent of Hobbes himself.[5]

The reasons for Idealism's influence in British intellectual life in the half century prior to the 1920s were many and varied and stemmed as much from religious and political concerns as philosophical.[6] But perhaps the chief philosophical assumption that the Idealists attacked was the claim that things can be understood apart from both their relation to other things and apart from the minds that perceive them. Mind and reality are not two distinct things, and we can

[4] Russell, *The Principles of Mathematics*; Moore, 'The Refutation of Idealism', *Mind*, 12 (1903), pp. 433–53.

[5] Hobbes's reputed claim "that if had read as much as other men, he should have knowne no more then other men" (John Aubrey, *Brief Lives*, Suffolk: The Boydell Press, 1975, p. 157) is very similar to Oakeshott's observation that "since there are no 'authorities' in philosophy, references of this kind [to one's 'sources'] would but promote a groundless trust in books and a false attitude of mind. A philosopher is not, as such, a scholar; and philosophy, more often than not, has foundered in learning" (EM 8).

[6] Useful studies of the history of British Idealism include Anthony Quinton's, 'Absolute Idealism' in *Thoughts and Thinkers* (London: Duckworth, 1982); Peter Robbins, *The British Hegelians 1875-1925* (New York: Garland, 1982); Kirk Willis, 'The Introduction and Critical Reception of Hegelian Thought in Britain 1830–1900', *Victorian Studies*, Autumn 1988, pp. 85–111.

only talk meaningfully about the world when we break down the misleading distinction between the knowing subject and a supposedly
external world. Knowledge and reality need to be understood, then, as
inextricably tied to an experiencing mind. Hence one of the guiding
assumptions of the British Idealists, following Kant and Hegel, was
that philosophy is driven by a search to account for nothing short of
experience as a whole. Philosophy has little room for specialization. As
Oakeshott would put it in the early pages of *Experience and Its Modes*:
"the character of philosophy forbids us to console ourselves with the
notion that, if we fail to achieve a coherent view of the whole field, we
can at least do honest work in the cultivation of one of its corners. Philosophy has no such corners; whatever we say is said, if not explicitly,
then ignorantly and implicitly, of the whole" (EM 7).

The attempt to account for knowledge and truth by paying attention to the experiencing mind took on different forms. Where, for
instance, Kant in the *Critique of Pure Reason* was content to try to determine what conditions must hold for our knowledge of the world to be
valid — thereby leaving something of a gap between the knowing
mind and things-in-themselves — Hegel sought to bridge this gap
through an entire history of world spirit. Though most of the British
Idealists gave Hegel his due they were on the whole suspicious of his
grand synthesis. No doubt this had much to do with their relatively
modest concern to counter the assumptions of an encroaching scientific
materialism and to defend a broadly spiritual conception of human
nature. But the ideas they took from Hegel were also translated into a
sceptical register in keeping with the dominant mood of British philosophy, at least since Hume. Both Green and Bradley, for instance, kept a
clear distance from some of Hegel's loftier claims.

So Oakeshott inherited a chastened or domesticated Hegelianism
which he contributed to in his own way. This is no more apparent
than in his treatment of the modes themselves. Though the Idealists
claimed that experience is to be understood as a coherent whole and
philosophy seeks as far as possible to give an account of the whole,
most of the time we experience the world in a partial, fragmentary
form. As Bradley put it, the whole of experience "is for the average
man an indefinite number of worlds, worlds all more or less real but
all, so far as appears, more or less independent".[7] Earlier Idealists
talked about these worlds variously in terms of abstraction, modality or
fragmentation. These worlds of experience are potentially endless, but

---

[7]   *Essays on Truth and Reality*, p. 31, cited in Boucher, 'Overlap and Autonomy: The
       Different Worlds of Collingwood and Oakeshott', *Storia, Antropologia e Scienze
       del Linguaggio*, 4 (1989), pp. 69–89, at p. 71

some, such as history, science, and practice have a clearer outline and more sophisticated nature than others and can more readily be subjected to philosophical analysis.

Hegel had also talked about forms of human consciousness, as manifested in activities such as art, religion, science and philosophy. For Hegel these forms of experience are not independent of each other but represent different stages in the evolution of world spirit. Philosophy is the highest form of human understanding because it incorporates at the same time as it transcends (*Aufhabung*) each of the earlier forms of human consciousness. There are traces of this view of philosophy in *Experience and Its Modes* where Oakeshott suggests that philosophy is the most satisfactory form of experience because it entails the rejection of the abstraction that characterizes most of human life. However, Oakeshott rejects the idea that the reason philosophy is superior to other forms of human consciousness is because it carries within itself the traces of all other levels or forms of experience. There is no hint of a teleological understanding of history in Oakeshott's argument and of all the British Idealists none was more insistent that the modes are independent of each other. To fail to recognize this and to transpose a form of reasoning appropriate in one mode but not another, involves a great intellectual confusion. It is to commit the fallacy of *ignoratio elenchi* — "the most fatal of all errors" (EM 5). Philosophy is finally the most satisfactory form of experience because it involves a questioning of the presuppositions that all other forms of experience depend on if they are to constitute a world of understanding at all. So Oakeshott's brand of Idealism carries further some of the sceptical themes that were there already within earlier British Idealism. Before turning to that great seventeenth century sceptic, Hobbes, more needs to be said about the general argument of *Experience and Its Modes*.

All experience, according to Oakeshott, entails thought. Thought is not merely one form of experience (as opposed to, say, perception or sensation) but is equivalent to experience itself. Further, experience is a unified whole, a completely coherent system involving no unquestioned or unsubstantiated assumptions. "What is given in experience is single and significant, a One and not a Many" (EM 20). Here Oakeshott is expressing the Monism characteristic of Idealist thought. Experience, on this view, is never a mere collection of ideas. Rather, it is an interconnected world of ideas, where no statement, proposition or 'fact' is isolated, independent or self-sufficient in relation, not only to other particulars, but to the whole.

Entailed in all experience is a process whereby "a given world of ideas is transformed into a world of ideas which is more of a world".

Moreover, "we proceed always by way of implication. We never look away from a given world to another world, but always at a given world to discover the unity it implies" (EM 30–31). Implicit in all experience is what is termed 'the concrete whole'. The concrete whole of experience is a perfectly coherent world of ideas. It is coherent as all abstraction has been overcome. It is also the complete world implied in, and therefore not separate from, the various abstract worlds. Experience contains that which the abstract worlds seek in order to become more coherent. It is "what they attempt but cannot achieve without surrendering their character as abstract worlds, without self-extinction"(EM 80). Wherever this process of attempting to arrive at what is concrete or coherent in experience "is pursued without hindrance or distraction", philosophic experience is achieved. Philosophy attempts to discover what is definitive, absolute and unconditional in experience. It is "experience without reservation or presupposition, experience which is self-conscious and self-critical throughout, in which the determination to remain unsatisfied with anything short of a completely coherent world of ideas is absolute and unqualified"(EM 82).

Most of our experience is, of course, non-philosophic. In order to specify the nature of philosophic experience more adequately Oakeshott contrasts it with what it is not. It is not arrested experience, that is, experience which is satisfied to order experience on the basis of certain unquestioned presuppositions. The world thus created rests on an abstraction as it is content "to construct and explore a restricted world of abstract ideas" in lieu of the search for a complete view of the whole (EM 70). All of these arrests in experience are termed modes, as they modify the character of experience as a concrete whole. The modes are not to be seen as separate from the whole as "an island in the sea of experience", but as the whole of experience from a modified or incomplete viewpoint (EM 71). Nor should they be seen as mere parts, which, if collected together make up the whole. No "collection or combination of such abstractions", he argues, "will ever constitute a concrete whole", because, "the whole is not made up of abstractions, it is implied in them; it is not dependent upon abstractions, because it is logically prior to them" (EM 78–9).

Here I do not want to discuss the specific arguments as to why each of the modes examined (history, science, practice) fail to contribute to what is finally satisfactory in experience since this would take me beyond the limited purpose of this chapter. It is enough here to recognize that each of these modes, though themselves offering legitimate, if limited, explanations of experience have no contribution to make to philosophy itself. What is of interest to the analysis at hand is that Oakeshott reads Hobbes's conception of knowledge in similarly modal terms. On Oakeshott's reading Hobbes defines philosophy in contrast to experience, science, and faith. There are indeed some striking and suggestive parallels between Oakeshott's Hobbes and Oakeshott himself when Hobbes's 'system' is seen in the light of the argument of *Experience and Its Modes*.[8]

The first contrast to observe is that between philosophy and experience. Experience is unmediated, concerned with particulars not universals and so, within its limits, can be defined as absolute knowledge; "mere, uncritical 'knowledge of fact'" (Intro xxiv [RP 241]).[9] In contrast to experience, which, according to Hobbes, "concludeth nothing universally", philosophical knowledge, according to Oakeshott's reading, is concerned with knowledge of universals and with a knowledge of causes. Hobbes says it is "the natural reason of man flying up and down among the creatures, and bringing back a true report of their order, causes and effects" (cited in Intro xxv [RP 243]). Further, Oakeshott claims that philosophy for Hobbes is thoroughly conditional: "From beginning to end there is no suggestion in Hobbes that philosophy is anything other than conditional knowledge, knowledge of hypothetical generations and conclusions about the names of things, not about the nature of things". Moreover, "philosophy may be defined as the establishment by reasoning of true fictions" (Intro xxvi–xxvii [RP244–5]).

Oakeshott also contrasts Hobbes's view of philosophy with both theology and science. On this reading, Hobbes's view of philosophy (or reason) as knowledge of causes excludes "the consideration of the universe as a whole, things infinite, things eternal, final causes and things known only by divine grace or revelation; it excludes what Hobbes comprehensively calls theology and faith. He denies not the existence of these things, but their rationality" (Intro xx [RP 237]). In contrast, science is only imperfectly distinguished by Hobbes from philosophy. "The distinction", says Oakeshott, "is that between knowledge of things as they appear and enquiry into the fact of their appearing, between a knowledge (with all the necessary assumptions) of the phenomenal world and a theory of knowledge itself" (Intro xxii [RP239]). His concern with the latter is what distin-

---

[8]   For the moment I am simply interested in highlighting some of the general features of Oakeshott's reading of Hobbes, not its accuracy.

[9]   Needless to say, this is the complete antithesis of Oakeshott's Idealist argument that experience is not contrasted to thought it *is* thought.

guishes him from the scientists of his day. Indeed, when the world is described in mechanistic terms it is not because Hobbes thought it was in fact a machine, but because this is the appropriate level of abstraction for considering the causes of things. The machine analogy is generated not by observation but by reasoning. He is therefore, according to Oakeshott, a "scholastic, not a 'scientific' mechanist" (Intro xviii–xxi [RP236–8]). Hobbes's philosophy lies not in any doctrine about the nature of the world but in his understanding of the nature of philosophical knowledge. In terms of this system even man can be described as a mechanism (Intro xxx [RP 249]), but it is inaccurate to find in his thought the origins of anything like a science of politics (Intro xxiii [RP240]).

For both Oakeshott and Oakeshott's Hobbes philosophical truth is created and maintained by human artifice. Though, of course, where Oakeshott claimed that philosophy is absolute because it supplies what is satisfactory in experience, according to Oakeshott, philosophy for Hobbes is thoroughly conditional. However, this contrast is misleading. Philosophy, for Oakeshott, supersedes abstraction not because it supplies foundations to activities that would otherwise lack them, but because it refuses to rest content with the explanation of experience that any one mode offers. As soon as it ceases to be self-critical it ceases to be philosophical. Further, as will be seen below, Oakeshott went on to argue that philosophy transforms the things observed at other levels of experience — that is, transforms the nature of the things, not merely their appearance. In this sense, philosophy can be said to be concerned with establishing 'true fictions'. Above all, Hobbes, on Oakeshott's reading, sought to circumscribe the powers of reasoning. His rationalism is at best tentative, and arises from his attempt to impose a conditional intelligibility on existence which sense experience alone, because of its chaotic, random nature, is incapable of producing.[10]

---

[10] For an interesting critique of Oakeshott's reading of Hobbes on this see Seifert, "The Philosophy of Hobbes: Text and Context and the Problem of Sedimentation", *The Personalist*, 60 (1979), 177–85. Here the author claims that Oakeshott has a mistaken view of Hobbes's philosophy. That is, for Hobbes, philosophy was not radically hypothetical, but merely conditional — that is, mediated, unlike sense experience. Further, the author claims that the exclusive equation of philosophy with natural philosophy is misconceived — "But this is not to say that it is not more [than "the natural reason of man, busily flying up and down among the creatures, and bringing back a true report of their order, causes and effects"], or that natural reason yields only the indemonstrable, or hypothetical kind of knowledge found in natural philosophy; and to say that it does amounts to denying what Hobbes considered to be the most important accomplishment — the founding of a demonstrable science of politics" pp. 179–80. Hobbes equates political philosophy

There seems, then, to be a certain affinity between Oakeshott's modal view of experience and the distinctions he detects in Hobbes between philosophy, science and theology. This apparent similarity needs to be treated with caution. As Oakeshott points out, the distinction drawn by modern philosophers between philosophy and science was not made in Hobbes's day. Oakeshott is therefore able to make the distinction between science and philosophy more explicit than does Hobbes. Where Oakeshott's Hobbes contrasts philosophy (or reasoning, since it deals with cause and effect) with empiricism (science), Oakeshott himself, in *Experience and Its Modes*, contrasts philosophy as the critical probing of presuppositions with science as the world of measurement and quantity — the world *sub specie quantitatis*. Nevertheless, what is central to Oakeshott's reading, clearly distinguishing him from other accounts — notably other Idealist philosophers — is the rejection of the view that Hobbes is a scientific reductionist.[11]

---

with geometry, ie. both are demonstrable — because we make them ourselves. In contrast, natural philosophy is indemonstrable, ie. hypothetical. What actually gives coherence to his system "is his conception of demonstration, or 'teaching'", ie. science is best taught when its subjects are arranged in increasing order of complexity — civil society is therefore to be taught last, and is to be understood in terms of the new understanding of the universe — "In this respect Hobbes's thought is guided more by the principles of rhetoric than by those of logic, by the *ars disserendi* rather than the *ars demonstrandi*" pp. 182–3. For further criticism of the type of philosophical system Oakeshott attributes to Hobbes see Ted H. Miller, 'Oakeshott's Hobbes and the Fear of Political Rationalism', *Political Theory*, 29 (2001), 806–832. I will return to this criticism at the end of this chapter.

[11] Though Oakeshott does not take up the issue of the relationship between history and poetry in Hobbes it is interesting to note that the distinction was made by the latter. According to Strauss, Hobbes's turn to history in the so-called humanist phase of his thought should be seen in terms of the general turn away from scholasticism in the sixteenth and early seventeenth centuries. History is efficacious in promoting virtue in a way that scholastic precept is not. In his introduction to Thucydides Hobbes states that, "the principle and proper work of history (is) to instruct and enable men, by the knowledge of actions past, to bear themselves prudently in the present and providently towards the future . . . " (EW, vol. viii, p. vii. cited in Strauss, p. 80). Hobbes therefore subscribes to a view of history that Oakeshott terms the practical past — the appropriation of the past for present purposes. Strauss suggests that the contrast between history and poetry is strongest in the humanist phase of Hobbes's thought. Where history is concerned with truth, poetry is concerned with fancy. In the *Answer to the Preface of Gondibert* (1650 — the end of his humanist phase) Hobbes can assert that unlike history and philosophy, "the subject of a poem is the manners of men . . . manners presented, not dictated; and manners feigned, as the name of poesy imports, not found in men" (EW. vol.iv, p445). Further, "as the truth is the bound of historical, so the resemblance of truth is the utmost limit of poetical liberty" (*ibid.* pp. 451–2) According to Strauss, Hobbes subsequently turns away from history, and sense experience generally, as the

Though the lines drawn between the different modes are not the
same, and though for Oakeshott, unlike Hobbes, to talk of unmediated, ie. sensory, knowledge is meaningless, what unites
Oakeshott's argument with his reading of Hobbes is the pre-emi-
nence of the idea of modality.[12] As Gerencser has argued, Oakeshott is
able to assimilate much of what he finds in Hobbes because there is a
basic philosophical sympathy between them.[13] Oakeshott's circum-
scription of reason through this modal framework is clearly reminiscent of the late medieval tradition Hobbes inherited of sharply
demarcating the boundaries between reason, faith and experience. For
this reason J.L.Auspitz could plausibly write that *"Experience and Its
Modes* reads as if William of Occam had undertaken to redo Hegel".[14]

---

contours of his new science of politics become clearer in his mind. In his preface
to the translation of Homer he no longer draws the distinction between poetry
and history. Interestingly for us, here Hobbes describes poetry in a way
remarkably reminiscent of Oakeshott's idea of poetry as the activity of
'contemplating and delighting', where images of 'fact' or 'not-fact' are
irrelevant (see Oakeshott's 'The Voice of Poetry in the Conversation of
Mankind' in RP at p. 516). According to Hobbes, the 'design' of poetry "is not
only to profit, but also to delight the reader . . . the work of an heroic poet is no
more but to furnish an ingenuous reader, when his leisure abounds, with the
diversion of an honest and delightful story, whether true or feigned" (EW. vol. x
p. iii).

[12] In chapter 3 of *Leviathan* "Of the Consequences or Train of Imagination",
Hobbes draws a distinction between regulated and unregulated trains of
thought which reinforces this idea of modality. Hobbes claims that regulated
thought is more constant than that which is unregulated because it is directed by
"desire, and design" (Lev 14). Unlike other beasts man has the capacity to search
out all the effects of a particular cause. "In sum, the discourse of the mind, when
it is governed by design, is nothing but *seeking*, or the faculty of invention, which
the Latins called *sagacitas*, and *solertia*; a hunting out of the causes, of some effect,
present or past; or the effects, of some present or past cause . . . Sometimes a man
knows a place determinate, within the compass whereof he is to seek; and then
his thoughts run over all the parts thereof, in the same manner as one would
sweep a room, to find a jewel; or as a spaniel ranges the field, till he finds a scent;
or as a man should run over the alphabet, to start a rhyme" (Lev 15). As with
Oakeshott's modes of history, science and practice, which, as will be seen
shortly, he refers to as determinate modes of experience, Hobbes is here
suggesting that knowledge only comes into existence when the mind imposes
on experience a logical sequence. Though the modal specifications are different,
nevertheless, for both Oakeshott and Hobbes knowledge is something
achieved, not merely given. It is an act of invention or imagination and not the
property of the things themselves.

[13] For further discussion of these connections emphasizing especially Oakeshott's
nominalist reading of Hobbes see Gerencser, *The Skeptic's Oakeshott*, ch.4. I will
say more on this nominalist reading in the following chapter.

[14] "Individuality, Civility, and Theory: The Philosophical Imagination of Michael
Oakeshott", *Political Theory*, 4 (August, 1976), 261–294, at p. 288.

III

Having outlined the connections between the modal 'system' developed in *Experience and Its Modes* and Oakeshott's account of Hobbes's philosophical system we need to examine the way that Oakeshott develops his conception of political philosophy. As will be seen shortly Oakeshott's reflections on Hobbes were central to working out this conception and many of the ideas discussed in the introduction to *Leviathan* are developed at greater length in other writings at the time. It is ironic that one of the most distinguished political philosophers of the twentieth century made the claim in his first major treatise, *Experience and Its Modes*, that political philosophy was an example of pseudo-philosophical experience. This view is subsequently revised, but before looking at these revisions we need to understanding why Oakeshott's early conception of political philosophy did not quite fit his modal framework.

All of the modes examined in some depth in *Experience and Its Modes* are examples of what Oakeshott calls determinate modes. They are self-contained and independent worlds of experience which, so long as their respective presuppositions are not subjected to criticism, offer themselves as complete explanations of the whole of experience. "History, Science and Practice, as such, and each within its own world, are beyond the relevant interference of philosophic thought" (EM 332). Whenever the attempt is made to question the underlying presuppositions of these worlds the character of these worlds as independent, sovereign worlds is undermined.

There are, however, certain abstract forms of experience, which arise when experience is inadvertently arrested. Ethical and political philosophy and theology are all examples of experience that is arrested yet, unlike History, Science and Practice, fail to offer an adequate explanation of experience on their own terms. They are indeterminate as they fail to acknowledge the world to which they rightly belong. In the case of ethical and political philosophy the world they demand to be judged by is philosophy. Here the example that he examines is ethical thought.[15]

The distinction is made here between ethical thought and the practice of making judgments of value which represent distinct activities and belong to two separate worlds of experience. Ethical thought is concerned with determining the definitions of moral concepts. It seeks to understand what is meant by notions such as

---

[15] Often termed "Moral Philosophy", which according to Oakeshott, indicates its character as qualified or limited philosophical thought — according to him an oxymoron, see EM 335.

"good", "right", or "ought". Judgments of value, in contrast, are wholly orientated towards the transformation of practical life that involves the attempt to alter the world of what currently exists "to realise what is seen to be valuable" (EM 336–40). It is to make the world of 'what is' conform to the world of 'what ought to be'. Ethical thought, or moral philosophy, forms no part of the world of practice. It does however take as its subject matter the judgements of value made in the world of practice. It constructs ethical theories from ordinary notions of "right", "wrong", "ought", "ought not", etc. However, it views these ideas from the concrete totality of experience. The activity of philosophical definition has no connection with the world of practice since "to define a concept is to exhibit its reference to reality" (EM 342). In the process of definition the concept itself undergoes transformation. It is not simply the same concept viewed from another perspective. Ethical concepts are not therefore *sui generis*, constituting an independent world that makes no reference to reality. They are not irreducible concepts, definable on their own terms. Since all concepts make some implicit reference to the totality of experience they are, therefore, all definable (EM 342).

In so far as ethical thought and political philosophy belong to worlds at all they belong to the world of philosophy. However, they are both abstract as they fall short of pursuing what is completely satisfactory in experience and settle for viewing "one particular mode of experience — practical experience — from the totality of experience" (345 EM).

In *Experience and Its Modes* Oakeshott had marginalised the activity of political philosophy. There it was argued that as soon as ethical or political reflection takes on the task of defining everyday concepts used in practice it invariably transforms those concepts to the point where they no longer play any role in guiding the conduct of life. Once transformed, the concepts cease to be merely designated concepts, which mistakenly take themselves to be separate from the concrete whole of experience (see EM 45, 52–3, 70–1, 268), and become philosophical definitions. Political and ethical thought, to the extent that they are instances of philosophical reflection, lose their connections with ordinary ethical and political ideas and remain abstract and incomplete activities, since they are content only to consider one abstract mode of experience and ignore their relations with the whole of experience. However, to claim that philosophy is the only form of experience which is finally satisfactory because it is purged of all abstraction, incoherence and presupposition is really only to have said that philosophy is nothing if not self-critical. That is, philosophy is defined in terms of what it is not — abstraction.

IV

By defining political philosophy as pseudo-philosophical activity Oakeshott argued himself into a position which he soon reconsidered. It was in the years immediately prior to and after the Second World War — at the same time as he was reading Hobbes very closely — that Oakeshott turned his attention to working out a conception of political philosophy.[16] As he makes explicit in one of his essays of the time, Oakeshott's reflections on Hobbes served as something of a catalyst for his own reflections on what is entailed in an adequate account of a philosophy of politics (RPM 119). Throughout his career Oakeshott continually returned to the question of the nature of the philosophical enterprise, each time working out his ideas afresh. One of the most important periods where he gave special consideration to the philosophical project, here in its relation to political activity, was the point at which he worked out his important interpretation of Hobbes's philosophy. Of course, to establish historical contiguity is not to establish philosophical identification. It is nevertheless manifestly clear that Hobbes's work was vital to Oakeshott's formulation and that *Leviathan*, along with Plato's *Republic*, Spinoza's *Ethics* and Hegel's *Grundlinien der Philosophie des Rechts*, are each said to be the product of what Oakeshott considers to be true philosophical reflection (RPM 150).

In the introduction to *Leviathan* (1946) Oakeshott made the claim that political philosophy is a different order of enquiry from other forms of reflection on politics. It does not rest content with simply making coherent the world of practical life. On the contrary, it seeks to establish the connections between the world of practice and "the entire conception of the world that belongs to a civilization" (224 RP). This ambitious project requires more than the inadvertence of merely disallowing the process of reflection to rest content at any one point "and more than the mere acceptance of the two worlds of ideas". For,

> (t)he whole impetus of the enterprise is the perception that what really exists is a single world of ideas, which comes to us divided by the abstracting force of circumstances; is the perception that our political ideas and what may be called the rest of our ideas are not in fact two independent worlds, and that though they may come to us as separate text and context,

---

[16] The important texts include, "The Concept of a Philosophical Jurisprudence" (1938), "The Concept of a Philosophy of Politics" (1946), "Political Philosophy" (1946–50), Review of J.D. Mabbott's, *The State and the Citizen* (1949).

the *meaning* lies, as it always must lie, in a unity in which the separate existence of text and context is resolved (RP 224).

The context that Oakeshott is referring to here is nothing less than the
entire history of political philosophy. When the masterpiece of political
philosophy (such as *Leviathan*) is read in this context it is secured
"against the deadening requirement of conformity to a merely abstract
idea of political philosophy" (RP 225). Political philosophy then is the
attempt to establish the connections between politics and eternity: "it is
the whole intellectual history organized and exhibited from a particular angle of vision" (RP 225). Despite the fact that its limited angle of
vision is determined by its subject matter, political philosophy is no
longer to be seen as a form of arrested experience. Oakeshott seems to
have left behind the argument that nothing save unhindered philosophical experience supplies what is satisfactory to the concrete whole
of experience. In exploring the connections between politics and eternity the political philosopher offers a consideration of the way in which
the political order contributes to the deliverance of mankind from its
universal predicament that expresses itself differently in different
circumstances (RP 225–6).

For Oakeshott, the political philosopher finds his starting place in
everyday political concepts. However, as a philosopher he is not
content with foreclosing reflection and working with the conditional
certainties necessary for the conduct of practical life, rather, he
attempts to find "*an explanation or view of political life and activity from the
standpoint of the totality of experience*" (RPM 126). This understanding of
the philosophical enterprise is adumbrated in "The Concept of a Philosophical Jurisprudence" (1938) (CPJ) in respect of law, and "The Concept of a Philosophy of Politics" (1946?) in relation to politics.[17]

In "The Concept of a Philosophical Jurisprudence" Oakeshott
defines philosophy as the process "of coming to know more fully
and more clearly what is in some sense already known" (CPJ 346).
Contra Plato, we never begin the philosophical enterprise in a state
of ignorance. Rather, as he was to begin *On Human Conduct*, we live in
a world of intelligibles, of things in some sense understood. This may
consist of incoherent, unorganized ideas, but it is never a state of unremitting nescience. Reflection is prompted by the perception that what
is known is in some sense incomplete and ambiguous and political philosophy is guided by the determination to relate political activity to
experience as a whole. He reiterates the argument presented in *Experi-*

---

[17] Since the philosophical enterprise is discussed in virtually identical terms it is
      safe to assume that what he says about a philosophical theory of law is
      interchangeable with politics and vice versa.

ence and Its Modes in relation to ethical concepts that political life and activity are not to be considered *sui generis* and the task of the political philosopher is, first, to distinguish political activity from other forms of activity and, second, to relate it to the complete map of experience. This is achieved by a process of philosophical definition, by taking the concepts of ordinary political experience and making them more coherent and intelligible. The aim "is to arrive at concepts which, because they presuppose nothing, are complete in themselves" (RPM 127).

The concepts thrown up in practical life which invite reflection are the starting place, not the foundation, for philosophical thought. Further, the positive teaching produced by philosophical reflection should not be seen as the philosophical foundation of politics. There are in fact no foundations since the concepts themselves are transformed in the process. The concepts not only look different when seen from different perspectives, they are different concepts. To suggest that they are the same thing seen from different perspectives is a form of positivism.[18] Importantly, this 'anti-foundationalist' view of philosophy is thoroughly consistent with the 'system' he attributes to Hobbes. Hobbes's putative connection with subsequent positivist thinkers is entirely rejected by Oakeshott.

According to Oakeshott, a philosophy of politics is not the attempt to work out the implications for political activity of a preconceived 'philosophical doctrine'. It is simply the process by which ordinary political concepts are transformed when thought is allowed to take a certain course unhindered by the distractions of conditional certainty. As he expressed it in *Experience and Its Modes*, it seeks to define what is otherwise merely designated.

A prime task of any adequate philosophy of politics will be the explanation of political activity in terms of value. That is, concepts such as 'law', 'government' and 'sovereignty' are more concretely defined when they are understood in terms of the purposes they serve, and this is already to have begun to transform the concepts.[19] However, ethical or normative concepts ('good', 'bad', 'right', 'wrong', 'ought', 'ought not' etc.) are not *sui generis*. They contain presuppositions which philosophy seeks to unravel, thereby defining the concept in more concrete terms. Its final goal is to establish the connections between political activity and the concrete whole of experience.

We get some idea of what this means towards the end of the essay where he makes the point that the transformation of ordinary political concepts will not provide prescriptions for use in political activ-

[18]   Review J.D. Mabbott, *The State and the Citizen*, in *Mind*, 58 (1949), 378–89, at p. 383.
[19]   Hobbes, he suggested, recognized this — RPM 133.

ity, because philosophical concepts by nature have nothing to say about the specific ends or purposes pursued in practical life. The practical view is superseded; the ought becomes an is, or the merely imperative becomes the more comprehensive indicative. The view of political life changes radically from what appeared at the level of ordinary political life. It is worth quoting him here at some length:

> Not only is it useless to expect from a philosophy of politics any explicit judgment about what ought to be the end in political activity; but the whole notion of political life as activity for the achievement of certain ends is superseded by a view of political life in relation to the totality of experience. Activity implies change, and change an identity which does not change; and, as I understand it, the business of philosophy is to conceive change and activity, not merely as what they are for commonsense — more change and identity — but concretely, as abstract aspects of a genuine, and therefore changeless, totality. And a philosophy of politics is an attempt to get away from what political life appears to be for commonsense — activity for the achievement of some end — to a view of the character of political life from the concrete standpoint of the totality of experience (RPM 136–137).

Though modified, Oakeshott's account of the totality of experience is essentially the Idealist notion of the concrete universal or the absolute. This is why he is able to claim, in the context of elucidating Hobbes's thought, that "the human predicament is a universal appearing everywhere as a particular" (RP 226). Moreover, this is why he is able to interpret, and hence appropriate, Hobbes in the manner that he does. Indeed, it has profound implications for the way in which past political philosophy is read. Whenever political thought reaches a properly philosophical perspective it says something of universal significance. The human predicament, despite manifesting itself in a variety of ways, is a coherent whole that is impervious to change. For the man of practice, as indeed for the historian, this is largely a meaningless notion, since both assume the reality of change. Where the latter's business is to explain change in the historical past, the former invariably must deal with its present reality in the conduct of life. Change is a presupposition of practical life: "What cannot change cannot, for practice, be a fact" (EM 263). However, when seen from the gaze of eternity, from the philosophical perspective, the human predicament is a changeless whole.

The political philosopher is concerned with establishing the unity of text and context which all experience implies yet is left divided in most of its modes. The text is "the permanent character of political activity" (RPM 151), not as a *thing* that possesses meaning in and of itself but by virtue of being related to a context — "the permanent *it* is what it *becomes* when given a place in an intelligible universe" (RPM

151). Political philosophy attempts to resolve the distinction between text and context, to bridge the gap between politics and eternity. It "is saying something concerned with political activity such that, if true, things will be as they are; not as they were when we first caught sight of them, but as they permanently are" (RPM 152).

It was worthwhile pointing out that there is an important distinction between Hobbes and Oakeshott on the question of definition. For Oakeshott, philosophical definition is the end point of the enquiry, whereas Hobbes suggests that philosophical enquiry begins by first determining precise definitions and then reasoning from cause to consequence:

> The use and end of reason, is not the finding of the sum and truth of one, or a few consequences, remote from the first definitions, and settled significations of names, but to begin at these, and proceed from one consequence to another. For there can be no certainty of the last conclusion, without a certainty of all those affirmations and negations, on which it was grounded and inferred (Lev. 26)

The failure of philosophers in the past to arrive at a true civil philosophy is attributed by Hobbes to a failure to establish the definitions required to build such a philosophy:

> For there is not one of them that begins his ratiocination from the definitions, or explications of the names they are to use; which is a method that hath been used only in geometry; whose conclusions have thereby been made indisputable (Lev. 27)

Where Oakeshott suggests philosophy begins with commonsense concepts and transforms them in the process of definition, Hobbes claims that the philosopher must bypass the 'absolute knowledge of fact' which he terms experience and reason from clear, stable definitions.

However, again the affinities between the two are more important than the differences. Central to both is the idea that philosophy is independent of ordinary, practical experience and the conclusions of the former are not to be judged by the criteria of the latter. Both philosophers maintained that the establishment of truth involves an act of imagination. Knowledge is created and supported by human artifice. For Oakeshott, the discourses or modes of science, history and practice generate their own distinctive criteria for assessing what is to be counted as fact. Similarly for Hobbes there is no knowledge which is absolute. Even science "is not Absolute, but Conditionall", and is simply opinion which has been organized and given definitions. "No man", Hobbes argues, "can know by Discourse, that this, or that, is, has been, or will be; which is to know absolutely: but onely, that if This be, That is; if This has been, That has been; if This shall be: which is to know conditionally; and that not the consequence of one thing to another; but of one name of a thing, to another name of the same thing" (Lev 40). Further, "to know truth, is the same thing as to remember that it was made by ourselves by the common use of words".[20]

Though, according to Hobbes, "there is no conception in a man's mind, which hath not at first, totally, or by parts, been begotten upon the organs of Sense", the senses are ultimately unreliable and so incapable by themselves of generating knowledge. Scientific knowledge is not empirical but hypothetical. Mathematics was to provide the ideal model of the new science. As Leo Strauss was to state Hobbes's position: "we have absolute certain or scientific knowledge only of those subjects of which we are the causes, or whose construction is in our power or depends on our arbitrary will . . . The construction must be conscious construction; it is impossible to know a scientific truth without knowing at the same time that we have made it."[21] The consequence of this is that we can never come to know the world through science. As Strauss put it: "The universe will always remain wholly enigmatic".[22] On the basis of this Strauss makes the claim that Hobbes made a break not only with the Schoolmen but with the pre-modern nominalists who taught "that the 'anticipations' by virtue of which we take our bearings in ordinary life and in science are products of nature". The upshot of Hobbes's abandonment of this doctrine is the denial of the "natural harmony between the human mind and the universe".[23] For Strauss the gap that Hobbes opens between nature and the human mind is one of the central sources of the crisis of modern political philosophy, and much of Strauss's intellectual career can be understood as an attempt to close this gap by recovering what he termed the 'classic natural right' teachings of ancient political philosophy.

Strauss is only able to make this judgment because he takes as normative a mind-independent conception of reason that he attributes to the classical political thought of Plato and Aristotle. Strauss is not alone in identifying Hobbes's scepticism with a perceived 'crisis of modernity'. From a different perspective, but with a related set of concerns about the modern condition, Hannah Arendt makes very similar judgments about Hobbes's place in the broad tradition of

[20] *De Cive*, The English version, Howard Warrender (ed.) (Oxford: Clarendon Press, 1983), ch. 18, p. 254.
[21] *Natural Right and History* (Chicago: University of Chicago Press), p. 173.
[22] *Ibid.*, p. 174.
[23] *Ibid.*, p. 174–5.

Western political thought. For Arendt, the radical doubt that formed the background to the scientific revolution was instrumental in leading to what she calls 'world alienation' or the loss of a common world — the world as it appears to common sense. The new science of the seventeenth century sought to find an Archimedan point — a vantage point beyond the senses — from which to view the world. But, she claims, the "perplexity inherent in the discovery of the Archimedean point was and still is that the point outside the earth was found by an earth bound creature, who found that he himself lived not only in a different but in a topsy-turvy world the moment he tried to apply his universal world view to his actual surroundings".[24] This turn inward in the attempt to meet the challenge of scepticism gave rise to an interest in experimentation by which human beings sought to discover the secrets of an alienated nature. What began in a theoretical attempt to establish certainty by moving beyond the senses in due course gave rise to the technological attempt to control nature and the triumph of a new conception of man as *homo faber*. For Arendt, no one did more than Hobbes to bring this new understanding of science into the political realm: "Hobbes's attempt to introduce the new concepts of making and reckoning into political philosophy — or, rather, his attempt to apply the newly discovered aptitudes of making to the realm of human affairs was of the greatest importance; modern rationalism as it is currently known . . . has never found a clearer and more uncompromising representative . . . The political philosophy of the modern age, whose greatest representative is still Hobbes, founders on the perplexity that modern rationalism is unreal and modern realism is irrational — which is only another way of saying that reason and reality have parted company." Arendt immediately went on to suggest that Hegel's subsequent attempt "to reconcile spirit with reality (*den Geist mit der Wirklichkeit zu versöhnen*), a reconciliation that is the deepest concern of all modern theories of history, rested on the insight that modern reason foundered on the rock of reality".[25]

For Oakeshott, there is no such 'crisis of modern political philosophy' because he accepts, and indeed builds on, Hobbes's subject-centered conception of reason and truth. It should be stressed that Oakeshott's philosophical sympathy with Hobbes was not unqualified. In the next chapter I will suggest that Oakeshott (at least

---

[24] *The Human Condition* (Chicago and London: University of Chicago Press, 1958), p. 284.
[25] *Ibid*, p. 300,1.

in his early phase) distanced himself from the radically subjective theory of the will that follows from Hobbes's thoroughgoing nominalism. Despite this, there is much in Oakeshott's sceptical brand of Idealism that is consistent with ideas undoubtedly there in Hobbes but which have been obscured by the latter's identification with a tradition of scientific naturalism. Oakeshott agrees with both Arendt and Strauss on the radical nature of Hobbes's scepticism, but he disagrees that this signals the crisis of either modern politics or modern political philosophy. Moreover, he stands with Hobbes rather than Hegel on the question of the need to find a reconciliation of spirit and nature in a philosophy of history. Shortly I will say something on the 'historical element' (to borrow a phrase from one of Oakeshott's early essays) that becomes increasingly important in Oakeshott's later political thought, but Oakeshott never claimed that historical understanding was more than one of many ways in which the world could be understood.

V

In his contribution to Oakeshott's *Festschrift*,[26] W.H. Greenleaf explored some of the interesting affinities between post-Wittgensteinian ordinary language philosophy and Idealism and the similar implications each has for political philosophy. For instance, he noted the way in which each conceives philosophy to be a second order enquiry which transforms the phenomena of ordinary or first order experience. They both reject the proposition that philosophy discovers new facts about the world that form the foundation to be built upon. For linguistic philosophers such as Austin, Ryle, and Hare, following Wittgenstein, this involves clarifying the meaning of words which in everyday speech are often used in ambiguous, even contradictory, ways. The meaning of words is determined by the use made of them in different contexts and Greenleaf points out how similar the Idealists' talk of modes of experience (in particular Oakeshott's notion of tradition, which is central to his account of the practical mode) is to the Wittgensteinian idea of 'forms of life'. On this view, truth is wholly conventional. It is a function of language not of objects. There is no truth outside language. According to Wittgenstein, "(t)here is no outside; outside you cannot breathe".[27]

[26] "Idealism, modern philosophy and politics", in *Politics and Experience: Essays presented to Michael Oakeshott on the Occasion of his Retirement* (Cambridge: Cambridge University Press, 1968), Preston King and B.C. Parekh eds.
[27] *Philosophical Investigations*, cited in *ibid.*, p. 118.

There are clearly many similarities between these two schools of thought, the exploration of which is beyond my intention.[28] However, it is of some significance that recent commentators have discovered in Hobbes ideas about language that are said to anticipate those of Wittgenstein and Austin. Terrence Ball, for instance, suggests that the linguistic turn "was taken in political theory long before it was taken in philosophy, and that the first to take it in political theory was none other than the first self-consciously scientific thinker, Thomas Hobbes . . . ".[29] On this reading, because man has language he has reason since language "is the medium that makes reason and science possible."[30] Moreover, "(w)ords and concepts are our inventions and have only such meaning as we give to them. Because the world of mutual meanings and shared significations — our world — is our own creation, we can know it in a way that we can never know the world of nature".[31]

Language can be abused and distorted, something which is all too likely in creatures of passion, motivated by pride and ambition, thereby intensifying, in a sense creating, the chaos of the state of nature. But it also provides the remedy to this predicament. That is, it provides the material out of which a civil science can be constructed, showing men the way to peace. It is both a constitutive cause as well as a solution to the predicament. It is, however, an artificial remedy, superfluous to creatures immune from the destructive effects of distorted communication (to borrow from Habermas). The upshot of this is that by making Hobbes's analysis of language central to his account of the generation of scientific knowledge, Ball, like Oakeshott, is able to resist the positivist reading of Hobbes, and to assimilate aspects of his thought to modern linguistic analysis.[32]

Without forcing the point, it is possible to see an interesting three way connection between this anti-naturalist Hobbes for whom truth is a creation of linguistic convention, the Idealist Oakeshott for

---

[28] The similarities between Wittgenstein and Oakeshott have also been explored by Hanna Pitkin in *Wittgenstein and Justice* (Berkeley, Los Angeles and London: University of California Press, 1972), see esp. pp. 51–4.

[29] "Hobbes's Linguistic Turn", *Polity*, 17 (1985), pp. 739–60, at p. 740.

[30] *Ibid.*, p. 748.

[31] *Ibid.*, p. 751.

[32] See also Geraint Parry "Performative Utterances and Obligation in Hobbes", *Philosophical Quarterly*, 17 (1967) and David R. Bell, "What Hobbes does with words", *Philosophical Quarterly*, 19 (1969). Boucher claims that Collingwood in fact anticipated this linguistic reading of Hobbes and arrived at a theory of language similar to but independent of Wittgenstein. See Boucher, *Social and Political Thought of R.G. Collingwood*, pp. 135–140, where I discovered these references to this aspect of Hobbes interpretation — at p. 275.

whom nature has no meaning outside the world or discourse of science, and those who have taken over from Wittgenstein the idea of a form of life without which language becomes meaningless. In the chapters that follow we will see the way Oakeshott appropriates much that he finds in Hobbes, but it should be stressed that he is only able to do this because there is a basic affinity in their respective intellectual systems. Had earlier Idealists paid closer attention to those aspects of Hobbes that Oakeshott takes to be central, they might have found more common ground with him than a superficial reading suggests. At the end of this chapter I will suggest, however, that what Oakeshott chooses to ignore in Hobbes may be as significant for his project of reinventing Hobbes as that which he highlights.

VI

Prior to this it is necessary to say a few things about the way in which Oakeshott's conception of the philosophical or theoretical enterprise develops in the later part of his career. It is in *On Human Conduct* that Oakeshott next develops a sustained account of the nature of theoretical understanding. Though many of the themes discussed in the earlier treatment of philosophy and its relation to the modes or voices are reiterated here there are some important modifications that seemed to me to reflect broader changes in Oakeshott's theory broadly understood. In the pre-war and immediate post-war periods Oakeshott's philosophical reflections on politics were principally devoted to working out an authentic conception of political philosophy. He was concerned with what it meant to think philosophically about politics and he had not yet turned his attention in a sustained way to working out his substantive political (or civil) philosophy — the theory of civil association which was given its definitive treatment in *On Human Conduct*, 'The Rule of Law',[33] and 'The Vocabulary of a Modern European State'.[34] Many of the key features of this find an early expression in his writings on Hobbes, as will become apparent over the next two chapters, but these works are ostensibly, at least, interpretations of another philosopher's ideas.

Thus far Oakeshott's writings on political philosophy proper are rather abstract. He has marked out a place for political philosophy as a legitimate intellectual endeavour but he has not yet said a great deal about the precise subject matter of political philosophy. We are

---

[33] In *On History* (Oxford: Basil Blackwell, 1983).
[34] In *Political Studies*, 23 (1975), 319–41, 409–14.

told that political philosophers transform common sense or ordinary understandings of politics but we are not told much about the content of these understandings — which ones does the political philosopher make the subject of his inquiry? It's up to the political philosopher to choose his subject matter, to mark out his territory, and in other writings this is precisely what Oakeshott does.

As is well known, one of Oakeshott's deep and abiding interests was history. He studied history as an undergraduate, taught history at Cambridge between the wars, and most importantly, some of his most original writings were on the philosophy of history. These writings may yet come to be considered Oakeshott's most enduring philosophical legacy. His early writings on the philosophy of history were considered by no less an authority than Collingwood to be "the high-water mark of English historical thought upon history".[35] In his review of *Experience and Its Modes*, Collingwood was even more enthusiastic in his praise, suggesting that the chapter on history was "the most penetrating analysis of historical thought that has ever been written".[36]

But as well as writing philosophically about the nature of historical understanding he was also working out his own interpretation of European moral and political history. As Luke O'Sullivan has shown,[37] this was a long-term interest of Oakeshott's, stretching back to his early intellectual career. But it is in the post World War II years that this interpretation of the European past was worked out in some depth. I will say more about the detail of this reading of the past in the next chapter because it is central to Oakeshott's account of individuality, which in turn is crucial for understanding his theory of civil association. At this stage I am simply interested in its implications for Oakeshott's conception of philosophy or theory as such.

---

[35] *The Idea of History* ed. J van der Dussen (Oxford: Oxford University Press, 1994) originally published 1946.

[36] "Oakeshott and the Modes of Experience" in *The Cambridge Mind*, ed. E.Homberger (Boston: Little Brown, 1970), pp. 132–4, originally published in *The Cambridge Review*, February 16, 1934. Collingwood also suggested in this review that Oakeshott "writes of history like an accomplished historian who, driven into philosophy by the problems of his own work, has found the current philosophies impotent to cope with their philosophical implication", pp.133,4.

[37] "Michael Oakeshott on European Political History" in *History of Political Thought*, 21 (2000), 132–151.

Oakeshott is quite clear in these writings[38] that though he is interested in presenting a kind of 'historical description' (RP 365) he is not writing history 'properly so-called' (PFPS, 19). In his discussion of the rationalist disposition — itself an historical identity — he claims that the historian must seek "to escape that gross abridgment of the process which gives the new shape a too early or too late and a too precise definition, and to avoid the false emphasis which springs from being over-impressed by the moment of unmistakable emergence. Yet that moment must have a dominating interest for those whose ambitions are not pitched too high" (RP 18). Though Oakeshott's reading of the past never pretends to conform to his rather austere account of historical enquiry it does nevertheless claim to have historical plausibility. That is, the rival understandings of the state as *societas* and *universitas* and the moral dispositions concomitant to them are not mere inventions, they are ideal characters which are elicited from historical experience. Though they are deliberate abridgments, they are not mere inventions which are imposed on the past (MPME 3).

So there is a certain reading of the past going on here that is neither strictly historical nor philosophical. It is instructive here to mention the list of authors he chooses to discuss, for instance, in *Morality and Politics in Modern Europe*. Of the political theory of individualism he includes Locke, Kant, Smith, Burke, Bentham, and Mill. The collectivists include, Calvin, Bacon, Owen, Saint Simon and Marx. Of all of these political theorists, only Kant is credited with offering a properly philosophical perspective (MPME 58, 64). Perhaps more indicative of his intention here is his omission of Spinoza, Hobbes and Hegel, each identified by Oakeshott as thinkers whose writings represent a properly philosophical perspective (MPME 14). In these lectures, as in the last essay of *On Human Conduct*, Oakeshott adopts an attitude to his subject matter neither purely philosophical nor historical, at least according to the criteria he sets out in *Experience and its Modes* and elsewhere. Since his discussion centers on ideal characters or idioms of reflection that include many authors whose writings fall short of philosophical reflection, it cannot properly be called a philosophical

---

[38] The most important of these writings are: *Morality and Politics in Modern Europe: The Harvard Lectures* (MPME) ed. S.R. Letwin (New Haven and London: Yale University Press, 1993), *The Politics of Faith and the Politics of Scepticism* (PFPS) ed. T.Fuller (New Haven and London: Yale University Press, 1996), "The Masses in Representative Democracy" in *Rationalism in Politics* ed. T. Fuller (Indianapolis: Liberty Press, 1991), originally published in *Freedom and Serfdom: An Anthology of Western Thought*, ed. A.Hunold (Dordrecht: Reidel, 1961), "The Moral Life in the Writings of Thomas Hobbes", in *Rationalism in Politics*, and the final essay of *On Human Conduct*.

enquiry. Nor is it properly history since, in *Morality and Politics in Modern Europe*, he quite self-consciously employs what he terms abridgments elicited from the past, the very thing he elsewhere argues historians should avoid (MPME 3, RP 18). It seems to be a hybrid mode of experience. In terms of the tightly argued position elaborated in *Experience and Its Modes* Oakeshott appears to be guilty of a form of *ignoratio elenchi*.

What Oakeshott seems to be doing here is creating a kind of 'text' which can become of the subject of philosophical or theoretical treatment. As I mentioned in the introduction, David Boucher suggests that here Oakeshott invokes a philosophical past. According to this view the ideal characters (*societas* and *universitas* or the state understood as civil or enterprise association) explored in the final essay of *On Human Conduct* have nothing "to do with history at all: they are philosophical constructions philosophically conceived and presented 'on the analogy of human history'".[39]

This reading makes the final essay of *On Human Conduct* as well as "The Masses" consistent with Oakeshott's modal view of experience. However, it seems in these works that Oakeshott's fidelity to modality is subordinate to other tasks, which do not easily fit within Oakeshott's modal framework, and that they each contain, in various degrees, instances of historical, philosophical and, indeed practical modes of experience. The ideal characters have some, not merely contingent, connection with history because they are said to be elicited from a study of the course of events (MPME 3). I think that Boucher here wrongly conflates Oakeshott's philosophical traditions (Will and Artifice, Rational Will etc) identified in the introduction to *Leviathan*, which are conceived 'on the analogy of human history', with the ideal characters explored in *On Human Conduct*, "The Masses", *The Politics of Faith and the Politics of Scepticism*, and *Morality and Politics in Modern Europe* for which Oakeshott claims to have some historical plausibility. Further, as Boucher himself notes, Oakeshott claims that the cogency of these two moral dispositions "depends upon the identification of these dispositions as historic self-understandings" (OHC 325).[40]

Second, these writings are at least partly philosophical (or theoretical) in that they elucidate the teachings of past political philosophers. The last essay of *On Human Conduct*, for instance, discusses in

[39] "Politics in a Different Mode", p. 723. This last phrase comes from Oakeshott's introduction to *Leviathan* (RP 227), in reference to the tradition of Rational Will.

[40] See *ibid.*, p. 724n30. Though I disagree with Boucher on this particular point I should stress that I have found his writings on both Oakeshott and Collingwood extremely helpful in clarifying many of my own thoughts on these writers.

some depth the philosophies of Montesquieu, Bodin, and Hegel. Montesquieu is considered for his analysis of the state in terms of the idea of character and Bodin and Hegel for their substantive theories of civil association.

Oakeshott moves quite freely between describing the course of the development of these ideal characters (in some sense an enquiry into an historical past — not just any past) and giving an interpretation of some notable philosopher's teachings arising from their reflection on this experience. Most of the time Oakeshott is content to move between these two types of enquiry. However, as most commentators have noticed, he clearly slips into the practical mode when he claims, for instance, that the urge to impose on the state the character of a *solidarité commune* "is easily recognised as a relic of servility of which it is proper for European peoples to be profoundly ashamed", and that "no European alive to his inheritance of moral understanding has ever found it possible to deny the superior desirability of civil association without a profound feeling of guilt" (OHC 321).

Leaving aside for the moment the precise modal status that Oakeshott's reading of the past has, he is clearly marking out a topic that he wants to subject to theoretical reflection. Or, to put it in the terms used in *On Human Conduct*, he wants to interrogate the postulates of the ideal character civil association. I do not want to say a great deal here about what he describes in the early part of this work as theoretical understanding and how the modal theory is reworked in terms of the idea of idioms of understanding which exist within the two categorically distinct orders of explanation (practice and process). This has been well said elsewhere[41] and the detail of it is not central to my concerns.

There are nevertheless a few general points that can be made here that will take us back to Oakeshott's Hobbes. The first point to make is that what we might call Oakeshott's meta-theoretical task in *On Human Conduct* is a much more modest project than his earlier reflections on the philosophical enterprise and this stems from the subject matter that Oakeshott is reflecting on. Oakeshott suggests in the preface to this work that "the engagement to understand the Civil Condition in terms of its postulates" is the "central concern" of the book and what he says about theoretical understanding and what it is to theorize human conduct in the first chapter is "a consideration of some of the terms and presuppositions of that engagement" (OHC, vii).

---

[41] For a recent careful and comprehensive treatment see Terry Nardin's *The Philosophy of Michael Oakeshott* (University Park PA: Pennsylvania State Press, 2001), ch 3.

To reiterate, what Oakeshott is reflecting on is the ideal character civil association whose features have been abstracted from an historical experience. So the task of the theorist of civil association is not to try to build a bridge between politics and the "whole world of ideas that belongs to a civilization", it is rather to examine the postulates of a contingent historical identity.[42] But it is not only the theorist of civil association whose task is so circumscribed. So too is that of the theorist of human conduct. Unlike the philosopher, the theorist of human conduct is one who is "self-consciously conditional" and who recognizes that "nothing will come of questioning everything at the same time". He deliberately focuses his attention on one particular aspect of experience and seeks to understand it in terms of its postulates. The postulates themselves are left uncriticized. The theorist of moral conduct or civil association must "forswear metaphysics" if he is to elicit convincing theorems from these particular 'goings-on'. Though the theoretical enterprise is potentially endless, the theorist of human conduct or civil association has to know how to refrain from asking certain kinds of questions — those that will too rapidly take him to his 'heavenly home' (OHC 25)

In *On Human Conduct* Oakeshott seems to have worked out a place for theoretical activities such as political (or civil — given Oakeshott's highly circumscribed conception of politics in *On Human Conduct*)[43] philosophy and ethics different from that developed in *Experience and Its Modes* and the subsequent pre and post war period. The theorist of human conduct or civil association engages in a legitimate, if qualified, activity. He is not a pseudo-philosopher who explores an indeterminate arrest in experience, but a "self-consciously conditional theorist". However, he is distinguished from the political philosopher of the middle period by his concern to "forswear metaphysics". He is aware that the theoretical engagement, if left to follow its own course, would eventually seek to grasp the whole of experience and moral conduct and civil association would recede from view. To invoke a metaphor he uses in an earlier essay,[44] in *On Human Conduct* Oakeshott is content to attach himself to one level of the tower and elucidate the theorems of moral conduct and civil association as they appear from this vantage

---

[42] As Nardin notes (*The Philosophy of Michael Oakeshott*, p30n15), the notion of an ideal character is reminiscent of Weber's ideal types and indeed it has much the same provenance — the nineteenth century concern to describe the nature of an historical identity or historical individual.

[43] For a discussion of this see Glenn Worthington, "Oakeshott's Claims of Politics," *Political Studies*, 45 (1997) 727–38.

[44] The tower metaphor is used in "Political Philosophy" (1946–50?), in *Religion, Politics and the Moral Life*.

point. Further, though he is aware of both the world of practice and the whole world of a civilization — ie. eternity — his concern is not to reunite these two worlds but to leave them distinct and explore the terrain of the former on its own terms.

I think this more circumscribed conception of theory has a great deal to do with what might, with only some exaggeration, be termed the 'historical turn' in Oakeshott's political thought. This is not for a minute to suggest that Oakeshott became in any meaningful sense an historicist. He consistently maintained that historical understanding was just one form of human understanding among many. He never sought, like Croce or Collingwood, to effect a translation of all knowledge into a kind of historical understanding. And though in *On Human Conduct*, for instance, Oakeshott is theorizing an historical experience this is not to be confused with history as a mode or idiom of human understanding.

The other point to make here is that there was never any particular moment in Oakeshott's intellectual career when this form of historical understanding could be said to have supplanted his other concerns in the way, say, that Aubrey claims Hobbes was set on the path to developing a new science of politics by 'discovering' Euclidean geometry. Oakeshott was always interested in both history as a form of human understanding, as well as constructing his own reading of the past. But he was clearly wanting to do certain things with the past that went beyond what he himself understood by an historical interest in the past.

One of the criticisms that is often made about Oakeshott's writings on the philosophy of history is that — despite his claim that he is simply thinking philosophically about what historians actually do when they are doing history — they are so prescriptive and disallow so many of the sorts of judgments historians routinely make about the past that they seem to make historical understanding an unachievable aim.[45] In some ways almost the opposite could be said of Oakeshott's early formulation of philosophy (and subsequently political philosophy) in the sense that it left so much unsaid about what philosophers philosophize about. What Oakeshott seemed to be doing in constructing his civil philosophy was at once freeing up the strictures he elsewhere places on 'the activity of being an historian' and, at the

---

[45]   For an example of this kind of criticism see Gertrude Himmelfarb's essay 'Does History Talk Sense?', in *The New History and the Old* (Cambridge MA and London: Harvard University Press, 1987) originally published in *The American Scholar*, Summer 1976.

same time bringing down from the heavens, the activity of the philosopher/theorist.

As mentioned previously, Oakeshott's interpretation of Hobbes undergoes alterations in the light of all this. Whereas in the introduction to *Leviathan* Hobbes is said to have been the foremost representative of the *philosophical* tradition of 'will and artifice', in the "Moral Life" he is said to have philosophically systematized an *historical* idiom of moral experience — "the morality of individuality". Here Oakeshott says that for Hobbes to have done other than reflect on this experience, to reflect, say on "the morality of communal ties or the morality of the common good would have been an anachronism" (RP 298). While the concept of anachronism has meaning in a historical understanding of the past it has no relevance in a past that is conceived philosophically where "past and present are comparatively insignificant" (CPJ 359). Seen from the philosophical perspective, Plato, Hobbes and Hegel for all intents and purposes can be considered contemporaries.

This philosophical view of the past clearly recedes in Oakeshott's later writings and is replaced by a conception of the past, closer, but not identical, to history and serviceable for philosophical or theoretical reflection. By the time Oakeshott works out his civil philosophy in a thoroughgoing manner he has a clearly demarcated field of inquiry located in history. It is not insignificant that the epigraph to the chapter on the Civil Condition in *On Human Conduct* comes from that great statement of the precedence of historical understanding, namely, Vico's *La scienza nuova*:

> In the night of thick darkness enveloping ancient times there shines the eternal never-failing truth beyond all doubt: that the civil condition is certainly a human invention and that its principles are therefore those of human intelligences.[46]

Though for Vico, unlike Hobbes, history is the pre-eminent form of human knowledge, the reasoning underlying this claim is precisely that made by Hobbes about his own civil science based on geometry — we know it is secure knowledge because we ourselves have made it.

---

[46] I have used Oakeshott's quotation of this text cited on p. 108 of *On Human Conduct*. It comes from section 331 of Vico's *New Science*. Vico immediately goes on in this passage to argue that philosophers for too long have sought to understand what is ultimately unknowable — nature — and should turn their attention to those things that can be known — such as the civil world — because they are the product of human intelligence.

Since nature is God's handiwork we can never know it in the way we know the artifacts of our own intelligence.[47]

Vico is often credited with inaugurating a new age of historical consciousness that finds something of an apotheosis in Hegel. And Hegel, as will be seen more fully in the following chapter, saw in Hobbes's writings a great breakthrough in the development of modern subjectivity. No doubt, it was a theory of the subject that was inadequate, but Hegel gives Hobbes a crucial place in his history of mind. We have seen that Oakeshott also wants to find an appropriate context for understanding Hobbes and the contexts he chooses are both philosophical and historical. The shift from the former to the latter clearly mirrors developments in Oakeshott's own theory itself. Though he rejects a teleological conception of history, Oakeshott's various interpretations of the past, no less than Hegel's, form an integral part of his own political theory.

VII

Earlier in the chapter it was suggested that one of the factors uniting Oakeshott's view of philosophy with his reading of Hobbes is the idea that philosophy departs from commonsense concepts. For Oakeshott, the implication of this is decidedly conservative. Philosophy is a different level of knowledge from that with which the practitioner works and so has no contribution to make to the world of practice. In his writings which reflect on the activity of philosophy/theory, Oakeshott is insistent that there is an unbridgeable gap between philosophy or theory and practice. In *On Human Conduct*, for instance, he suggests that the theorist betrays his calling when he attempts to apply in practice the theorems generated at the theoretical level of understanding. He becomes a theoretician if he thinks that theorizing is concerned with turning theorems into principles that can be applied in conduct. Oakeshott's disdain for the theoretician is unreserved. He is 'offensive', a deplorable character with no respectable occupation, "a fraudulent tutor", and he issues counterfeit certificates (OHC 25–6). Many of these

---

[47] The classic study of this connection is Arthur Henry Child, *Making and Knowing in Hobbes, Vico, and Dewey* (Berkeley: University of California Press, 1953). There are also some illuminating pages on this in Arendt's *The Human Condition* (p. 294ff.) in the context of the rise of *homo faber*. Arendt in fact points out that it was only relatively late in Vico's career (with the publication of the *New Science*) that he advocates history as the proper study of mankind. In an earlier work (*De nostri temporis studiorum ratione*) he had advocated a study of the new moral and political sciences based on geometry. His reasoning was the same as he would subsequently apply to history — because it is a science of our own making we can be sure of it (see *The Human Condition*, pp. 283, n. 298).

criticisms are consistent with Oakeshott's depiction of the Rationalist who seeks to replace the practical knowledge acquired through experience with the sort of technical knowledge that can be learnt apart from the activity it seeks, misguidedly, to master.

We need to ask, however, if this is Hobbes's understanding of his own philosophy, and if not, what this signifies about Oakeshott's reading. As will be seen in chapter 5, Oakeshott condemns Bacon as one of the pre-eminent theoreticians of the enterprise state. Bacon was a theoretician and not a theorist because he sought to make his intellectual system serve utilitarian ends. This ultimately stemmed from his failure to distinguish between a theory of knowledge and the world itself (epistemology and ontology). It may be true that, in this regard, Bacon missed what Hobbes saw and that Oakeshott is right to resist their identification. But Hobbes clearly understood his philosophy to be of utilitarian value. To choose just one example of this, at the conclusion to the second book of *Leviathan*, Hobbes (after an allusion to Plato's desire to see philosophy and rulership merge)[48] expressed the "hope, that one time or other, this writing of mine may fall into the hands of a sovereign, who will consider it himself, . . . without the help of any interested, or envious interpreter; and by the exercise of entire sovereignty, in protecting the public teaching of it, convert this truth of speculation, into the utility of practice" (Lev. 241).

It may be, as Seifert has suggested[49] that the failure of Oakeshott to acknowledge the utilitarian message of Hobbes's philosophy arises from Oakeshott's equation of civil with natural philosophy. That is: the subject of natural philosophy, nature, because it is the artifice of God, cannot be known by man. It is hypothetical knowledge, dealing in conjectures and probabilities. However, by constructing a civil science based on the demonstrable methods of geometry, the hypothetical nature of physics, the most fundamental branch of natural philosophy, is superseded, enabling man to imitate the creative power of God. And for Hobbes, God is first and foremost a being of power.[50]

---

[48] Oakeshott also refers to Plato in the course of a discussion about the proper relation between theory and practice. But Oakeshott wants to defend the 'cave dwellers' from the pretensions of the philosopher who thinks he can return to the cave and replace their knowledge with a set of theorems that belong to an entirely different world of understanding (see OHC, 27–31)

[49] See note 10 above.

[50] See Seifert, "Text and Context", p. 180. For further discussion of Hobbes's separation of natural and civil philosophy see, for instance, Ball "Hobbes's linguistic turn", and Tom Sorell, "The Science in Hobbes's Politics", in *Perspectives on Thomas Hobbes*, G.A. Rogers and Alan Ryan eds. (Oxford: Clarendon Press, 1988).

On Seifert's reading, man is able to imitate God and bring into being that which was not because he is in the possession of knowledge which, though conditional, is demonstrative — not hypothetical. And as John Dewey put it,

> (t)he end or object of science is power, control, for if we know the generation or cause of things, we have it in our power to determine them. The question of the scientific character of morals and politics is, then, a question of the possibility of enduring social security and safety — "peace".[51]

On this reading Hobbes may in fact exhibit more of the character of the theoretician than Oakeshott allows.[52] Indeed, as Ted Miller has recently argued,[53] Hobbes's point in distinguishing science from prudence was largely to demonstrate its superiority in guiding practice. Science gives us a degree of control over the world that mere prudence can never match. For the present I do not want to do more than point to this difficulty in Oakeshott's reading of Hobbes. It is, however, worth keeping in mind as Oakeshott consistently maintains that philosophy has no part to play in the guidance of practice. Oakeshott's silence over this feature of Hobbes's thought may be as important in his project of appropriating the latter to his own views as his explicit verdicts. In other words, his assimilation of Hobbes's view of philosophy to his own may be as much by omission as by commission.

VIII

If we return to the point where this chapter began it is possible to conclude that Oakeshott's later modal impurity is actually a result of his attempt to conduct a philosophical or theoretical enquiry on politics which was only possible by revising the meticulously crafted account of experience presented in *Experience and Its Modes*. To say

---

[51] "The Motivation of Hobbes's Political Philosophy", in Schneider and Waldman, *Thomas Hobbes in his Time*, (Minneapolis, 1974), p22, cited in Seifert, "Text and Context", p. 179.

[52] See also the first chapter of *De Corpore* where Hobbes, in the manner of Oakeshott's theoretician, asserts that "(t)he end of knowledge is power; and the use of theorems (which, among geometricians, serve for the finding out of properties) is for the construction of problems; and, lastly, the scope of all speculation is the performing of some action, or thing to be done". More specifically, "the utility of moral and civil philosophy is to be estimated, not so much by the commodities we have by knowing these sciences, as by the calamities we receive from not knowing them. [ie. civil war, which arises from] . . . there being but few in the world that have learned those duties which unite and keep men in peace, that is to say, that have learned the rules of civil life sufficiently. Now, the knowledge of these rules is civil philosophy" (*English Works*, Vol. 1, pp. 7–8).

[53] 'Oakeshott's Hobbes and the Fear of Political Rationalism', esp. 813–6.

that philosophical experience is simply experience purged of abstraction and conditionality is to leave unanswered the question, 'What, if anything, can philosophy say anything meaningful about?' Despite his claim in *Experience and Its Modes* that philosophy is experience at its most complete, satisfactory level, because it is distinct from all the other worlds of experience it can say nothing to any of them without committing *ignoratio elenchi*. It is a skeleton in need of a body. His subsequent account of the nature of political philosophy and his substantive theoretical account of civil association and its history, developed in his interpretation of Hobbes and worked out most fully in *On Human Conduct* provides the flesh which gives the body its distinctive shape. I will more fully discuss these issues in the conclusion to this work. At this point it is sufficient to be cognizant of some of the difficulties raised for Oakeshott's depiction of modality by his substantive forays into political theory.

Chapter 2

Will, Agency, Individuality

The 'private individual' is an institution of the greatest value; the philosopher's business is to discern the nature of his individuality.[1]

Human individuality is an historical emergence, as 'artificial' and as 'natural' as the landscape. In modern Europe this emergence was gradual, and the specific character of the individual who emerged was determined by the manner of his generation . . . The emergence of this disposition to be an individual is the pre-eminent event in modern European history.[2]

I

Of all the points which set the philosophical Idealists against Hobbes and the individualist tradition that he is said to have inspired, none was more stark than the issue of human subjectivity. To the extent that Idealism in Britain was a moral and religious movement it rejected the conception of the individual as a utility-maximizing creature underlying both the new science of political economy and the moral philosophy of utilitarianism. It was generally held that Hobbes's apparent psychological egoism helped lay the groundwork for these intellectual movements. During the nineteenth century there was, in fact, a fairly stable consensus on this aspect of Hobbes's thought and the link was made between him and the utilitarians as well as those who were engaged, more generally, in the attempt to build a science of society and politics from first principles.[3] In lining themselves up against these developments the Idealists implicitly distanced themselves from

[1]   Oakeshott (1949), review J.D. Mabbott, *The State and the Citizen*
[2]   Oakeshott (1961), 'The Masses in Representative Democracy'
[3]   For a discussion of the utilitarians and their fellow travelers, the sovereignty theorists, see Mark Francis, 'The Nineteenth Century Theory of Sovereignty

Hobbes. However, as will be seen shortly, it wasn't simply that all the Idealists rejected Hobbes's theory outright. The claim that they tended make was that he had developed a one-sided account of the human subject and that his reduction of the will to appetite needed to be transcended in a theory of the true or rational will. To some extent Oakeshott shared this estimation of Hobbes, but his reasons for rejecting Hobbes's theory of volition were not quite the same as other Idealists and, moreover, Oakeshott subsequently came to regard Hobbes's individualism as a strength rather than a weakness of his theory.

In this chapter I will take up and extend some of the themes developed in the last in order to elucidate Oakeshott's theory of agency. It has been noted previously that Oakeshott understood Hobbes's moral and political philosophy primarily in terms of his theory of knowledge. Likewise, Oakeshott's theory of knowledge is not peripheral to his theory of agency, but is largely derived from it. As he constantly returns to the nature of understanding throughout his career, Oakeshott also at various stages attempts to elucidate the nature of human agency from a philosophical or theoretical perspective.

I will therefore trace Oakeshott's formulation of the will from the early period, prior to the second world war, through the immediate postwar years, to the final period where he offers his most extensive treatment of the topic in *On Human Conduct*. We will find that though certain consistent themes emerge and no radical break is made from one formulation to the next, the theory shifts in significant, though often subtle, ways. I endorse Robert Orr's observation that, "we are inquiring, not into possibilities of stark consistency and inconsistency, but into eddies and drifts discernible in one composite picture that might not be discernible in the other".[4]

This account of the development of Oakeshott's theory of agency will, of course, be carried out in conjunction with his reading of Hobbes, focusing on the way in which the early criticisms of Hobbes's theory of volition give way to a theory of moral individuality that closely parallels Oakeshott's own theory. These two con-

and Thomas Hobbes', *History of Political Thought*, vol. 1 no. 3, Autumn (1980), 517–40.

[4]   "A Double Agent in the Dream of Michael Oakeshott", *The Political Science Reviewer*, Spring 1992, 44–62, at p. 50. I am sympathetic with Orr's treatment of the body of Oakeshott's work — especially the classification into distinct phases. However I disagree that in discussing his conception of agency the early (pre "Rationalism in Politics") account can be easily set aside because it is concerned with a theory of knowledge, not action, as Orr suggests (see p. 50). For the reasons outlined above, and as will become clearer as the chapter proceeds, Oakeshott's theory of knowledge is central to his theory of agency.

cerns — Oakeshott's account of human agency and the will, and his reading of Hobbes on this — will be examined in tandem throughout this chapter.

II

Towards the end of his extensive 1937 review of Leo Strauss's *The Political Philosophy of Hobbes* Oakeshott argued that,

> although Hobbes set an example followed in one way or another by almost every later political thinker of starting with will instead of law, he never had a satisfactory or coherent theory of volition, and the whole Epicurean tradition to which he belonged did not bear fruit until this lack was remedied, and the remedy was, in fact, the union of a reconstituted natural law theory with Hobbes's Epicurean theory — a union indicated in such phrases as Rousseau's 'General Will', Hegel's 'Rational Will' and Bosanquet's 'Real Will'. The most profound movement in modern political philosophy is, as I see it, a revivification of the Stoic natural law theory achieved by the grafting upon it an Epicurean theory; it springs from the union of the two great traditions of political philosophy inherited by Western Europe from the ancient world. (HCA 147, 8)

From the perspective of the recently arrived 'Rational Will' tradition Oakeshott makes the judgment that Hobbes's theory of volition is incoherent as it stands. It is necessary however, to determine the precise reasons for this judgment since they are not exactly those offered by other philosophical Idealists.

In his *Lectures on the History of Philosophy* Hegel set the tone for subsequent Idealist readings where he clearly identifies Hobbes, and other English philosophers such as Bacon and Locke, with the hedonistic tradition of Western thought stretching back to the Roman Epicureans and the Greek Cyrenaics.[5] For Hegel, the Hobbesian state of nature is a condition "like that of the animals — a condition in which there is an unsubdued individual will."[6] Despite this we find in the *History of Philosophy* a reading of Hobbes sympathetic to Hegel's account of the emergence of modern subjectivity. In contrast to the prevailing view that authority, whether in the form of Holy Scripture or positive law, is external, an ideal set before the individual, Hobbes, according to Hegel, "sought to derive the bond which holds the state together, that which gives the state its power, from principles which lie within us, which we

---

[5] For a good discussion of Hegel's critique of hedonism see Judith Shklar, *Freedom and Independence: The Political Ideas of Hegel's Phenomenology of Mind* (Cambridge: Cambridge University Press, 1976), pp. 102–5.

[6] *Lectures on the History of Philosophy* (Routledge and Kegan Paul, 1896), trans. E.S. Haldane and F.H. Simpson, Vol. 3, p. 317.

recognize as our own."[7] He is also said to have derived the principles of monarchical power from universal determinations,[8] and to have recognised that the natural state where individual wills are pitted against one another is "not what it should be, and must hence be cast off."[9] Nevertheless, on Hegel's reading, Hobbes's identification of the will with appetite ultimately renders his theory defective. For Hegel the self only achieves true freedom when arbitrary willing is superseded — that is, when the will chooses its ends in a rational or intelligent manner; when the universal is chosen over mere subjective preference. Only here does the content and the form of the will coincide, since, "when I will what is rational, then I am acting not as a particular individual but in accordance with the concepts of ethics in general. In an ethical action, what I vindicate is not myself but the thing."[10] In other words, the completely indeterminate subjective side of the will which "has an infinite aspect in virtue of its form"[11] is connected with the determinate content of the will, that is, the external act of the will which is chosen in accordance with the concrete universal and in so choosing the will realizes its potential. Hegel has claimed to have restored the proper place of Reason in the formation of the free will, though at a fundamentally new level to that which Hobbes's chief target, the scholastics, had drawn it.

The dominant, if not exclusive, reading of Hobbes by Idealist philosophers, following Hegel, centered on the claim that he was perhaps the seminal figure in the history of modern hedonist thought. Conscience, rationality and the moral ties that bind individuals together, so the argument runs, are mere chimera and are reduced by Hobbes to mere animal appetite. From Coleridge[12] to Collingwood philosophical Idealists placed Hobbes at the centre of the modern hedonistic theory of human motivation. On T.H. Green's reading, for instance, feeling is said to be the exhaustive mode of consciousness, and reflection its mere servant. "'Conscience,' the rational will, and the actual fabric of moral custom and law", can all be explained in terms of feeling. According to Green, feeling forms the basis of all the

---

[7]   *Ibid.*, p. 316
[8]   *Ibid.*, p. 317.
[9]   *Ibid.*, p. 318.
[10]   *Philosophy of Right* (Oxford: Clarendon Press, 1952), trans T.M.Knox, p. 230, addition to Par 15.
[11]   *Ibid.*
[12]   For Coleridge's discussion of Hobbes see, for example, *Biographia Literaria*, ch. 5, in *The Collected Works* (Routledge and Kegan Paul — UK, Princeton University Press, US, 1983), Kathleen Coburn and Bart Winer (eds.), Vol. 7, No. I, 91ff, *Table Talk*, in *ibid.*, Vol. 14, No. II, Carl Woodring (ed.), 1990, Appendix H, par 325, p. 145, *The Friend*, in *ibid.*, Vol. 4, No. 1, Barbara E Rooke (ed), 1969, p. 32, 166ff.

dominant ethical theories from Hobbes down, though with him we get a most stark and uncompromising formulation:

> With Hobbes, the feeling on which morality rests is the mere animal appetite, the sense of want, with the impulse to appropriate that which will satisfy the want. This appetite, however, has to lose its merely animal character before it will account even for the state of universal warfare in which, according to Hobbes, society begins. '*Homo homini lupus,*' but the wolf eats when he is hungry, and has done with it.[13]

Base appetite, supplemented with the capacity to calculate in instrumentalist terms offers an explanation for the origin of positive law and "of the judgment 'I ought'", which, Green argues, "Hobbes finds simply in the command of a ruler". The ruler is none but "the appetite of some one strong enough to enforce its satisfaction, in submission to which the appetites of others gain more than they lose". Further, "appetite, transformed (it is not explained how) into deliberate self-interest, is thus the source at once of the idea of duty, and of the 'moral sentiments,' or the affections which dispose us to realise the idea."[14]

Rather than completely rejecting Hobbes's theory, writers such as Hegel, Green and Collingwood[15] saw in hedonism a necessary if insufficient explanation of volition. Equally inadequate is the account of morality which separates moral reasoning from the phenomenal world of action in the manner of Kant or, indeed, any account which holds moral qualities to be radically separated from the human agent. According to post-Kantian Idealist thought the deficiencies of these respective moral theories are only superseded where the individual actively identifies his will with the complex of community life where Reason is said to reside. As Oakeshott suggests, this is indicated in Rousseau's General Will, Hegel's Rational Will, Bosanquet's Real Will, but also, we may add, in Bradley's notion of "My Station and Its Duties",[16] and Collingwood's attempt to discover an encompassing theory of mind.[17]

Though Oakeshott claimed Idealist thinkers such as Hegel and Bosanquet had made significant advances on Hobbes on the question, and though, as will be seen, he clearly draws on a similar reservoir of resources, the actual place of freedom in Oakeshott's topography of

---

[13]   Green, *Works* (London: Longmans, 1885–8), ed. Nettleship, Vol. 3, pp. 97–8.
[14]   *Ibid.*
[15]   For Collingwood's reading of Hobbes, see David Boucher, *The Social and Political Thought of R.G.Collingwood* (Cambridge: Cambridge University Press, 1989), pp. 71–80.
[16]   *Ethical Studies* (Oxford University Press, 1927).
[17]   See especially *The New Leviathan* (Oxford: Clarendon Press, 1942).

human experience is, with the possible exception of Bradley, quite unlike that given by earlier Idealists. For Oakeshott, it is meaningless to talk about freedom in any mode other than practice: "Freedom I take it, is a practical idea, an idea which has relevance in the practical world of activity and nowhere else" (EM 267n). Since practice is an arrested mode, and therefore makes no contribution to what is ultimately satisfactory in experience, everything constituting practical experience, everything that makes it a world, including freedom, from the absolute standpoint of philosophy is shown to be entirely contingent. Unlike Hegel, Bosanquet, and Green who made human freedom central to their entire metaphysical systems, Oakeshott claims that it is not a necessary aspect of experience, but a mere postulate of an arrest in experience. Practical truth and freedom are inseparable: "wherever the one is, the other will be found also" (EM 268n). From Oakeshott's viewpoint these thinkers are guilty of an *ignoratio elenchi*, of illegitimately transposing the criterion of truth in one mode to experience as a whole.[18]

Moreover, because Oakeshott had a different reading of Hobbes's theory of volition he had a different estimation of what made it inadequate. In his 1935 review essay on contemporary Hobbes literature Oakeshott makes the point, in contradistinction to these earlier Idealists, that what is generally taken to be Hobbes's uncompromising view of human selfishness is in fact the logical conclusion of his theory of knowledge and is not the premise of his moral theory.

> His premise is a doctrine of solipsism, a belief in the essential isolation of men from one another, and expounded as a theory of knowledge. This isolation, it is true, is modified by 'the most noble and profitable invention of all other,' speech; but it remains a merely artificial modification. And when this genuine premise of Hobbes's argument is appreciated, the attribution to him of the doctrine of the essential selfishness of man is seen at once to be mistaken. Others have held an egoistic view of human nature, and have based that view upon their observation of human behaviour; but no such argument is to be found in Hobbes. His doctrine is that each man is unavoidably shut up within the world of his sensations; and there is no more meaning in speaking of him as 'selfish' than there is in speaking of anything else that is monadically conceived as selfish — the universe as a whole, or an electron. (TH 275)

Oakeshott also claimed in this essay that "the true nature of Hobbes's individualism has yet to find its expositor, we still have to wait for the interpreter who will show us that this individualism is based, not upon any foundation in moral opinion at all, but upon a theory of knowl-

---

[18]   Noel O'Sullivan, *The Problem of Political Obligation, in Green, Bosanquet and Oakeshott* (New York and London: Garland Press, 1987), p. 108, has a similar discussion on this.

edge, upon a thorough-going nominalism and an almost as extreme solipsism." (TH 272) While it is unclear whether Oakeshott ever saw himself as this interpreter it cannot be doubted that Oakeshott consistently saw Hobbes as nothing other than a towering figure in the history of modern individualism; an individualism arising from the nominalist glasses through which he viewed the world. According to Oakeshott, Hobbes's civil philosophy "is based, not on any vague belief in the value or sanctity of the individual man, but on a philosophy for which the world is composed of *individuae substantiae*." (RP 280)

Since, according to Oakeshott, Hobbes's theory of volition is in fact derived from his theory of knowledge it is reasonable to assert that it was precisely the latter, ie. the radical solipsism and nominalism, which was found wanting. Oakeshott's reasons for claiming Hobbes's theory of volition to be inadequate should be seen in terms of the theory of practical knowledge fully elaborated in *Experience and Its Modes*. In practical life the world is viewed *sub specie voluntatis*, and Oakeshott's theory of the will, consistent with the way he reads Hobbes at this stage, is tied to his understanding of the achievement of practical knowledge. It is from this perspective that Hobbes's theory of volition is said to be inadequate. Oakeshott contends that radical solipsism is capricious because it fails to acknowledge the world it implicates. Mere activity, which is not conditioned by the world of value, or, if it does assert value, recognizes it only as subjective preference, is a vicious abstraction. In light of Oakeshott's account of the nature of practical experience and his nominalist reading of Hobbes it is not difficult to see why at this stage he found Hobbes's theory of volition inadequate.

Specifically, Oakeshott rejects the view, entailed by a nominalist reading of experience, that practice is no more nor less than a collection of mere opinions. Whether they be "personal or social estimates of value" defenders of this position deny that such opinions can ever constitute a world of moral or practical knowledge. In *Experience and Its Modes* Oakeshott described this position in the following way:

> Nothing, it is said, is more frequent than a difference of opinion on these questions of moral value: what one judges to be good, another considers bad; what one believes to be right, another thinks wrong; what one holds to be admirable, another finds despicable. The most elementary lesson of life is the necessity of recognizing these irreducible differences; a life passed in an attempt to reconcile them would indeed be febrile and fruitless. And what is true of moral judgments is true, no less, of all practical judgements whatever; they belong to no world and recognize no criterion of coherence. (EM 254)

There is perhaps no more intrepid enunciator of this position than Hobbes himself. One reference will suffice:

> But whatsoever is the object of any mans Appetite or Desire; that is it, which he for his part calleth *Good*; And the object of his Hate, and Aversion, *Evill*; And of his Contempt, *Vile* and *Inconsiderable*. For these words of Good, Evill, and Contemptible, are ever used with relation to the person that useth them: There being nothing simply and absolutely so; nor any common Rule of Good and Evill, to be taken from the nature of the objects themselves; but from the Person of the man (where there is no Common-wealth;) or, (in a Commonwealth,) from the Person that representeth it.(Lev. 32)

Though the solipsistic predicament of man in Hobbes's world may be susceptible of qualification via the artificial contrivance of language, its fundamental nature is, according to Oakeshott, not open to change. Even allowing for the mitigating effects of language (or other artificial institutions such as the Sovereign) on man's predicament, judgments of value, according to Hobbes, are only ever "used with relation to the person that useth them". The judgments of the mind are not corrigible according to the arrangements of objects in the world since world (or object) is invariably other than mind (subject). There is an intimate relation between Hobbes's uncompromising scepticism and his theory of human volition. Man can be considered a willful being precisely because knowledge of the world is inaccessible to him. As Leo Strauss suggested, he "can be sovereign only because there is no cosmic support for his humanity . . . only because he is absolutely a stranger in the universe".[19]

Though Oakeshott's world of practice is also a world of human artifice, according to the view asserted in *Experience and Its Modes* it is possible to infer that Oakeshott found Hobbes's position inadequate because judgments of value according to the latter never rise above the level of mere opinion to the world of practical knowledge. Such a view, says Oakeshott, "is open to a fatal objection". For,

> (i)f anything were a matter of *mere* opinion there could be no difference of opinion. It belongs to the character of a mere opinion that it can never be contradicted: in the region of mere opinions, what one asserts the other never denies. Yet not only does this view of practical experience assert the possibility of a difference of opinion, but it is obliged to assert it. A 'mere opinion', in this sense, must fall outside possible experience. Everywhere there is the possibility of contradictory opinions, and where these are possible we have left behind a collection of mere opinions and have, at least, entered a world of opinions. (EM 254)

[19] *Natural Right and History*, p. 175.

To deny the proposition that opinions constitute knowledge, however rudimentary, is to deny that opinion is a component of experience, since, according to Oakeshott, all opinions make some implicit assertion of reality (EM 255).

An integral component of Oakeshott's world of practice is the concept of valuation, since practice involves the transformation of 'what is' into 'what ought to be'. Values are neither 'objective' nor 'subjective' in the way that these terms are usually understood. The world of value is not a world external to the practical world (as a traditional natural law theory might have it). Values do not lie beyond the mind awaiting discovery. But neither are ideas 'subjective' in the sense that they are simply products of the mind projected onto a 'real' world which is wholly other than mind.[20] Subjectivity, according to Oakeshott, is only an aspect of judgment, not its sufficient condition. "All judgments of value demand to be universally recognized". If everything were a matter of mere opinion or mere preference then there could be no judgments of value, since

> the question whether or not a man was correct in asserting something to be valuable would resolve into the question whether or not he had correctly assessed his condition of mind. And a dispute about judgments of value would be not only futile, but meaningless and impossible (EM 276).

Oakeshott's rejection of Hobbes's theory of volition arises, not from a hedonistic reading of Hobbes's theory, but from Hobbes's inadequate depiction of the nature of practical experience. Seen from the perspective of the argument of *Experience and Its Modes*, Hobbes's understanding of experience would seem to be nothing but a set of random, chaotic, unmediated encounters with an external world, incapable of generating true knowledge. This of course is wholly at odds with Oakeshott's contention that every experience implies a world of coherent, integrated ideas. Practical knowledge, as is the case with the worlds of history and science, is only possible because each so called 'fact' implicates, and can only exist in relation to, such a world of ideas. Clearly, the theory of volition constructed in *Experience and Its Modes* draws on ideas common to earlier Hegelian theories. Moreover, despite his subtle, but significant, divergence from other Hegelian

---

[20] Though Oakeshott develops a fact/value distinction of sorts (ie. the distinction between the world of 'what is' and the world of 'what ought to be') he completely rejects the Weberian version of this which underlies some recent 'subjectivist' or 'emotivist' ethical theories. See, for instance, J. Mackie's *Ethics* (Harmondsworth: Penguin, 1977).

readings of Hobbes's understanding of the will,[21] Oakeshott's own theory of volition nevertheless reflects the judgment common amongst these writers concerning the inadequacy of Hobbes's account.

In the introduction to *Leviathan* Oakeshott reiterates the argument that Hobbes's individualism does not arise from a conviction that human beings are essentially egoistic beings; rather, it springs from the nominalist philosophy of late medieval scholasticism, "with its doctrines that the reality of a thing is its individuality, that which makes it *this* thing, and that both in God and man will is precedent to reason". Accordingly, "his civil philosophy is based, not on any vague belief in the value or sanctity of the individual man, but on a philosophy for which the world is composed of *individuae substantiae*" (Intro lv [RP 280]). The predicament of man in the state of nature is a consequence of his being "by nature, the victim of solipsism; he is an *individua substantia* distinguished by incommunicability" (Intro liv [RP279]). All his relationships with other individuals are purely external: "Individuals may be collected together, may be added, may be substituted for one another, but can never modify one another or compose a whole in which their individuality is lost . . . Neither before nor after the establishment of civil society is there any such thing as the *People*, to whom so much previous theory ascribed Sovereignty" (Intro lv–lvi [RP 280-1).

---

[21] Oakeshott's departure from the traditional reading of Hobbes on this seems to lie in the different emphasis Oakeshott gives to the intellectual tradition that Hobbes is said to belong to. It is significant that Oakeshott reads this particular tradition in terms of the master conceptions 'Will and Artifice' and not, as his predecessors had done, in terms of ideas such as hedonism/egoism. To the tradition that Oakeshott recounts "Epicurus was an inspiration rather than a guide" and though it was nourished by Roman law, the "politico-theological ideas of Judaism," and Augustine it was reinvigorated from the fourteenth to the seventeenth centuries in the ideas of late scholastic nominalism (Intro, p. liii). On Oakeshott's reading Hobbes's closest intellectual affinities are to Duns Scotus, Ockham and the theologians of the fifteenth and sixteenth centuries who grappled with problems arising from the new found status of the individual, rather than to Epicurus, Machiavelli (contra both Collingwood and Strauss), and subsequently, Bentham and the utilitarians. Accordingly, Oakeshott places less significance (and certainly no *moral* significance) on Hobbes's equation of will and appetite [*Leviathan*, ch. 6, p. 38, *De Homine*, XI, 2, in *Man and Citizen*, Bernard Gert (ed), (New York: Anchor Books, 1972), pp. 63,4] than other writers since, according to Oakeshott, what many have regarded as egoism in Hobbes's theory of man "turns out to be neither moral nor a defect; it is only the individuality of a creature shut up, without hope of immediate release, within the world of his own imagination" (Intro, p. liv).

III

The general lines of Oakeshott's early reading of Hobbes's individualism are now quite clear. Hobbes is perhaps the foremost exponent of the tradition of political thought that takes its bearings from the concepts of will and artifice. These two concepts in Hobbes's thought are intimately connected. Human beings are radically volitional creatures precisely because they create and impose intelligibility, order and authority on an otherwise chaotic, confused universe. More than any other writer, Oakeshott says, Hobbes is responsible for passing on the doctrine of individualism of late scholastic nominalism to the modern world (Intro lv [RP 280]). However, the inadequacies of this tradition of political thought are only overcome (at least according to its followers) in the tradition which takes as its master conception Rational Will.

What emerges from Oakeshott's categorization of the history of political philosophy into three distinct traditions is that Oakeshott, by identifying himself with the Rational Will tradition, still finds problems with Hobbes's theory of volition. Indeed, at much the same time as he makes these observations about Hobbes he criticizes J.D.Mabbott's book, *The State and the Citizen*, for taking an atomistic form: "Each self is what it is, and not another thing. Its relations with other selves may determine what it does, but not what it is". As Oakeshott reminds us, this may be a fact of practical experience (this, of course, was also the claim he made in *Experience and Its Modes*), but it does not tell us much about the nature of the individual, who he is and where he comes from. "The 'private individual'", Oakeshott tells us,

> is an institution, a social, indeed for the most part a legal, creation, whose desires, emotions, ideas, intelligence, are social in their constitution. Nothing, I take it, is more certain than that this individual would collapse, like a body placed in a vacuum, if he were removed from the 'external' social world which is the condition of his existence.

The philosopher (unlike the practitioner) cannot rest content with the claim that the individual is simply that which is separate and unique, rather, his "business is to discern the nature of his individuality."[22] The entire body of Oakeshott's work at this time — as he develops his critique of rationalism and positive account of the idea of tradition — reinforces the claim that the individual is a thoroughly social being. Based on these claims it appears that Hobbes's radical individualism as a theory of agency is still clearly inadequate to the needs of contemporary political philosophy. The radical, solipsistic individualism of Hobbes stands in need of qualification, and Oakeshott's development of the

---

[22] Review J.D. Mabbott, *The State and the Citizen*, *Mind* 58 (1949), 378–89, at 386–7.

idea of tradition, subsequently explored in terms of the idea of a practice, extends the diagnosis of post-Hobbesian philosophers such as
Hume, Burke, and Maine, and provides the ground for a more comprehensive theory of individualism than that which Hobbes left behind.

IV

The original introduction to *Leviathan* (1946) is notable for the emphasis
it places on Hobbes's voluntarism, which, according to Oakeshott,
arises not from a moral doctrine about the sanctity of the individual,
but from a radical nominalism. In this the 1946 introduction is consistent with the 1930s essays on Hobbes. However, in "The Moral Life in
the Writings of Thomas Hobbes" (1962), as indicated by the title,
Oakeshott seeks to uncover the moral doctrine he sees at the heart of
Hobbes's theory. This is a significant change from his 1930s view that
Hobbes's "individualism is based, not upon any foundation in moral
opinion at all, but upon a theory of knowledge, upon a thorough-going
nominalism and an almost as extreme solipsism" (TH 272,). Rather
than seeing Hobbes's radical individualism as an inadequate theory of
volition Oakeshott comes to regard this as the great virtue of his
thought. Hobbes is the philosopher, *par excellence*, of the morality of
individuality, which, along with the morality of communal ties and the
morality of the common good, constitutes one of the three major idioms
of moral discourse to be found in the last thousand years of European
history (RP 295–298). As we will subsequently see, Oakeshott revised
the introduction to *Leviathan* (1975) in important ways in keeping with
his reading of Hobbes in "The Moral Life" as well as his own later
moral theory.[23]

In "The Moral Life" (1962), Oakeshott deploys the second of his
tripartite schemata in terms of which Hobbes's work can be understood. In this case he identifies three major idioms of moral conduct
existing in the last thousand years of European history. These idioms are not the prescriptions of the moralist, telling us how we
ought to behave, but are interpretations of who in fact we are.[24] The

---

[23] It should also be stressed that since much of the original introduction was carried
into the revised version, Oakeshott's various writings on Hobbes in certain respects
remain unchanged. As with his own philosophy no radical break is ever made with
the past. Nevertheless the new emphasis on the moral aspects of Hobbes's theory
that emerges in this later period — 1960s–70s — is far from insignificant. In the
following chapter I will look much more closely at the changes Oakeshott makes to
his introduction to *Leviathan*.

[24] Here he makes the claim, I think for the first time, that we are what we believe
ourselves to be, as opposed to the view prominent in the immediate post war

distinct idioms he identifies are as follows: the morality of communal ties; the morality of individuality; the morality of the common good.

The conditions necessary for individual choice are absent from the first of these idioms. Here morality appears as ritual rather than rules. "What ought to be done is indistinguishable from what is done; art appears as nature". The undivided unity of the first conception breaks down in the second — the morality of individuality. Here separate selves are recognized as sovereign, independent centers of activity and choice, related to other selves in terms of this individuality, not in terms of a common enterprise: "Morality is the art of mutual accommodation". The third idiom also acknowledges the existence of separate selves, only here individual moral choice is subservient to the claims of the community, which is united in terms of a single, common enterprise. The latter provides the grounds upon which individuals are related. Though "the lion and the ox are distinguished from one another . . . there is a single approved condition of circumstance for both: the lion shall eat straw like the ox". Whenever there is a conflict between the individuality that is here recognized and the claims "of this single approved condition of human circumstance", commonly called the 'good of all', or the 'social good', the former always gives way to the latter (RP 296–7).

For Oakeshott, the moral philosopher does not create his moral theory *de novo*, but takes his precepts from ordinary moral practice and seeks to discover its rational ground. Since western Europe in the seventeenth century saw the flowering of an emerging human character distinguished above all by this feeling for individuality — "the independent, enterprising man out to seek his intellectual or material fortune, and the individual human soul responsible for his own destiny — this unavoidably became for Hobbes, as it was for his contemporary moralists, the subject matter of moral reflection" (RP 298).

Since the "Moral Life" is chiefly concerned with exploring what Oakeshott takes to be Hobbes's theory of moral obligation in contrast to some competing interpretations I will leave substantial discussion of its contents until the next chapter. For now it is sufficient to note that the emphasis in Oakeshott's reading of Hobbes is substantially different from the original introduction to *Leviathan*. This is not to say that there is no discussion of Hobbes's moral theory in the earlier work. Oakeshott consistently rejects the claim that Hobbes's the-

---

essays that we are what we have become. This is a subtle but significant alteration and it prefigures the anti-naturalist view he elaborated in *On Human Conduct*. Orr also makes this observation — though not about this particular instance, see "Double Agent", p. 51.

ory of moral obligation is equivalent to self interest. His theory of obligation is a true *moral* theory since it arises from an act of will. In contrast, "self interest is a rational, not a moral, obligation" (Intro lx).[25] Nor is it the case that Oakeshott comes to regard Hobbes's epistemology as anything like a peripheral aspect of his system. Despite this, the introduction is notable for the manner in which it down plays the moral components of Hobbes's theory in favour of the epistemological and it is only in "The Moral Life" that the moral theory is fully explored.

In "The Masses in Representative Democracy" Oakeshott works out in more detail the history of modern European moral experience that he briefly mentioned in "The Moral Life."[26] Using Burckhardt as his guide, Oakeshott charts the story of modern individuality and the reactions it has provoked from those unequal to its challenges. The vicissitudes of this story are "exceedingly complex", but roughly speaking modern individuality has its origins in the transformation of conditions of life existing in late medieval Europe. Until roughly the twelfth century the individual as such was an unknown character. To quote Burckhardt, "man was conscious of himself only as a member of a race, people, party, family or corporation — only through some general category".[27] Likewise Oakeshott suggests that all activities, as well as rights, decisions and responsibilities, were communal in character: "What differentiated one man from another was insignificant when compared with what was enjoyed in common as members of a group of some sort" (RP 365). This is the morality of communal ties. The modern individual emerged from the break up of these tightly integrated communities of medieval Europe. Beginning in Italy in the twelfth and thirteenth centuries and subsequently gradually spreading throughout the rest of Europe, the individualist disposition transformed all aspects of European life and thought: "it gathered to itself an appropriate understanding of the office of government, it modified political manners and institutions, it settled itself upon art, upon religion, upon industry and trade and upon every kind of human relationship" (RP 367). Importantly it also had its reflection in moral theory where the central problem revolved around the question, How does this self-directed being come to have duties to others of his kind?, and the further task of determining the nature of these duties. According to Oakeshott, this task is

---

[25] These distinctions will be explored in the next chapter.

[26] He calls this 'history' a work of 'historical description'. The exact relation between this and his rather austere understanding of historical inquiry is a matter that must be passed over for the present.

[27] *The Civilization of the Renaissance in Italy*, (Penguin Classics, 1990), trans. S.G.C. Middlemore, p. 98.

paramount in Hobbes, "the first moralist of the modern world to take candid account of the current experience of individuality".

> He understood a man as an organism governed by an impulse to avoid destruction and to maintain itself in its own characteristic and chosen pursuits. Each individual has a natural right to independent existence: the only problem is how he is to pursue his own chosen course with the greatest measure of success, the problem of relations to 'others' of his kind (RP 367)

The same problem presents itself to Spinoza, Kant, indeed most moral theorists of the seventeenth and eighteenth centuries. Human life for these thinkers is *inter homines esse*, and morality is the art of mutual accommodation.[28]

According to Oakeshott's treatment of this story there arose in reaction to the emergent individual a creature of altogether different caste of mind, the 'individual *manqué*'. Unlike the character of the individual, the individual *manqué* was not equal to his fortune. He was afraid of the responsibility that went with this condition and longed for the warmth and security of communal life. Since it was not possible to turn the clock back to a pre-modern era the only way to establish his preferred manner of living was to undermine everything the individual stood for. He was not content that government simply concern itself with ruling, that is, establishing common rules enabling individuals with diverse activities and interests to accommodate themselves to one another, but required it to transform its *modus operandi*. The mass man since he "had feelings rather than thoughts, impulses rather than opinions, inabilities rather than passions", demanded leadership in order that a substantive condition of things be imposed on all regardless of their preference: "the lion shall eat straw like the ox". This is the morality of the common or public good, and it always asserts itself by undermining the morality of individuality:

> 'Self love', which was recognised in the morality of individuality as a legitimate spring of human activity, the morality of the 'anti-individual' pronounced to be evil. But it was to be replaced, not by the love of 'others', or by 'charity' or by 'benevolence' (which would have entailed a relapse into the vocabulary of individuality), but by the love of 'the community' (RP 375).

The morality of individuality and the morality of the common good are the two dominant traditions of moral experience in modern European history and Oakeshott makes no attempt to conceal his preference for the former and contempt for the latter. Interestingly he distances Ratio-

---

[28] See also the early pages of 'The Voice of Poetry' in RP where this 'morality of mutual accommodation' is elaborated further.

nalism, which he tends to equate with liberalism,[29] from the individualist tradition that he explores in essays such as "The Masses". (The link
between Rationalism and anti-individualism will be explored in chapter 5). In the essay "Scientific Politics" Oakeshott suggested that British
parliamentary government (unlike the parliamentary institutions of
America and Continental Europe) had its origins in the Middle Ages,
before the tide of Rationalism spread itself over Europe. Parliamentary
government and the experience of individuality arose prior to their
codification into the ideology of liberalism and Oakeshott argues that
they belong to different traditions.[30]

In these essays Oakeshott's emphasis moves from an account of
agency where the existence of separate selves are a mere postulate of
practical experience to the view that individuality is a precarious,
essentially modern, achievement. That is, he shifts from a philosophical account of individuality to a form of explanation which
Oakeshott presents (in a broad sense) as history. However, his
account of the modern individualist disposition betrays, on his own
understanding of historical explanation, a decidedly non-historical
attitude. A properly historical attitude to the past can only become
operative if moral judgment is left to one side (see RP 178–9). Yet
Oakeshott clearly celebrates and commends as morally superior the
modern individualist disposition and condemns everything that
poses a threat to it. Since it is a historical disposition, and history is
the realm of the contingent, there is no guarantee that it will survive
into the future. It must therefore be fought for in the present and, as
will become clearer in chapter 5, this is Oakeshott's intention in his
construction of this historical schema.

It is finally in *On Human Conduct* that Oakeshott gives a full account
of individuality from both a philosophical and a historical perspective.
In the first essay he returns to and extends themes first outlined in *Experience and Its Modes* and developed in his immediate post-war essays
which centered on the invariably traditional nature of human activity.
In the final essay he fully elaborates a history of the modern European
state made intelligible by relating it to the context of modern moral

---

[29] "Scientific Politics", *The Cambridge Journal*, 1 (1947–8), 347–58, at p. 350. Reprinted in
       RPM.
[30] *Ibid.*, p. 357. See also RP 366 where Oakeshott claims that "(b)y the middle of the
       sixteenth century they [the conditions favourable to individuality] had been so
       firmly established that they were beyond the range of mere suppression". At a
       theoretical level it may be said that Hobbes reflects this pre-Rationalist
       experience of individuality, and Locke the transformation of this experience
       into a doctrine or ideology. See further ch. 5 for further discussion of the
       tradition of Locke.

experience as outlined in these later essays. As I will argue in the next chapter, in the discussion of the different senses of freedom in Oakeshott and Hobbes, these two accounts do not always fit together without tensions or ambiguities. We must, however, now turn to his account of agency as it is worked out in what, for convenience sake, I have called the final phase of Oakeshott's political theory. In particular the first essay of *On Human Conduct*.

V

In a perceptive essay on the development of Oakeshott's idea of agency Robert Orr[31] points to the change in vocabulary from Oakeshott's immediate post war essays where he launched his attack on Rationalism to the later phase of his career where he composed *On Human Conduct* and *On History*. In the earlier phase a quasi-naturalistic reading of the human agent was presented. He had a familiar home, was the carrier of local sentiments, affections and prejudices and all human activity was understood to involve participation in the "prevailing sympathy" of traditional under-standings (see RP 127). Orr points out that the *pro* words of this period included the following: habit, tradition, concrete, affection, activity, unselfconscious. In contrast, words such as conscious, self-conscious, reflection, premeditation, abstract, even intelligence, take on decidedly negative connotations.[32] In *On Human Conduct* this vocabulary is partly reversed along with a conceptual shift in the idea of agency. The keystone of the reformulated account is the idea of intelligence which is defined in strict contrast to a naturalistic reading of human agency. The agent is free because he is a reflective intelligence, not the manifestation of a natural process. The world for him is an understood world and he is free, "not because he has 'free will', but because he is *in* himself what he is *for* himself". Freedom is inherent in agency and 'it lies not only in his ability to make statements expressing his understanding of himself, but also in the world's being for him what he understands it to be" (VLL 19). Learning, Oakeshott now claims, is not "acquiring habits or being trained to perform tricks or functions; it is acquiring something that you can use because you understand it" (VLL 22).[33] And relationship in terms of a practice is "an understood relationship, capable of being engaged in only in virtue of having been learned" (OHC 55).

[31] "A Double Agent in the Dream of Michael Oakeshott", *Political Science Reviewer*, Spring 1992, 44–62.
[32] Orr, "Double Agent", pp. 52,3.
[33] See also OHC 20.

Oakeshott makes the point that his specification of the idea of a practice should be read as a corrective to what he had earlier written about 'tradition' and "that if such changes are read back into what I had written earlier they make it more exact."[34] It is worth asking what it was that Oakeshott found inadequate about what he had earlier theorized under the rubric of tradition and why in particular his theory of agency becomes so thoroughly infused with intelligence and understanding. We may get some clues to this reformulation from questions Peter Winch posed to Oakeshott's dual account of the moral life. In *The Idea of a Social Science*[35] Winch suggested that Oakeshott's postulation (in "The Tower of Babel" 1948) of two ideal constructions of the moral life, one conceived as a habit of affection and behaviour and the other as "the reflective application of a moral criterion" in terms of either ideals or rules, represented a false dichotomy of human behaviour. Following Wittgenstein, Winch argued that all human behaviour is rule governed and to be able to follow a rule (unlike acquiring a habit) is to understand, whether implicitly or explicitly, the type of actions that follow from rules. Winch disputes Oakeshott's claim that purely customary, habitual (non-reflective) behaviour is given to change and adaptability because "*the possibility* of reflection is essential to that kind of adaptability."[36] For behaviour to be rule governed, and not merely conditioned, the possibility of alternative courses of action must be available. That is, the agent "must be able to understand what it would have been like to act differently. [In contrast] (t)he dog who balances sugar on its nose in response to its master's command has no conception of what it would be to respond differently (because it has no *conception* of what it is doing at all). Hence it has no alternative to what it does; it just responds to the appropriate stimulus."[37]

Oakeshott clearly seems to have taken these criticisms on board and in *On Human Conduct* the dualism does not appear in terms of the contrast between reflective or non-reflective human behaviour, but between human conduct, which is the expression of intelligence, and other, non-intelligent occurrences. Agents are free because their response to a situation is an expression of intelligence, in contrast to any non-intelligent process, such as a cause or a law of nature. The

---

[34] "On Misunderstanding Human Conduct: A Reply to My Critics", *Political Theory*, 4 (1976), p. 364.
[35] (London: Routledge and Kegan Paul, 1958).
[36] *Ibid.*, p. 63.
[37] *Ibid.*, p. 65.

first essay of *On Human Conduct* is concerned above all with fully and systematically developing this account of human agency.

At the same time as he is developing this account of human conduct he is talking about Hobbes's theory of agency in very similar terms. At the outset of "The Moral Life" he distinguishes human conduct from natural necessity. Morality is only possible, he says, when "human behaviour is free from natural necessity; that is, when there are alternatives in human conduct" (RP 295). But the similarity of Oakeshott's theory of agency to his later reading of Hobbes is best exemplified in an essay entitled "Logos and telos" which was a review of Thomas Spragens' *The Politics of Motion: the World of Thomas Hobbes*, written in the same year *On Human Conduct* was published. Here Oakeshott is concerned with refuting the claim that Hobbes's understanding of human beings could be reduced to a simplistic mechanistic model of matter in motion. Though certainly motivated by motives such as fear and pride, these should not be seen as the unconditional causes of the civil condition. For Oakeshott the predicament Hobbes "is considering is uniquely human although the condition it generates is, in some respects, common to all moving bodies; it calls for an answer in terms of uniquely *human conduct*" (RP 357 emphasis added). The creation of rule-based association governing the lives of free individuals can only be the product of intelligent action, and this, says Oakeshott, "has no counterpart in a universe composed of bodies characterized solely by inertial motion"(RP 358). Further, Hobbes's account of civil association "turns upon the assumption that human beings are what they believe themselves to be" (RP 358). Oakeshott has here clearly added something to his account of volition in the introduction to *Leviathan* where will, not self-consciousness, was the defining characteristic of agency (RP 280).

Though there is a clear overlap here between Oakeshott and his interpretation of Hobbes, the account of agency developed in *On Human Conduct*, in terms of conventions and practices, clearly adds something to Hobbes's individualism. Practices, of which language is the prime example, are necessarily common and agents learn to pursue their private ends at the same time as they learn the conditions of a common moral practice. Moral agency is a complex whole in which both prudential and moral considerations interact simultaneously. Since, as Wittgenstein demonstrated, the idea of a private language is nonsensical, moral agency is inevitably common.

> What is called "moral autonomy" does not require moral choice to be a gratuitous, criterionless exercise of a so-called "will" (an isolated *meum*) in which a lonely agent simultaneously recognizes or even creates a "value"

for which he is wholly responsible and places himself under its command, thus miraculously releasing himself from organic impulse, rational contingency, and authoritative rules of conduct. .... his "moral autonomy" lies, first, in his character as an agent (that is, in his action or utterance being a response to an understood want and not the consequence of an organic impulse), and secondly, in his action or utterance as self-disclosure and self-enactment in a contingent subscription of his own to the conditions of a practice (which cannot tell him what to do or say) recognized in terms of its authority (OHC 79).

Oakeshott repeatedly rejects subjectivist interpretations of the self and argues that self-understandings are always mediated by various overlapping practices. Individuals in Oakeshott's theory are not the radically isolated beings that he had earlier attributed to Hobbes's theory, rather, they come to understand themselves and their actions in the context of various practices. Indeed, morality is 'objective' in the Hegelian sense of being justified by the criteria contained within an ongoing moral practice.

Though there are still echoes of an Hegelian position here it needs to be stressed that Oakeshott's account of freedom has moved some distance from his earlier 'Rational Will' formulation. A recent commentator has termed Hegel's ethical theory "historicized naturalism" which "is founded on a conception of human nature that has implications for what human beings need, what is good for them, what fulfils or actualises them".[38]

For Oakeshott, in contrast, one of the central components in his theory of agency is the idea of contingency. Individuals can be said to be free when they are able to choose from a variety of optional ends. When an agent chooses ends that are particular and contingent, which he invariably does, he is acting freely. Oakeshott is here rejecting the view that a truly free act is one that conforms either to Nature, Reason or proceeds from knowledge of our 'true' selves. This account of freedom largely depends on a basic scepticism towards such privileged knowledge. There is no 'true' self lurking

---

[38] Allen W. Wood, *Hegel's Ethical Thought*, (Cambridge: Cambridge University Press, 1990), p. 33. Clearly Hegel regards human nature as essentially conditioned by history and therefore without a settled or fixed nature. However, Hegel is careful to distinguish between the actual (ie. what is rational) and the merely existent. Existing states in many respects fall short of the full rationality of things as grasped by philosophy. Implicit in the contingent and transitory world lies intimations of what is rational, and "reason's actuality in the world consists in the exercise of the capacities of existing things, the fulfilment of essential tendencies in them", Wood, *Hegel's Ethical Thought*, p. 12.

beneath the surface which we come to know by an act of clairvoyance.[39]

In this scepticism about the claim that we can discover our true self underlying the mere facade of our various interpretations Oakeshott most resembles Hobbes and the voluntarist tradition of which he is the great exemplar. As Leibniz pointed out, the central issue of Hobbes's disputation with his continental critics was the question whether the justice of a thing consists in the mere fact that God wills it or whether God wills it because it is intrinsically just.[40] By upholding the former contention Hobbes drew the accusation that his universe is simply the product of a contingent, arbitrary will. Moreover, since reason only leads to the conclusion that God exists (ie. the first cause of all subsequent causes) and does not reveal his nature, it is meaningless to suggest that the nature of the temporal sovereign, established solely by an act of will on the part of the subjects, somehow reflects the divine. In a similar way, Oakeshott's understanding of practices as internally authoritative stems from a kind of 'negative capability' — the recognition that the human condition is one of mystery and uncertainty, and this is something to be cultivated and enjoyed, unlike the Rationalist who treats it as a puzzle to be solved (see RP 6). Reason rather than authority is destructive of individuality and the individual is free because "he is in himself what he is for himself" (VLL 19) and not because his will conforms to the 'true' nature of things whether accessed by Reason or revelation.[41] This theme will be discussed further in the following chapter.

---

[39] It is worth contrasting Oakeshott here with a philosopher like Charles Taylor who is also deeply indebted to Hegelian modes of thought. For Taylor human agency is marked by the capacity to choose our particular ends from what he terms second order desires (which he takes from Harry Frankfurt's 'Freedom of the will and the concept of a person"). That is, what marks distinctively *human* agency is the ability to make, what Taylor calls, strong evaluations of our particular desires. Elsewhere he talks about 'hypergoods' or 'horizons of significance' which provide interpretive glasses whereby our particular actions are made meaningful from a broader moral perspective. See "What is human Agency?" in *Human Agency and Language: Philosophical Papers 1* (Cambridge: Cambridge University Press, 1985). On 'hypergoods' see *Sources of the Self: The Making of the Modern Identity* (Cambridge: Cambridge University Press, 1989), pp. 63–73. On 'horizons of significance' see *The Ethics of Authenticity* (Cambridge and London: Harvard University Press, 1992), esp. pp. 35–41.

[40] See Mark Goldie, "The Reception of Hobbes" in *The Cambridge History of Political Thought 1450–1700* (Cambridge: Cambridge University Press, 1991), 589–615, at p. 589.

[41] This link between a sceptical theory of knowledge and individualism has been worked out most fully, at least amongst recent theorists, by Richard Flathman who has drawn on Hobbesian, Oakeshottian and Wittgensteinian ideas (amongst

In both Oakeshott, and in Oakeshott's interpretation of Hobbes, freedom at this stage (ie. prior to a consideration of authority relationships) is not a quality to be found only in certain acts, nor is it even, as many modern champions of negative liberty have taken it to be, the supreme and governing good of the state. It is simply an inescapable feature of human conduct. Oakeshott's account of free agency as the exhibition of intelligence is similar to Hobbes's idea that the will is free so long as it not hindered by external obstacles. That is, the type of freedom inherent in agency is not diminished by being constrained or coerced. A person complying with an extortionist's wishes may be constrained, but because his actions are not 'caused' he is not on this account acting unfreely. Oakeshott's contention that freedom is intrinsic to human conduct appears to be similar to the point that Hobbes used against those of his rivals who urged that freedom could only be secured under a form of republican self government. In contrast Hobbes made the point that a man can be said to be free whenever he "is not hindered to doe what he has a will to". He is free so long as there are no external barriers preventing him from acting according to his will. As Oakeshott himself put it in his revised version of the introduction to *Leviathan*; "(H)uman freedom is a quality of conduct itself, not of will. To find no external stop in doing what he has a will to do is to be a free man" (RP 264).[42] For Oakeshott also, this formal freedom is inherent in agency and is not dependent on what sort of 'state' one lives in.[43]

Though both Oakeshott and Hobbes are in agreement that freedom is consistent with constraint there is clearly a difference here on the question of the connection between causation and freedom. Oakeshott is not saying, as does Hobbes, that free agency is compatible with everything having a cause. On Oakeshott's reading, agency

---

others) to develop his own, strong voluntarist, version of liberalism. See esp. *Willful Liberalism. Voluntarism and Individuality in Political Theory and Practice* (Ithaca and London: Cornell University Press, 1992). See also his *Thomas Hobbes: Skepticism, Individuality and Chastened Politics* (Sage, 1993), which develops many of the themes first explored by Oakeshott, from whom Flathman says he has learnt most about Hobbes (p. 174).

[42]   This is not in the original version.

[43]   Oakeshott suggested that this conception of 'free' agency "does not distinguish one agent from another and it does not entail any particular mode of association; it is the postulate alike of relationships of master and slave, of commanding and obeying, of ruling and being ruled . . ." (OHC 235). In the following chapter I will explore the different levels of freedom in Oakeshott and their relationship to different types of association (civil and enterprise).

is incompatible with causation, though not with constraint.[44] Hobbes, of course, claimed that liberty and necessity are consistent:

> Because every act of mans will, and every desire, and inclination proceedeth from some cause, and that from another cause, which causes in a continuall chaine (whose first link in the hand of God the first of all causes) proceed from *necessity*. So that to him that could see the connexion of those causes, the *necessity* of all mens voluntary actions, would appear manifest (Lev 263).

In contrast to Hobbes here, one of Oakeshott's central contentions is that conduct is free precisely because mind itself operates in the realm of the contingent. Necessity belongs to nature, not to the world of human action. The dualism that Oakeshott employs here, as Orr suggests, is clearly reminiscent of Kant's distinction between the noumenal and phenomenal worlds.[45] The former being the realm of rationality and freedom, the latter necessity and hence unfreedom. However, for Kant, as indeed for Hegel, this distinction implies a choice. Not all human action operates according to the dictates of rationality. It is, for that reason, tied to a condition of unfreedom. Oakeshott's point, in contrast, is that all conduct is intelligent, hence free. There is no rational kingdom of ends which stands over against other forms of human conduct. Intelligence is simply a postulate of conduct, common to master and slave alike.

VI

This intermingling of Hegelian and Hobbesian conceptions of agency has led Paul Franco, for instance, to claim that Oakeshott sought to develop a theory of volition which, while still working within the parameters of the 'Rational Will' tradition, offered itself as a more convincing account than that left by Bosanquet. That is, by combining these two traditions of thought the defects in each could be overcome. We are left with a theory of Rational Will purged of teleological notions such as 'self-realization'.[46] Though I tend to endorse this reading it needs some qualification since Oakeshott's later theory of agency is not entirely devoid of teleological overtones. This stems from the distinct forms of freedom in Oakeshott's account which are related to the range of subject matter he is grappling with in *On Human Conduct*.

---

[44] See Liddington , "Freedom in a Modern State", p. 300.

[45] See Orr , "Double Agent", p. 58.

[46] *The Political Philosophy of Michael Oakeshott*, pp. 102, 178. See also "Michael Oakeshott as Liberal Theorist", *Political Theory*, 18 (1990), 411–36, esp. pp. 416–419.

Though I suggested in the previous chapter that Oakeshott's understanding of political or civil philosophy changes as he reflects on a particular historical experience, the first essay of *On Human Conduct* is ostensibly driven by straightforward philosophical or theoretical (rather than historical) concerns. It is an attempt to describe in theoretical terms the (apparently) universal features of human agency. The content of this agency and the practices that give it its distinctive character may change through time but Oakeshott has given us an account of its underlying form or structure which is, presumably, timeless. As he might have put it earlier in his career, it is a universal which appears everywhere as a particular. In the final essay of *On Human Conduct*, where the themes outlined in, for instance, "The Masses", *Morality and Politics in Modern Europe*, and "The Moral Life" are taken up and extended, he has clearly moved to the realm of the contingent. The morality of individuality and collectivism are *historical* dispositions. Though human agents are always 'free' in a formal sense, it was in the early modern period that human beings became conscious of themselves as individuals with the capacity to be self-directed. Here, according to Burckhardt, "man became a spiritual *individual*, and recognized himself as such".[47] In a very similar vein Oakeshott says,

> (w)hat has to be reckoned with is a historic disposition to transform this unsought 'freedom' of conduct from a postulate into an experience and to make it yield a satisfaction its own, independent of the chancy and intermittent satisfaction of chosen actions achieving their imagined and wished-for outcomes (OHC 236).

This disposition to cultivate and enjoy individuality is a form, (for Oakeshott the highest form), of self-enactment.[48] It is a response to what he terms "the ordeal of consciousness" (OHC 243). The celebratory account of this disposition indicates that Oakeshott has reintroduced, via the backdoor, an element of teleology into his argument. The best life is one in which self-sufficiency, independence and a Montaigne-like ability to know how to belong to oneself is cultivated and enjoyed.

This normative form of individuality is also a feature of Oakeshott's Hobbes, setting it apart from some other notable interpretations. Among Hobbes scholars Oakeshott is famous for making the claim that pride rather than fear is the true source of Hobbes's moral theory. As will be seen in chapter 5 this 'aristocratic' reading of Hobbesian individuality is quite unlike the 'bourgeois/posses-

---

[47] *Civilization of the Renaissance in Italy*, p 98.
[48] I will elaborate the distinction between what Oakeshott terms 'self-disclosure' and 'self-enactment' in the discussion of religion in chapter 4 below.

sive individualist' versions given by Strauss,[49] Arendt,[50] and MacPherson.[51] It also goes well beyond the more recent claim by Quentin Skinner that the best way to understand Hobbes's use of the term liberty is as a rhetorical strategy to subvert those claims to liberty (such as the classical republican view) which, Hobbes thought, aroused civil contention and stood in the way of a proper theory of sovereignty.[52]

Though Oakeshott never goes so far as to suggest that Hobbes's civil philosophy either depends on, or is designed to encourage, this form of noble individuality,[53] it is notable that Richard Flathman, whose interpretation of Hobbes owes most to Oakeshott, does take Hobbes's ideas in this direction. Addressing the question as to why Hobbes uses voluntarist notions such as consent and contract when all they seem to do is place a barrier between subjects and their duty to acknowledge and obey natural law and provide (theoretically at least) so many pretexts to exempt ourselves from what these laws prescribe, Flathman suggests that the answer can be found in Hobbes's privileging of the idea of "individuality and individual self-making". Flathman continues: "Obligations or any other binding requirements that owed nothing to, that depended not at all upon, the individual's own desires and beliefs, ends and purposes, would unacceptably diminish those on whom they are imposed."[54] Flathman freely acknowledges that he

---

[49] *The Political Philosophy of Hobbes.*
[50] esp. *The Origins of Totalitarianism*, ch.5.
[51] *The Political Theory of Possessive Individualism*, (Oxford, 1962)
[52] Quentin Skinner, "Thomas Hobbes on the Proper Signification of Liberty", *Transactions of the Royal Historical Society* 40 (1990), 121–151. Here Skinner makes the point that Hobbes uses a deliberately broad definition of liberty — ie. freedom as equivalent to movement — to explode the meaning of the term and thereby rob it of its antinomian consequences. Oakeshott's depiction of human agency in the first essay of *On Human Conduct* as inherently free is equally capacious. But it seems to me that the normative sense of freedom developed in the final essay of *On Human Conduct* is more important for understanding the theory of civil association developed in the second essay of this work.
[53] His claim is that Hobbes sought to provide people with the appropriate motivation for adhering to authority, knowing that the vast majority of human beings are security seeking creatures. That is, Hobbes "felt constrained to write for those whose chief desire was to 'prosper' [ie. to seek material security *a la* bourgeoisie]" even though he "understood human beings as creatures more properly concerned with honour than with either survival or prosperity" (RP 344). Though in a lengthy note at the end of "The Moral Life" Oakeshott explores the possibility that this noble individuality might provide a solution to the problem of the creation of the contract (see RP 344–350).
[54] *Thomas Hobbes*, p. 72.

takes the arguments beyond Hobbes himself.[55] But he suggests that the paradoxes and tensions in this aspect of Hobbes's argument can be overcome if we see them in terms of a distinctive notion of *virtù* that Hobbes wanted to encourage. In other words, despite his animadversions directed towards Aristotle and his seventeenth century followers, there are nevertheless teleological overtones in Hobbes's moral theory. This is not a teleology that is located in nature, but there is a preference in Hobbes for a certain type of human individual. I have no intention of making a judgment about this reading of Hobbes. However, the general point that Flathman makes here is the same sort of point I will go on to make about Oakeshott's own theory of civil association. I will suggest that the criticisms that have been made about this theory regarding its non-instrumental or purposeless nature can be countered when it is understood as that form of association that privileges the idea of individuality which Oakeshott takes to be central to the modern moral experience.

VII

By way of bringing this chapter to a conclusion I want simply to refocus the general point made earlier on the ambiguities of Oakeshott's Hobbes and the way these are reflected in his own modal ambiguities. In the introduction and the previous chapter I pointed to some of the difficulties that potentially arise from the different contexts Oakeshott employs when writing about Thomas Hobbes. In exploring the developments in Oakeshott's theory of agency via his reading of Hobbes this chapter has pointed out the tensions in both his reading of the latter and the way this is reflected in his own account of volition. These distinct frameworks, the philosophical, the historical, as well as the practical, are present throughout his career, the latter two gaining prominence from the late 1950s until the publication of *On Human Conduct* where they are all given full expression. The distinction between Hobbes the radical nominalist whose theory of volition sprang from a theory of knowledge and the Hobbes in whom prideful individuality appears as a sought after moral ideal is clearly reflected in the different degrees, or experiences of freedom examined in *On Human Conduct*. Oakeshott's 'history' of modern individuality, with its celebratory moral tone, is a

---

[55]   The purpose of his book, says Flathman, is "to do to (or for) Hobbes what he for the most part did to his philosophical predecessors, to wrench him out of his historical context, to thrust him into ours, to make his texts speak to questions of present philosophical and especially moral and political concern" (p. xxi). Flathman's response to Hobbes is simply a more explicit version of Oakeshott's understanding of the philosophical and practical pasts.

clear example of the intrusion of the practical into the historical past. Though the experience of modern individuality may not, *pace* Hegel, be the teleological end point of world history, nevertheless, Oakeshott, by ignoring the strictures of historical enquiry, makes this past live in the present and serve the interests of issues with contemporary practical and philosophical relevance. These tensions, it seems, are never finally resolved by Oakeshott. What is clear, however, is that Oakeshott's reflections on Hobbes's theory of volition were central to his own philosophy of agency and he has remained true to his intention of making past philosophy speak to the present.

In chapter five I will look more closely at the tensions between the individualist and anti-individualist characters and the profound implications for Oakeshott's understanding of civilization that arise from them. In the next chapter I will examine the relations between the different senses of freedom I have touched on here as well as giving a full account of the nature of obligation, both moral and civil. Since, for Oakeshott, civil obligation is a species of the genus moral obligation I have chosen to consider both in one chapter. Again, as I will argue, this is paralleled in his reading of Hobbes.

Chapter 3

Authority, Freedom, and Civil Association

I

For many contemporary political thinkers the conditions of modernity seem to pose unique challenges to both the theory and practice of authority. The loss of a unifying set of beliefs and values capable of structuring both public and private life is a story so often told it does not bear repeating. But it is noteworthy that for a number of prominent twentieth century political philosophers who have offered various diagnoses of the modern predicament Hobbes has been accorded a fairly prominent — even emblematic — role in leading us to this dubious situation. Hannah Arendt, for instance, went so far as to suggest that the understanding of authority that has shaped the political history of the West since ancient Rome has now "vanished from the modern world" and so grave is the crisis of our time that "(p)ractically as well as theoretically, we are no longer in a position to know what authority really *is*."[1] What we have in its place is an ersatz form of authority that is a barely concealed form of *macht*, *gewalt*, or *herrschaft*. For Arendt, Hobbes was instrumental in inaugurating this modern understanding of the political order as nothing but the accumulation of power relations, and the Leviathan model of the state is for her the antithesis of an authentic political or public sphere.[2]

---

[1] 'What is Authority?' in *Between Past and Future* (New York: Viking Press, 1968), 91, 2.

[2] See *The Origins of Totalitarianism*, ch. 5. For further discussion see Ernst Vollrath, "Hannah Arendt: A German-American Jewess Views the United States — and

Leo Strauss has a different reading of the tradition of the West, but he too sees Hobbes as one of the major instigators of the crisis of modern authority. Specifically it was Hobbes's replacement of natural law with natural right that, for Strauss, represents a break with the classical view that reason is the proper determinant of political order. Strauss points out that sovereignty (who should rule?) only becomes a problem when the precedence of reason is called into question. Hobbes's "supplanting of 'law' by 'right'"[3] shifted the problem of sovereignty into the forefront of modern debates about authority where — despite the efforts of Rousseau and Hegel to overcome it in a theory of the general or rational will — it remains.

The other major twentieth century thinker who is worth mentioning in this regard is Carl Schmitt who also wrote extensively about Hobbes at the same time as he was grappling with the problem of modern authority. There are interesting points of connection between Schmitt and Oakeshott in as much as they both combine a deep interest in Hobbes with a concern about modern rationalism. But importantly, they conceptualize this rationalism completely differently and fundamentally disagree about Hobbes's place in its development. They also want to recover quite divergent features of Hobbes's philosophy in their own attempts to counter modern rationalism. Broadly speaking, Schmitt turns to Hobbes to uncover the irrational and mythical basis of authority as a means of combating contemporary liberalism — the rule of law, individualism, pluralism, pacifism — which he equates with rationalism. For Schmitt, the modern liberal attempt to control power, if allowed to run its course, entails the end of politics itself — the "age of neutralizations and depoliticizations". Schmitt's reading of Hobbes on this is ambiguous and he eventually came to the view — after a curious dialogue with Leo Strauss[4] — that Hobbes's thought runs in different directions and it contains both the source of the very liberalism that has led to the modern crisis of authority as well as its antidote.[5]

As different as these writers are from each other, what nevertheless marks all of their reflections on modern authority is a sense of

Looks Back to Germany", in *Hannah Arendt and Leo Strauss: German Emigrés and American Political Thought after World War II* (Washington and Cambridge: German Historical Institute and Cambridge University Press, 1995) eds. P. Kielmansegg, H. Mewes, E. Glaser-Schmidt .

[3]   *The Political Philosophy of Hobbes*, p. 160.
[4]   See Heinrich Meier, *Carl Schmitt and Leo Strauss: The Hidden Dialogue*, trans. J. Harvey Lomax (Chicago: University of Chicago Press, 1995)
[5]   I have explored these themes in 'Leviathan as Myth: Michael Oakeshott and Carl Schmitt on Hobbes and the Critique of Rationalism', *Contemporary Political Theory*, (2002) 1, 349–369.

crisis. No doubt their sense of crisis (not unlike Hobbes) is partly a reflection of the times they lived through. But they all talk in terms of radical, and sometimes irretrievable, breaks with experiences or ideas whose loss impoverishes modern political life generally. Consequently, authority in the modern world is suspect. Related to this, they are also generally critical of most, if not all, expressions of modern individualism.[6] Not unlike Alasdair MacIntyre's more recent lament about the modern world's lost sense of virtue[7], these writers were all engaged in various versions of the old battle between the ancients and the moderns largely (but not exclusively and not without qualification) taking the side of the ancients.[8]

Though Oakeshott certainly felt that modern politics and authority were threatened by forces of one sort or another (a theme I will take up in chapter 5) he tended not to describe the modern condition as crisis ridden or as constituting anything like a radical break with the past. Indeed, he thinks that Strauss makes too much of Hobbes's supposed break with tradition,[9] and he suggests that Arendt's otherwise brilliant and suggestive interpretation of intellectual and political history is prone to exaggeration.[10]

This no doubt has something to do with Oakeshott's esteem for the British liberal political tradition. But perhaps more importantly, given that he is broadly in the Hegelian camp he is favourably disposed to the modern experience of individuality. Though the disposition to be an individual is sometimes expressed in a banal or impoverished form — especially in its economistic or 'possessive individualist' versions — it is anything but an illegitimate form of human conduct and, with Hegel and Constant, Oakeshott stands firmly on the side of modern liberty. A theory of authority that is adequate to the needs of the modern condition must take this experience seriously. When Oakeshott turns his attention to questions of

---

[6]   For further discussion on this see Horst Mewes, "Modern Individualism: Reflections on Oakeshott, Arendt, and Strauss", *The Political Science Reviewer*, XXI, Spring 1992, 116–147.

[7]   *After Virtue: a study in moral theory* (London: Duckworth, 1985).

[8]   Schmitt is something of an exception to this in that he took his bearings not from the ancient world but from the medieval catholic church.

[9]   See 'Dr Leo Strauss on Hobbes' in HCA.

[10]   See Oakeshott's review of Arendt's *Between Past and Future*, in *Political Science Quarterly*, 77 (1962), 88–90. Oakeshott says the following of *Between Past and Future*: 'Writing at this level of generalization, the peaks are apt to appear higher and the valleys deeper than they are; the differences between Greek and Roman and between ourselves as we are and ourselves as we were larger; and the degree to which a disposition of thought has managed to impose itself greater, than it really is'.

authority generally, and Hobbes more particularly, he does not write as if modern individuality — 'the pre-eminent event in modern European history' (RP 370) — poses a threat to, or stands in the way of, an authentic conception of authority. On the contrary, it provides the occasion to work out a conception of authority appropriate to the age.

The purpose of this chapter is to trace the developments in Oakeshott's theory of authority. Since many of the important themes underlying his theory of civil association are worked out in his lengthy essays on Hobbes[11] much of the chapter will be taken up with an analysis of the theory of obligation contained therein. In order to clarify Oakeshott's own position on Hobbes I will relate it to some other dominant interpretations of Hobbes's theory of obligation. This will not by any means be exhaustive, but will simply locate the key features of the debate in order to assess the distinctiveness of Oakeshott's contribution and to shed light on his own theory of authority. Since Oakeshott's theory of civil authority is inextricably tied to his moral theory I will discuss both in this chapter. There will necessarily be some overlap with the previous chapter since the question of will (agency) is central to both his reading of Hobbes's theory of obligation and his own theory of civil association.

In general terms, between 1929 and 1983 (his first and last essays directly dealing with the question) Oakeshott's account of authority altered in significant ways. As with his theory of agency it is possible to see his theory of civil association emerge in his essays on Hobbes in the middle of his career. As I will show below, Oakeshott's early theory of authority demonstrated much affinity with the political thought of earlier Idealist philosophers. Despite this, he never shared their estimation of Hobbes. Even in his early period, when he could most plausibly have followed their line, Oakeshott was a very sympathetic reader of Hobbes. This can, at least in part, be explained by the fact that Oakeshott wrote at a time when Hobbes had received renewed, generally favourable, interest, whereas for late nineteenth century readers he was not much more than "the somewhat dim figure in the positivists' calendar of saints."[12] However, as we have already seen, Oakeshott at this early stage maintains an important intellectual distance from Hobbes and identifies himself with the tradition of Rational Will which superseded the problems found in writers

---

[11]   Especially the introduction to *Leviathan* — original (1946) and revised (1975) versions — and 'The Moral Life in the Writings of Thomas Hobbes' (1962).

[12]   Oakeshott, review *Hobbes Studies*, ed K.C. Brown, in *English Historical Review*, 82 (1967), 123–5.

such as Hobbes. I will argue that this early position is subsequently greatly qualified. This becomes apparent when his own theory of authority is read in the light of his reading of Hobbes.

II

Though Oakeshott only fully developed his theory of civil association late in life, the question of civil authority was the subject of one of his first essays.[13] Before considering Oakeshott's treatment of Hobbes's theory of authority I will briefly discuss the argument of this essay as it reveals a philosophical perspective some distance removed from Hobbes and one that Oakeshott subsequently reworked at least partly through his engagement with the latter. The manner in which the argument advances is indicative of his early understanding of philosophical method. One commentator suggests that here "Oakeshott's Hegelianism reveals itself more as a philosophy of explanation . . . than anything else."[14] Though I tend to endorse this, I would also claim that arising from this is a recognizably Hegelian understanding of the state, which, though never in any sense repudiated, is transformed significantly in his later theory of civil association.

In this 1929 essay Oakeshott sets out to answer three general questions; "First, What do we mean by authority? secondly, What do we mean by the state?; and thirdly, Where, then, is the authority of the state?" (RPM 74). The philosopher removes the inconsistencies implicit in ordinary understandings of the term by transforming them into a coherent whole.[15] In order to determine what is itself authoritative we need to distinguish the cause of authority from its ultimate ground. Only the whole ground of authority will provide a sufficient definition, whereas the mere cause of authority is no more than an abstraction. The distinction is between that which produces or causes a belief and the reasons which ultimately ground a belief. Only the second can be authoritative, resting on nothing outside itself. Oakeshott rejects the common understanding of authority that takes it to be both external and coercive. By external he means that which takes the place of first hand experience, to be done away with where such experience exists. By coercive he means that which does not attempt to explain or per-

---

[13] "The Authority of the State", originally published in *The Modern Churchman*, 19 (1929–30), 313–27. Subsequently reprinted in *Religion, Politics and the Moral Life*. References are to the later edition.
[14] Paul Franco, *The Political Philosophy of Michael Oakeshott* (New Haven and London: Yale University Press, 1990), p. 78.
[15] Oakeshott employs here his method of arriving at a philosophical definition. See chapter 1 above.

suade. There is a certain ambiguity contained in this understanding. Authority, he suggests, cannot be both external and coercive, since

> if it be external, then it can be coercive in only a vague, metaphorical sense. For an external 'authority' can refer solely to the historical or psychological *cause* of belief, opinion or action, never to its whole *ground*, and it would be absurd to maintain that the power which actually compels a belief belongs merely to its cause. (RPM 75)

A belief has authority when it is sustained by adequate reasons. We may derive our beliefs from an external source — an expert, a parent, a schoolteacher, indeed, a tradition — but the ultimate ground of these beliefs is to be found in the judgment we make, either, of the adequacy of such sources, or in reasons unrelated to the source itself (RPM 78). A merely external authority "is a bare abstraction . . . it is a cause severed from a ground" (RPM 76). An external authority can only be said to be coercive in the negative sense that it fails to persuade. Whereas that which is authoritative is coercive in and of itself. It is a self-sufficient whole: "absolute, irresponsible, self-supporting and inescapable" (RPM 78). A belief is only inescapable, is able to compel action and thought, when it is supported by "our world of ideas as a whole" (RPM 79). This is the sole ground of an authoritative belief.

Far from being the antithesis of reason, authority is simply that which reason, as the ultimate ground of belief, compels us to accept. This is not, of course, the artificial reason of the *philosophe* whose genius "is a genius for rationalisation, for *making* life and the business of life rational rather than for *seeing* the reason for it, for inculcating precise order, no matter at what expense, rather than for apprehending the existence of a subtle order in what appears to be chaotic" (RP 139). Oakeshott here defines reason as "our world of ideas in so far as it is a coherent whole". Anything less than this is not authoritative, since an authority which we can escape is an imposter (RPM 78–9).

Oakeshott applies a similar procedure to understanding the state. A number of competing definitions of the state in ordinary usage are assessed and each found to be abstract and inadequate. A philosophical definition of the state cannot be considered satisfactory unless and until it supersedes these abstractions and considers it as a coherent whole. The philosopher's task is not randomly to choose one of these definitions since "pluralism run to seed is not an engaging spectacle", nor is it to add together a series of partial and incomplete definitions in the hope of constructing a complete account. It is rather to find a complete and convincing account of the state in the light of which these other conceptions appear as abstractions. The following accounts of the state are assessed: the state as a piece of territory, the state as a collection of legal or economic persons, the state as a secular whole, "or persons organised for secular purposes", the state as the political machinery of government.

All of these accounts point to important features of the state. Depending on their degree of abstraction, some are more adequate than others. The state understood as 'politically organized society' is less abstract than the state understood as 'secular society', "because the political whole more nearly supplies to our complete needs than the secular whole; the merely political man is more complete than the merely secular man" (RPM 84). However, none of these accounts are entirely adequate because they all imply something beyond themselves, namely, the concrete whole of which they are a part. The state cannot simply be identified with the government, rather, "it is the social whole which government implies and requires for its explanation; for to explain a thing is to think of it in terms of the whole which it implies" (RPM 83-4). To separate the 'political machinery of government' (which some take to be identical with the state) from society is an abstraction since the latter is implied by the former. It is to fall short of a complete explanation of the state. Because it is complete in itself, that is, it requires nothing beyond itself to explain it, the state is a concrete fact. Nothing short of this is adequate.

Since law is the ultimate voice of government, and authority is that "from which there is no possibility of appeal" it follows that law, from one viewpoint — that of the legal practitioner — is the ultimate authority in the state. For the practising lawyer or judge there is no authority outside the existing body of laws. However, this is simply a legal fiction, not a concrete fact. The authority of law and government is derivative, it rests on something outside itself, namely, "the moral and political opinions of its subjects" (RPM 86). Further, it is not sufficient to claim, with Locke, that authority resides in the consent of the people. Authority, since complete in itself, is independent of whether consent is given or withheld: "consent itself requires an authority upon which to rest" (RPM 86). There is no agent or set of agents, short of the state itself, to which authority can finally be attached. Though it is difficult to pin down, authority in the state is not illusory. He concludes as follows:

> The authority of the state is not mere government and law, nor is it founded upon a contract or any other form of the consent of the people, but resides solely in the completeness of the satisfaction which the state itself affords to the needs of concrete persons. Apart from its completeness, the state has no authority, for that only is authoritative, in the full sense, which is itself complete. Of this authority, and of no other, can it be said: *Non est potestas super terram quae comparetur ei* (RPM 87).

It is significant that Oakeshott concludes his first essay on authority with this clear reference to Hobbes, indicating a belief that Hobbes's purely legal conception of the state is an abstraction and therefore an inadequate explanation of the nature of authority. He is working here with a set of ideas developed by other Idealist political philosophers. Though analytically separable, the state and society are in practice a unified whole. Notably Oakeshott subsequently rejected the claim that his argument could be labelled Hegelian or Bosanquetian, suggesting that though he owed much to Hegel and Bosanquet he also found many of their arguments fallacious (RPM 87–90). No doubt Oakeshott would also reject the comparison with Green, but his attempt to distinguish between the source of authority and its ultimate ground bears a certain resemblance to the latter's *Lectures on the Principles of Political Obligation* (interestingly, the first of these goes under the title 'The Grounds of Political Obligation'). Green rejected John Austin's theory of sovereignty precisely because it failed to give a complete account of the grounds of authority in society. The authority of law, that is, the coercive part of the state, rests on the substantive conditions of social existence which it presupposes and whose end it serves. The business of law, says Green, "is to maintain certain conditions of life — to see that certain actions are done which are necessary to the maintenance of those conditions, others omitted which would interfere with them."[16] Law only has value for Green to the extent that it promotes the ethical ideal implicit in society.

Oakeshott's early estimation of the Idealist theory of the state is clearly expressed in a 1936 review, where he claimed that this theory "is the only theory of the state which has paid thoroughgoing attention to all the problems which must be considered by a theory of the state."[17] Though he went on to claim that it has yet to receive a satisfactory statement, it is clear that all subsequent theories of the state must build on the insights of writers such as Hegel, Green and Bosanquet. By siding with these thinkers Oakeshott apparently puts himself at odds with both the Hobbes-inspired Austinian school of jurisprudence and

---

[16] Green, *Lectures on the Principles of Political Obligation*, par. 13.
[17] Review Pfannenstill, *Bernard Bosanquet's Philosophy of the State*, in *Philosophy*, 11 (1936), 482–3.

Hobbes himself.[18] We saw in the previous chapter that at this stage Oakeshott judged Hobbes's theory of volition to be inadequate. This view changed during his subsequent interpretations of Hobbes. On the question of authority, also, there are to be found some indicative alterations. However, from the beginning, Oakeshott's reading of Hobbes on this stood in stark contrast to the interpretations offered by the sovereignty theorists and earlier Idealists.

In a 1934 review, Oakeshott makes the point that Hobbes does not succumb to the temptation "of that 'individualism' in political theory" which insists on separating the state from society. He says here that "the notion of the State taking up and directing a separable part of the life of society corresponds closely to the seventeenth century notion that when man entered political society he surrendered, not the whole, but a part of his natural rights — and it is a notion from which Hobbes might have rescued us if we had listened to him."[19]

So from an early stage Oakeshott is careful not to implicate Hobbes in his criticism of views contrary to his own position on authority. He never follows the view of Bosanquet and Green that Hobbes's sovereign rules merely by force (according to Bosanquet "in a will which is actual, but not general.")[20] Hobbes's theory of authority, says Oakeshott, "has suffered from its being isolated from the system of his thought" (TH 275). An accurate account of his theory of authority will only emerge by following through Hobbes's argument from its conceptual presuppositions — that is, his radical theory of knowledge permeates the whole of his thought. The authority of the sovereign is not a practical expedient, it is rather a logical necessity "exactly paralleled by the necessity of fixing the meaning of names if language is to serve any useful purpose at all"

[18] Oakeshott's rejection of analytical jurisprudence is also apparent in his later essay 'The Concept of a Philosophical Jurisprudence' (1938). Here, in a similar manner to the essay 'The Authority of the State', Oakeshott seeks to outline what an adequate philosophy of law must consist of. This is done by first assessing, then superseding, several incomplete, and therefore inadequate theories of law. In particular, he examines analytical jurisprudence, historical jurisprudence, the psychological interpretation of the nature of law, and finally the economic and sociological interpretations of law. Each of these are inadequate as philosophical explanations of law. A philosophical explanation of law must first of all be philosophical, that is, it must not rest on non-philosophical criteria. He then proceeds to spell out his understanding of philosophical method. It is nevertheless significant that here, though from a different perspective, Oakeshott distances himself from the school of Austin and his followers. In particular he refers to the more recent writers Salmon and J.C. Allen.

[19] Review O. Gierke's *Natural Law and the Theory of Society, 1500–1800* (trans. E. Barker), in *The Cambridge Review* 56 (1934–35): 11–12.

[20] *The Philosophical Theory of the State*, p. 98.

(TH 276). Because man is primarily a solipsistic creature of passion liable to conflict with others who share his world he requires a commonly recognized authority with the capacity to control men's external actions. What Oakeshott finds remarkable about Hobbes's theory of authority, "and what on any other interpretation appears as a mere contradiction," is its exclusive concern with the control of men's actions. Hobbes's sovereign has no concern with his subject's intellect or conscience, since "when a man is by himself, when he is speaking to himself, it is not necessary that the language he uses should be understood by others". According to Oakeshott, Hobbes's rejection of authority in philosophy, especially his rejection of Aristotle, far from being inconsistent with his view of the necessity of a common political authority, is actually entailed by it (TH 276). This is a view that Oakeshott consistently maintains and which is elaborated in his subsequent writings on Hobbes. Indeed, this distinction between different types of authority is central to his later argument that the authority of law is not a function of its desirability. I will not discuss this further here as it is central to much of the discussion to follow, however it is possible to see in this brief, early discussion of authority in Hobbes a contrast with the full-blown theory of state sovereignty expounded by Oakeshott in the essay 'The Authority of the State'.

III
Oakeshott on Hobbes's Theory of Authority

It is however, Oakeshott's substantial post war essays on Hobbes (the introduction to *Leviathan*, 1946 and 1975,[21] and "The Moral Life in the Writings of Thomas Hobbes", 1960) that are crucial to the theory of authority given full expression in *On Human Conduct* and "The Rule of Law."[22] It is to these writings that I will now turn.

We have seen that for Oakeshott the centrality of will in Hobbes's doctrine arises from a thoroughgoing nominalist theory of knowledge. The continuity of Oakeshott's reading of Hobbes becomes evident when we turn to the crucial theory of obligation. According to Oakeshott, the starting place for Hobbes's theory of obligation lies in his theory of the will. Obligation rests on nothing more than consent for there is "no obligation on any man, which ariseth not from some act of his own" (Lev 141). In what follows I will fill in the detail of

---

[21] The revised version of the introduction to *Leviathan* was originally published in *Hobbes on Civil Association* (Oxford: Basil Blackwell, 1975) and reprinted in the 1991 edition of *Rationalism in Politics*. My references are to the latter.
[22] In *On History and Other Essays* (Oxford: Basil Blackwell, 1983).

Oakeshott's reading of Hobbes on obligation. I will start by outlining the central features of the theory as it appeared in both the original and the revised versions of the introduction to *Leviathan* and in "The Moral Life". Perhaps the most immediately striking difference between the two versions of the introduction is the way in which Oakeshott systematically substitutes the terms civil association for civil society and *cives* for subjects. By itself this indicates a certain convergence with his own theory of authority as it is most fully developed in *On Human Conduct*. Along with these semantic changes Oakeshott made some significant alterations to the theory of obligation in response to criticisms made by Warrender and Brown. I will discuss some of these criticisms and the competing readings of Hobbes which they entail as this will help elucidate Oakeshott's own reading and the implications that thereby arise for his own theory of civil association.[23]

Oakeshott begins the crucial section on obligation in his introduction to *Leviathan* (Intro lviii–lxiv, RP 283–288) with the claim that much previous work on Hobbes had failed due to a proclivity on the part of scholars to extract a consistent doctrine from his writings when in fact such consistency is unlikely to be found in any seventeenth century writer (earlier he levelled a similar charge against Strauss — HCA 146–7). This was true of writers who attempted to extract a theory of political obligation solely from self-interest. The problem is not that such a doctrine cannot be found in Hobbes, but that it is found at the price of distorting Hobbes's thought as a whole by focussing on only one, undeniably important, aspect of the complete picture. The task for the interpreter of Hobbes is to seek to unite the multifarious, often conflicting aspects of his thought and present them in as complete an account of the whole as possible. Overemphasis on one dimension at the cost of any others prevents seeing the wood for the trees. The pitfalls of presenting an artificial unity are readily apparent to anyone aware of the subtle range of meanings found in Hobbes for words such as obligation, power, duty, forbid, command (RP 283).

In the original introduction Oakeshott deals with this problem by attributing to Hobbes four different senses of the word obligation, where obligation is taken to mean being bound, to be forbidden or to suffer impediment (Intro lix). The first, where a man is prevented

---

[23] Much of what follows covers similar territory to ch. 5 of Steven Gerencser's *The Skeptic's Oakeshott* which also looks closely at the changes from the original to the revised versions of the introduction to *Leviathan*. However, my focus is slightly different in that I spend more time detailing the differences between Oakeshott, Warrender and Brown. My discussion of the relationship between freedom and authority in Oakeshott's Hobbes and in Oakeshott himself is also slightly different.

from performing an action simply because of an external obstacle, such as the power of another man, is termed physical obligation. The second is internal and occurs whenever a man is prevented from acting because he deduces that the consequences of the act may be harmful. This is rational obligation. Oakeshott suggests that the labels rational and physical obligation are used for convenience because the sense of obligatoriness involved is of a different order from that arising from laws in the proper sense. The third type of obligation is termed moral and arises from an act of authority, which is (as outlined above) the product of a voluntary act. The creation of the Sovereign is an act of this type. On this account moral obligation does not exist in the state of nature. Only authority can curtail natural right since:

> an authority is a will that has been given a Right by a process called authorization, which (in turn) is the voluntary act of those who are to be morally obliged or bound by the commands of the authorized will. This voluntary act of authorization is a surrender (by mutual covenant) of the natural Right of each man, which, in a single act, creates and endows with authority an artificial Representative man or body of men who, in respect of the endowment is called Sovereign. The sole cause of moral obligation is the will of this Sovereign authority; the only sort of action to which the term moral obligation is applicable is obedience to the commands of an authority authorized by the voluntary acts of him who is bound. The answer to the question, Why am I morally bound to obey the will of this Sovereign? is, Because I have authorized this Sovereign, 'avouched' his actions, and am 'bound by my own act' (Intro lx)

The fourth and final sense of obligation, ie. political obligation (a term not used in the revised version) is said to be a combination of the first three.

> Civil society is a complex of authority and power in which each element creates its own appropriate obligation. There is the moral obligation to obey the authorised will of the Sovereign; there is the external physical obligation arising from force or power; and there is the internal rational obligation of self-interest arising from fear of punishment and desire of peace (Intro lxi).

A commonwealth is therefore a combination of these various elements each resulting from a separate motivation.

In the revised edition the distinctions physical, rational, moral, political are discarded and Oakeshott reformulates his account of obligation in general. Civil obligation is said to be one instance of moral obligation. This revision is partly an act of clarification. The terms rational and physical obligation Oakeshott no doubt felt had rather confused the overall sense of the picture of Hobbes he was trying to draw. However, as I will show below, there are also important alterations of substance made to the theory.

The problem faced by Hobbes scholars, identified by Oakeshott at the beginning of the section (RP 283, unchanged from original), is that in keeping with most writers of his time, Hobbes uses terms such as obligation in a variety of contexts for different purposes. For instance, in some places Hobbes suggests that the laws of nature are hypothetical theorems of natural reason which show men the means of securing peace. This is the sense Oakeshott attributes to Hobbes. Here they cannot be said to be laws in the proper sense. At other times however Hobbes suggests that the laws of nature are eternal and immutable (Lev ch. 15, 104), which has led some commentators to the conclusion that they are authentic laws which oblige all men in all times. If the latter conclusion is accepted then clearly moral obligation exists prior to the institution of the commonwealth. Hence Warrender makes the claim that for Hobbes:

> the laws of nature are eternal and unchangeable and, as the commands of God, they oblige all men who reason properly, and so arrive at a belief in an omnipotent being whose subjects they are.... Thus the duties of men in Hobbes's State of Nature, and the duties of both sovereign and subject in civil society are consequences of a continuous obligation to obey the laws of nature in whatever form the laws apply to the circumstances in which these persons are placed[24]

According to Warrender, though he made significant alterations to his predecessors, "Hobbes is basically a natural law philosopher."[25] Notably Warrender and Oakeshott are at one in rejecting the popular view that Hobbes equated authority and power. Whether established by institution or conquest, authority arises from an act of consent, "for in both cases the will of the subject decides the issue."[26]

However, where Oakeshott claims that obligation only comes into being by an act of willing, Warrender claims that the obligation to

---

[24] Warrender. *The political philosophy of Hobbes*, p. 322. cited in Greenleaf, "Hobbes: The Problem of Interpretation", p. 13.

[25] *Ibid.*, p. 36. A.E. Taylor earlier made the similar claim that Hobbes's moral theory, essentially a reworking of the Christian Natural Law tradition, is independent of his egoistic psychology. The most important aspect of his theory according to Taylor is the theory of obligation; "It is not a logical necessity of the system that we should accept the egoistic moral psychology. Even if we reject this psychology *in toto*, so long as we grant the premises that civil society rests upon a covenant to obey whatever shall be enacted as the 'law of the land,' and that breach of covenant is always a violation of duty, the conclusions he wishes to draw will follow", "The Ethical Doctrine of Hobbes", in Keith C. Brown ed., *Hobbes Studies* (Oxford: Blackwell, 1965), pp. 35–55, at pp. 44–45.

[26] *Ibid.*, p. 36.

obey all covenants is underwritten by the fundamental obligation to obey natural law.[27] The obligation to obey the sovereign is a continuation of the injunctions of natural law, such as seek peace, adhere to covenants made and summarised in the gospel law: *Whatever you require that others should do to you, that do ye to them.*

Though for Warrender's Hobbes "the duty of the citizen to obey the civil law springs from the consideration that he has made a valid covenant of obedience," this duty is only binding because it is a dictate of natural law that covenants be adhered to. These laws can however be suspended in certain circumstances. For instance, when there is inadequate security covenants cease to be obligatory. The obligatoriness of acting according to natural law is subject to the existence of, what Warrender calls, validating conditions.[28] In the absence of these the laws of nature are suspended. According to Hobbes, it is a law of nature "that men perform their covenants made" (Lev 93). However, for the first performer this law is suspended if he "has no assurance the other will perform after" (Lev 89). Further, it is only just to renege on a contract if the fear of adhering to it arises after the covenant has been made (Lev 90).[29] Since it is likely in the state of nature that events giving rise to such fears are common, most contracts are rendered invalid. Importantly however, some covenants are obligatory in the state of nature and "the function of the sovereign is not to make valid a covenant that was previously invalid, but to prevent (by taking away subsequent causes of fear) what is already a valid covenant from becoming invalidated."[30]

The major point at issue between Warrender and Oakeshott centres on what Hobbes takes obligation to mean. Of Oakeshott's fourfold categorization of obligation Warrender only recognizes two. That is, physical, which is only used by Hobbes metaphorically, and moral. For Warrender, political obligation is a short expression for the citizens' duty to obey civil laws, and is not a new type of obligation.[31] Oakeshott's rational, or pre civil obligation does not accommodate Hobbes's crucial distinction between obligation *in foro interno* and *in foro externo*. On Oakeshott's reading the laws of nature since they are merely theorems, or pieces of prudential advice, "oblige merely *in foro interno*" (Intro lix). J.M. Brown made a similar criticism, with the added suggestion that Oakeshott's difficulty here actually arises from his ear-

---

[27] *Ibid.*, p. 37.
[28] *Ibid.*, pp. 14–17.
[29] See *ibid.*, pp. 43–44.
[30] *Ibid.*, p. 44.
[31] *Ibid.*, p. 333.

lier claim that Hobbes's version of natural right begins with a right to all things, rather than the right to all things following from the natural right to preserve oneself. In trying to create a moral obligation where none formerly existed, Oakeshott, according to Brown, distorts Hobbes's intended meaning that the laws of nature are commanded by God and on that account are morally compelling.[32]

Oakeshott does address the predicament that concerned Hobbes of the Christian (or any adherent of a positive religion) who recognizes the laws of God to impose a real obligation. Where the first half of *Leviathan* detailed the universal predicament of mankind, the second half reinterpreted the argument in response to the transitory mischief of the age. For Oakeshott, Hobbes's discussion of the Christian commonwealth has no necessary bearing on the philosophical argument of the first half of the book. For the Christian these laws are laws in the proper sense, and therefore carry real obligations because they are commanded by God. It may be that they coincide with the theorems of natural reason, but they are not obligatory merely on this basis. "[U]nless and until they are transformed into laws by being shown to be the will of some authority," the determinations of reason cannot be said to be binding. According to this reading, "[t]here is, then, only one law, Natural and Divine; and it is revealed in Scripture". In an interesting footnote Oakeshott contrasts the laws of God for the Christian with what he says about natural law in the first half of the book. It is worth quoting in full:

> All that Hobbes says about Natural Law in the earlier chapters of the *Leviathan* is an irrelevant anticipation of the argument of the last two parts of the book. They are not, in fact, laws and are not part of the predicament except for Christians; and they have no relevance to the deliverance except in a Christian commonwealth. He might have brought to the surface at an earlier stage in the argument what he recognizes in the last two parts, but to do so would have involved a complete change of plan (Intro xlvi)

Both Warrender and Brown point out the difficulties entailed in this view pointing to relevant texts in Hobbes where these laws are said to be commanded by God independent of the recognition of Scripture.[33] Significantly, this footnote is removed from the revised version and, as will be discussed below, God is given greater prominence in Oakeshott's reworked sections on the theory of obligation and the generation of the commonwealth (these are the two sections that undergo substantial rewriting from the original).

---

[32] J.M. Brown, "A Note on Professor Oakeshott's Introduction to the *Leviathan*", *Political Studies*, 1 (1953), 53–64, at pp. 56–57.

[33] *Ibid.*, p. 63, Warrender, *Political Philosophy of Hobbes*, pp. 224–9, 333–4.

Brown and Warrender point to an important problem in Oakeshott's reading. That is, how, in the absence of a natural law theory of some sort, do the various parts of Hobbes's theory fit together, or does the theory in the final analysis collapse due to its internal inconsistency? According to Oakeshott "the covenant itself does not create a moral obligation: it is not itself morally obligatory and, not being a law (the will of the Sovereign), it does not itself make any conduct morally obligatory". However, "this and any other covenant may become morally obligatory if and when the Sovereign authority commands its observation" (Intro lx). As Brown suggests, this reading entails the contradictory claim that civil law is only obligatory because it is underwritten by a more fundamental civil law. However, Oakeshott's point is that by consenting to the creation of the Sovereign the covenantors become the authors of his actions. In the end the Sovereign's commands, whether or not consistent with the 'laws of nature', are authoritative only because they are authorized by the covenantors. Warrender finds this ultimately unsatisfying and a serious limitation on the explanatory value of Hobbes's theory of obligation.[34] It has to be said that one of the chief merits of Warrender's thesis lies in his attempt to make Hobbes's theory work. However, this is not the same as saying that Warrender's interpretation is superior to Oakeshott's (or any other) interpretation. It may be that Hobbes's Sovereign is finally held together by nothing more substantial than the covenantors' perception of their self interest. I will have more to say on this in due course.

IV

I now want to look at Oakeshott's response to these criticisms and the way his interpretation altered. Perhaps the most effective means of assessing the response is to look at the way in which the section 'The Theory of Obligation' was rewritten in the 1975 edition. I will also look at the way this is elaborated and objections answered in 'The Moral Life' (1962).

To be obliged, says Oakeshott, is to be bound or constrained. In the original version as we have seen, this constraint could be either internal or external; in the latter version it consists merely in external impediments (RP 284). Though a man may refrain from or undertake an action because he considers that to do otherwise would endanger himself, he cannot be said to be obliged to perform or not perform this action. So even when motivated by fear to act prudently

[34] *The Political Philosophy of Hobbes*, pp. 334–5.

(hence, for Hobbes, rationally) such action cannot be said to be obligatory.[35]

Far from being a natural property of man, reason is provoked into operation by passion and does no more than suggest convenient articles of peace. Its mood is indicative not imperative, since it is subservient to and generated by passion (see further RP 306). Man makes agreements with others in order to make more secure the satisfaction of his wants (RP 286), enabling at least a partial escape from the precariousness of mutual isolation.

It is in these original, evanescent agreements that the origins of moral conduct are to be found. The obligations they entail are genuine since they arise from an act of will. However, the only thing binding the parties to the contract is fear of the consequences of not obeying and at this stage where there exists no common adjudicator, neither party enjoys, to any meaningful extent, a greater capacity to enforce punishment for non compliance. Further reinforcement for these agreements may be found, when, for instance, both parties adhere to the maxim that honesty is the best policy. This is further strengthened if coupled with the belief that such maxims (termed by Hobbes the laws of natural reason) are recognized also as laws of God. There may be good reasons for obeying these laws (because of reward in heaven or because, if honest, a man's reputation will not suffer) but as long as there exists no common power there is no guarantee that either party will perform his part of the agreement. The first performer to any agreement makes himself vulnerable to the other party. Where there is no security, therefore, these 'laws' cannot be said to be obligatory. In this sense Oakeshott suggests the obligation arising from these transactions are "examples of pure but imperfect 'moral' obligation" (RP 287).[36]

Civil obligation like all other forms of obligation arises from a voluntary act (RP 287), and is therefore also a moral obligation. However it is different from the so-called pure but 'imperfect' type in at

---

[35] See Patrick Riley, *Will and Political Legitimacy: A Critical Exposition of Social Contract Theory in Hobbes, Locke, Rousseau, Kant, and Hegel* (Cambridge MA: Harvard University Press, 1982), ch2, for a good discussion of the contradictions in Hobbes. According to Riley, though Hobbes sought to base his theory of authority on consent/voluntary actions, his definition of will, consent and like terms was inadequate for the task. He marginalised these ideas by defining the will as the last appetite in deliberation. Because his naturalism undermines his theory of volition he cannot be said to have offered a consistent voluntarism. Riley endorses Oakeshott's early judgment that Hobbes's theory of volition was inadequate, yet his reasons for this conclusion clearly differ from Oakeshott's — see p. 201.

[36] Oakeshott discusses the transition of these 'laws' from rational theorems to moral obligations on pp. 309–312 RP.

least two important respects. First, the covenantors agree to establish a sovereign actor to whom they surrender both their right unconditionally to govern themselves and their power to act in accordance with this right. The establishment of a common authority, along with appropriate power necessary to enforce judgments, removes the insecurity of the state of nature as well as the reasons for not adhering to contracts entered into. Second, the obligation to obey the sovereign encompasses all other moral obligation. In authorising the sovereign to make and interpret laws the covenantors surrender their right to recognize the authenticity of all 'laws' save those of the Sovereign's making. Even the 'laws' of God only become authentic laws when enacted by the sovereign. Further, Oakeshott adds an extra section to the original description of the civil association where he argues that "in a *civitas* the *pax dei* is an integral part of the *pax civilis*" (RP 267).[37]

The question of whether or not there is valid law (the commands of an authorized law maker) outside the civil association Oakeshott suggests is largely irrelevant to the interpretation he offers since Hobbes wrote to men in civil association in order to show them the substance and foundation of their duties (RP 317). In response to the claim that his interpretation does not explain why the terms of the covenant must be kept, Oakeshott simply points out that by failing to identify desirable with dutiful action Hobbes was not speaking unintelligibly, but was simply circumscribing the use of the word duty. What finally holds the covenant together is the covenantors' perception of their self-interest. To act otherwise is not to act undutifully (unless it entails acting against the prescribed laws of the *civitas* — eg. treason) but self-contradictorily (RP 319–20). One commentator, sharing Oakeshott's nominalist reading of Hobbes, describes the laws of nature as 'assertoric hypothetical imperatives', which do not prescribe an end to be achieved, but assume the end and show the most likely means to its attainment.[38] On this reading the 'laws' of nature are more like doctors' orders. Since Hobbes assumes that all men, excepting lunatics, desire to preserve their lives, he need only spell out the most prudent means to attain this end.

So Oakeshott's claim in the revised version is that civil obligation is the same *sort* of obligation that exists in the state of nature, it "is a 'moral' obligation; it arises from a genuine surrender of *right*" (RP 288).

---

[37] In the original version this was discussed as a right, as opposed to a duty, of the sovereign — see Intro xlii.

[38] J.W.N. Watkins *Hobbes's System of Ideas. A Study in the Political Significance of Philosophical Ideas* (London: Hutchinson and Co., 1965), pp. 85–99.

It is not an entirely new form of obligation as he had claimed in the original version, but is simply a more encompassing version of an already
existing category of obligation. Like Warrender, Oakeshott holds that
civil obligation is the continuation of a type of obligation that existed in
the state of nature. However, though these rules of conduct may be buttressed by the recognition that they are the laws of God, they are not
dependent on their having divine sanction.[39]

The disagreement between Warrender, Brown and Oakeshott is
emblematic of the difficulty facing all Hobbes scholars.[40] As
Oakeshott points out (RP 332–338) there are many discrepancies in

[39]   It is worth noting here that Oakeshott does not quite represent Warrender's views
accurately. Warrender denies the view that Hobbes is specifically a Christian
natural law philosopher. Natural law is known to all who reason properly. It is not
obligatory simply by virtue of being recognised to be the will of God. Warrender
contends "that God was not necessary to Hobbes's system and that he could have
rested it simply upon the laws of nature as rational principles, which in any case he
regards as eternal and unchangeable (even by God)" , "Political Theory and
Historiography: A Reply to Professor Skinner on Hobbes", *The Historical Journal,*
22, 4 (1979), pp 931–940, at p 932. God is erected as a superstructure on the system of
natural law (see also "Hobbes's Conception of Morality", *Rivista Critica di Storia
della Filosofia*, XVII (1962), 434–49, reprinted in *Hobbes's Leviathan: Interpretation and
Criticism* (Wadsworth, 1969) B.H. Baumrin ed., 67–82, see esp. p. 74. See also "The
place of God in Hobbes's Philosophy", *Political Studies*, VIII (1960), 48–57). Belief in
God may reinforce Hobbes's system but its validity is not dependent on his
existence. All that results from removing God from his system is the loss of "a
certain formal analogy between civil law as command of the sovereign, and natural
law as command of God", leaving the substance of his teaching intact — "Political
Theory and Historiography", 932n8. Warrender therefore denies the view that
Oakeshott attributes to him, *viz.* that there can be no law without a known law giver
(see RP 324n66 and generally pp 322–332). Oakeshott's reconstrual may be truer to
Brown's position as it certainly is of F.C. Hood's *The Divine Politics of Thomas Hobbes*
(Oxford: Clarendon Press, 1964), but Warrender's reading of Hobbes on obligation,
because he rejects the volutarist thesis, is not tied to the presupposition that God
must exist. Warrender does suggest that in his early work he did not push this as
emphatically as he might have ("Political Theory and Historiography", 932). This is
perhaps an admission that he left an ambiguity in his early presentation of his thesis
which may explain Oakeshott's attribution to him of a view that he subsequently
denied. All this, however, is not central to my argument as I am principally
concerned with the way Oakeshott's theory altered in response to his consideration
of Warrender's and Brown's views and not whether or not his reconstrual of
them is in every way faithfully presented.

[40]   Oakeshott also disagrees with Strauss's reading of Hobbes's moral theory. I
have not considered it here as it does not provide the clear contrast that
Warrender's thesis does, and is therefore less useful to my purposes. Very
briefly, Strauss traced the origins of all obligation in Hobbes to the passion for
self preservation. All moral obligation is assimilated to justice which itself
springs from the fundamental right to self-preservation. To act justly is to act in
such a way to preserve oneself. To go further than this (ie. to try to be first in the
race) is vanity and is unjust. Vanity is the enemy of justice since it leads us go
beyond establishing the minimal conditions of peaceful coexistence. The

Hobbes's theory that cannot easily be put aside. Based on various key passages in Hobbes, Warrender has shown the possibility of extracting a plausible moral theory from Hobbes's writings at variance with both the traditional reading of Hobbes as well as the theory Oakeshott detects in him. In the end Oakeshott finds Warrender's theory inadequate because it relies on abstracting certain texts from the whole of his writings, thereby contradicting some of Hobbes's most cherished principles. Nevertheless, it may be said that Warrender's thesis draws on passages that are not incidental, but vital to Hobbes's argument and so they cannot easily be explained away. Though Warrender and Oakeshott emphasize what the other plays down, they are both in agreement that there is a real moral theory in Hobbes and this sets them apart from the once standard view that Hobbes's theory never rises above the determinations of self-interest.[41]

There appear to be (at least) two coherent and simultaneously existing moral theories in Hobbes's writings. Since it is beyond my purpose to resolve the seeming contradictions in Hobbes's thought it is enough here to note that Oakeshott's revised readings emphatically reject all elements of the natural law interpretation of Hobbes's thought. For Oakeshott, Hobbes's "Will and Artifice" moral theory represents not a reworking of the natural law tradition, but a departure from it. Notwithstanding Hobbes's language, which reflects his largely medieval cast of mind, his greatness as a moral theorist consists in the creation of a theory from the theological changes begun in the fifteenth and sixteenth centuries which laid the groundwork for the eclipse of natural law (RP 278).[42]

It is central to Oakeshott's nominalist interpretation that civil authority is a work of art not nature. It is the product of reasoning, not Reason. And reasoning is artificial, "an 'acquired' not a 'native' mental activity". The cause of a work of art is will, and what is dis-

---

difficulty with this reading, as Oakeshott points out, is that it fails to distinguish obligatory from merely permissible action. Rational conduct — that which is likely to preserve one's life — is not the same as moral, or obligatory conduct. I will have more to say on vanity (pride) and fear in Hobbes in chapter 5.

[41] For a discussion of what remains valid in Warrender's reading once the dust of criticism has settled see Glenn Burgess, "On Hobbesian Resistance Theory", *Political Studies* (1994), XLII, 62–83, esp. pp. 77–83.

[42] On the theological premises of the polemic against Hobbes see "The Reception of Hobbes" by Mark Goldie in *The Cambridge History of Political Thought 1450–1700*. This chapter supports Oakeshott's claim that Hobbes drew on central tenets of the voluntarist tradition of late scholastic nominalism. For many of his significant contemporaries this was the presupposition upon which they based their attack. Leibniz, for instance, suggested that even "Ockham himself was not more nominalistic than is Thomas Hobbes", p. 593.

tinctive about civil authority is that it is "artifice springing from more than one will" (RP 247). Man has within himself the resources to create authority and thereby overcome his natural predicament. "The saviour is not a visitor from another world, nor is it some god-like power of Reason come to create order out of chaos . . . The remedy of the disease is homeopathic" (RP 256). Oakeshott would undoubtedly endorse Hegel's observation that "Hobbes . . . sought to derive the bond which holds the state together, that which gives the state its power, from principles which lie within us, which we recognize as our own."[43]

The sovereign authority, once established, has the sole right to make, administer and adjudicate laws. Law, according to Oakeshott's Hobbes, "is a command, the expression of the Will of the Sovereign." In the revised introduction Oakeshott points out that not all commands are law, but only those that prescribe general rules of conduct applicable to all subjects (RP 262). The distinction between command and rule is an important feature of Oakeshott's own theory. There is also a subtle, but interesting, alteration in the wording on the question whether civil law can be either inequitable or unnecessary. Since the civil condition knows only one law, civil, no valid law can be considered unjust. However, in the first version the sovereign has the right and the duty (a right is what he may do, a duty what he must do — see Intro xl) "to make only such laws as are equitable and necessary." In general, inequitable laws are those that conflict with the theorems of natural reason, and unnecessary laws are simply those which restrict activity indifferent to the maintenance of peaceful coexistence (Intro xli). Though Oakeshott insisted that these considerations have no bearing on the authority of law, this reading does seem to indicate that the sovereign has an obligation, however vaguely specified, to frame laws that cohere with a standard independent of his own judgment. Importantly however, the configuration changes in the revised version. It is now the rights and 'faculties' of the sovereign that are specified. It appears that the Sovereign no longer has duties. If unnecessary laws or laws increasing rather than decreasing contention are enacted then they are to be deplored (RP 262), but for subjects there is no appeal, even to the vaguest conception of the Sovereign's duty, beyond civil law. In the revised version Hobbes is presented as a consistent and unequivocal voluntarist, purged of all traces of the natural law tradition.

Further indication of a shift away from natural law theory is found in the manner in which Oakeshott alters the section originally enti-

---

[43] *Lectures on the History of Philosophy*, Vol. 3, p. 316.

tled 'the rights and obligations of the subject' (Intro xliii–xliv) which subsequently reads 'the obligations and liberties of the subject' (RP 261, 264–5). The manner in which this section is rewritten has significant implications for Oakeshott's reading of Hobbes's theory of authority. It concerns the question of the extent of the subject's obligation to obey the civil law. Again since what this obligation depends upon is crucial to his own theory I will quote at length.

> [S]ince the contents of the commands of the sovereign authority (though not the authority of the commands) are derived, generally speaking, from the articles of peace, there are some things which, although they may in fact be commanded by the sovereign, are not obligations. For example, no subject is obliged to kill or injure himself, none (except as punishment) is obliged to suffer a greater deprivation of his natural liberty than any other, and there is no obligation to an authority that manifestly fails in its office of protection. *The appeal here is from what the law ordains to the end for which the legal order was instituted*; and when it succeeds freedom replaces obligation (Intro xliii, emphasis added).

On this reading the end for which the legal system is enacted provides the authority according to which the validity of any particular law is assessed. Though clearly the end (peace) here defined is a minimal one it is nevertheless an end, or a condition, which does not arise spontaneously, but must be created and maintained by substantive action, initially on the part of the covenantors and subsequently by the sovereign's law making activity. Law therefore has an instrumental relationship to this condition and those laws that conflict with it are not obligatory. In keeping with Oakeshott's own purposeless theory of civil association the altered account omits all discussion of law in terms of ends. There are certain rights (to protect oneself etc) that are not transferred when the contract is agreed to and *cives* are not obliged to act in such a way that threatens these rights. However the revised introduction is notable for the way in which all traces of instrumentality have been removed from Hobbes's civil association. The final sections of this chapter will largely be concerned with discussion of this crucial procedure/purpose distinction.

V
Authority and Freedom in Oakeshott's Hobbes

A central contention made by Oakeshott of his theory of civil association is that it preserves the link between belief and conduct. There is an intimate connection between authority and the freedom of agency. Since Hobbes is for Oakeshott a great exponent of civil association, it needs to be asked how this relationship is handled in Oakeshott's reading of him. Perry Anderson has suggested that Oakeshott took Hobbes for a model because "there is no place for rights in his [Hobbes's] scheme of things. Once the sovereign is constituted, subjects have only obligations. Here indeed there is no cant about consent: just a limpid statement of duty — obedience to civil authority."[44] Anderson seems to be invoking a reading of Hobbes that Oakeshott thought was a great mistake — i.e. the assumption that the authoritarian elements in Hobbes contradict the individualistic elements. It is true (in Oakeshott's Hobbes) that when individuals create the Sovereign they surrender their absolute freedom or right to govern themselves. This act "involves the replacement of freedom by law and right by obligation" (RP 276). Indeed, Oakeshott's own theory of civil association is distinctive among modern legal theories in its absence of a theory of rights. But for Oakeshott, Hobbes's authoritarian theory is paradoxical: he "is not an absolutist precisely because he is an authoritarian" (RP 282).[45] Though the relationship between freedom and authority is not quite the same in Oakeshott's theory of civil association as it appears in his interpretation of Hobbes, it is the same type of relationship. In the final section of this chapter I will assess the way in which Oakeshott connected an Hobbesian theory of authority with the insights of the "Rational Will" tradition in his theory of civil association.

Despite the fact that Hobbes's theory, according to Oakeshott, starts with will, not, as in the natural law theory, obligation and law (RP 277), it seems to be the case that in Hobbes something is given up when men consent to create a sovereign; their freedom is curtailed in that they forfeit their 'naturall liberty' to all things. Oakeshott follows this reading of Hobbes when he claims that the freedom of *cives* is curtailed to the extent that the laws compel them to do things they may not otherwise wish to do (RP 264). However, the curtailment of their freedom is something they have chosen. Even if the contract is entered into because of their fear of the consequences of not so acting the act itself cannot be said to be unfree. Accordingly Hobbes says, "Feare and Liberty are consistent" (Lev 137).

So for Hobbes there is a sense in which the laws governing civil society oblige us to act in ways we may not choose in their absence. However this obligation is not inconsistent with liberty (as Skinner

---

[44]   Perry Anderson, "The Intransigent Right at the End of the Century", *London Review of Books*, 24 September 1992, pp. 7–11, at p. 10.
[45]   The other point to make here is that Oakeshott downplays notions of contract and consent in Hobbes and replaces them with ideas such as recognition and acknowledgment — ideas which are central to Oakeshott's own theory of civil association. For a very good discussion of this element of Oakeshott's reading of Hobbes see Gerencser, *The Skeptic's Oakeshott*, pp. 111–8.

has put it) in the proper signification of the word. On the contrary the liberty enjoyed by subjects, though conditional, is one that all rational people would accept. That is, since the absolute right to everything required for self-preservation, including one another's bodies, has been relinquished, subjects no longer live in fear for their lives and property. The absolute liberty of the state of nature is liberty only in the most paradoxical sense.[46]

In what sense then is liberty affected in the transition from the state of nature to civil society? On Oakeshott's reading Hobbes says that though subjects surrender the absolute right to exercise their will in the pursuit of felicity, they do not give up their right to that pursuit. Rather, the giving up of that right is a condition of attaining 'true freedom'. Subjects give up their natural right to pursue felicity unconditionally and transfer certain rights to the Sovereign to act on their behalf. In particular the subject authorizes the Sovereign to establish the minimal conditions necessary for his pursuit of felicity. The freedom thus established, though conditional, can be said to be 'true' because it enables subjects to pursue felicity without (undue) concern that their lives may be violently ended by others unconditionally prosecuting their 'naturall liberty'. Accordingly, a net gain of freedom actually occurs (RP 265). The right that is given up "is the absolute right, on all occasions, to exercise one's individual will in the pursuit of felicity". However, "to surrender an absolute right to do something on all occasions, is not to give up the right of doing it on any occasion" (RP 282). The establishment of a sovereign authority is the creation of an artificial will whose rights, though unconditional, are limited (RP 261).

By purging all purposes from his reading of Hobbes's commonwealth Oakeshott opens himself up to a difficulty. If there is no end according to which the laws of civil association can be assessed, then there are no limitations to the areas of life to which law can be extended and, most importantly, no recourse for the subject against the sovereign. It is the end of securing peace that sets the limitations to sovereign authority. If the condition established by the sovereign actually increases, rather than diminishes, the contentions existing in the pre-civil state then subjects are released from their obligations. This is likely to occur if the sovereign oversteps his role and attempts to establish more than this minimal condition conducive to the pursuit of felicity. The sovereign may be, indeed must be, indifferent to the particular purposes that individuals pursue, but he cannot be

[46]   On this see also Quentin Skinner, "Thomas Hobbes on the Proper Signification of Liberty", at p. 133.

indifferent to the condition that supports and makes possible these pursuits without endangering his authority (his power — since it is natural, not artificial — is another matter which I discuss below).

In the original introduction Oakeshott's argument at times pointed in this direction. However, in the revised version unnecessary laws, ie. those that fail to cohere with the theorems of natural reason, are no longer spoken of as providing grounds for resistance. "In short, in civil association the validity of a law lies neither in the wisdom of the conditions it imposes upon conduct, nor even in its propensity to promote peace, but in its being the command of the sovereign and (although this is obscure) in its being effectively enforced" (RP 262). This revised reading certainly clarifies some of the discrepancies found in the earlier version. However, to repeat what was mentioned at the end of the last section, it may be asked whether Oakeshott's attempt to derive a consistent voluntarist theory of obligation in Hobbes has involved down playing other equally important features of his thought which lead to a substantially different moral theory. The problems that Warrender pointed to still confront Hobbes scholars.[47]

Moreover, Oakeshott's denial of any element of instrumentality in Hobbes's commonwealth removes the justification, if it previously existed, for viewing it as an example of an enterprise association. It seems that Oakeshott had not started to work out the distinction between civil and enterprise association until the late 1950s and this is reflected in the ambiguities in his original introduction to *Leviathan*.[48] Furthermore, in the later writings on Hobbes, civil association as an ideal character assumes a central interpretative role. It is an organizing category by which Hobbes's thought can be explained. To introduce into the interpretation of the commonwealth any element of instrumentality would corrupt the clear cut distinction Oakeshott draws between civil and enterprise association understood as ideal

---

[47] Recent commentators who argue along lines laid down by Warrender include Burgess, "On Hobbesian Resistance Theory", and Brian Trainor "Warrender and Skinner on Hobbes", *Political Studies* 36, (1988), 680–91.

[48] In 1951 for instance Oakeshott argued that what severely restricts the operational power of the *Leviathan* is the tightly circumscribed end for which it was established in the first place — "... there was no lust for government in Hobbes: the *Leviathan*, he thought, must be omnipotent, but he never imagined it omnicompetent. Intoxication with the opportunity which great power gives for doing great things was no part of the character of this *Leviathan*, whose limited but essential office was to be guardian of the peace. It was to operate, not arbitrarily, but by rule of law, and whatever was not forbidden was to be allowed. Supreme power was never more narrowly hedged or more finely directed to a special purpose, while being left with its necessary supremacy unimpaired". "Reminder from Leviathan".

characters. This has clear implications for the task he sets himself in *On Human Conduct*.

Despite these fluctuations and difficulties Oakeshott was consistent in his rejection of the conventional view that Hobbes began with a theory of radical individualism which his authoritarian theory of civil association ends up destroying (RP 281). To authorize a sovereign to act on my behalf does not, he argues, "destroy or compromise my individuality". The act of authorization does not entail the establishment of a general will.[49] The wills of subject and sovereign remain separate. Though there is a common object of will there is no common will (Intro lvi [RP 281]).

Further, the authority of law actually preserves individual freedom in a way other forms of absolutism do not. As mentioned above, to give up the absolute right to act according to natural liberty is not to give up the right to continual felicity. Rather, the pursuit of felicity simply has conditions attached to it. The *Leviathan*, according to Oakeshott, is not "a designed destruction of the individual; it is, in fact, the *minimum* condition of any settled society among individuals" (Intro lvi [RP 282]). As Hobbes himself put it in a manner reminiscent of Oakeshott's own theory of non-instrumental law: "The use of Laws (which are but Rules Authorised) is not to bind the People from all Voluntary actions; but to direct and keep them in such a motion, as not to hurt themselves by their own impetuous desires, rashnesse, or indiscretion, as Hedges are set, not to stop Travellers, but to keep them in the way" (Lev. 227).

Hobbes's radical individualism is not, as is sometimes assumed, compromised by his theory of authority. According to Oakeshott, Hobbes's authoritarianism actually preserves individualism since "law as the command of the Sovereign holds within itself a freedom absent from law as Reason or custom: it is Reason, not Authority, that is destructive of individuality" (RP 282). Michael Foster[50] makes a similar claim on this point when he argues that the subjective freedom characteristic of the modern state lies in the character of positive laws which are both objective, in the sense of being clear to the understanding of the subject, and general or abstract. A law can only be carried out if it is recognized, if it becomes an object of a person's understanding. This is not true of custom which is adhered to irrespective of its transparency to the understanding. Positive law is authoritative because it is

---

[49] See OHC 152 for Oakeshott's claim that civil association is not to be identified with a 'general will'. This will be discussed further below.

[50] *The Political Philosophies of Plato and Hegel* (Oxford: Oxford University Press, 1935), pp. 113–121.

recognized. Unlike custom or habit it implies subjectivity. According to Foster the second basic feature of a command is that it is abstract or general. No command specifies the precise details according to which it must be carried out. In every "act determined by a command there must always be a sharp line of distinction between the essence of what is commanded and the indifferent details of its execution". Again this is unlike habitual conduct or "a Nomos imparted by habituation" which is determined by "the tradition which gives it birth."[51] Oakeshott's interpretation of law as command is based on precisely these distinctions. Law, he claimed,

> is a command, the expression, not of reason, but of will. And a command implies liberty in the person commanded. First, it implies a liberty of mental activity, for it cannot be carried out by an automaton, but only by one who is mentally aware of it and understands it. And secondly, it implies a liberty of initiative; for all commands are abstract and general, are indifferent to the details of their execution, and assume the ability in the subject to fill in the detail and translate the generality into an act in which this generality is fulfilled. In every act commanded there lies a part which is not commanded; or rather, the object in a command is never a concrete act but always an abstract generality. The relation of sovereign authority to subject, where the right of the one is to command and the obligation of the other to obey, is not one that excludes liberty, but actually implies it. For, however large a portion of the acts of a subject are under the control of command, there remains inside every act of obedience an area of unassailable liberty (Intro xliv).

The section from which this passage is taken is rewritten in the revised version. As noted earlier, according to the revised reading not all commands are law. Despite the altered wording the link between law as command and freedom is central to Oakeshott's Hobbes, and it reappears in modified form in Oakeshott's theory of authority in which the distinction between law and command is central to the distinction between civil and enterprise association.

The significance of the above quotation is twofold. There is here the germ of the idea given full elaboration in *On Human Conduct* that general rules of conduct are indifferent to the purposes of agents. Further, what is presupposed in this understanding of law is the crucial idea that humans are self-interpreting beings. In Oakeshott's terms they are agents, they are in themselves what they are for themselves. Authority, that is, recognized general rules of conduct, and not power, protects rather than diminishes free agency. Automatons or mere

---

[51] *Ibid.*, p. 115

receptacles of pleasure and pain have no need for law since it is meaningless to them. Power is the only salvation for such creatures.[52]

Because Oakeshott, like Warrender, makes a clear distinction between power and authority in Hobbes, he is able to claim, not only that Hobbes had a true moral theory as opposed to a theory of mere coercion, but that the latter's theory of civil association preserves, rather than diminishes, individual freedom. However, without the means to ensure that the terms of the covenant are agreed to, this authority is impotent. In the state preceding all contracts or agreements each man enjoys a natural right to all things that is constrained only by his lack of adequate power "to do that which he has a will to do". Because a man's power is, in this state, uncertain, yet he has a right to all things, "Might and Right are never the same thing" (unlike God whose power, since irresistible, is equal to his right). What is transferred in the establishment of the contract is the authority to prosecute this right. Obligation arises from this act of authorization. There is "no obligation on any man, which ariseth not from some act of his own" (Lev 141, see RP 285). The power that is transferred is derivative. It is necessary in order to ensure that the terms of the contract are adhered to.

The only way the Sovereign's authority can become effective is if a sufficiently large number of individuals are inclined to subscribe to the terms of the contract: "for the Sovereign's power is only the counterpart of his subjects' disposition to obey" (RP 347). The covenantors must subsequently act in such a way that is consistent with their acknowledgment of the authority of the contract. Where the authority relationship between subjects and sovereign is both unconditional and artificial, the power relationship is conditional and natural. The Sovereign is simply the acknowledged recipient of the accumulated power, or natural right, that the covenantors previously exercised in the state of nature. Despite being juridically absolute the Sovereign's practical ability to govern is in fact potentially very weak.[53]

Hobbes's commonwealth is a civil association because it is first and foremost an authority-based association. Power is restricted to punishing breaches of the covenant. As soon as power is employed to impose substantive performances on subjects the Sovereign

---

[52]   The connection between Foster and Oakeshott is also noted by Franco, *The Political Philosophy of Michael Oakeshott*, p. 247, n. 63.

[53]   For a discussion of just how weak the Sovereign potentially is see Flathman's *Thomas Hobbes: Skepticism, Individuality and Chastened Politics*, pp. 95–128. It should be noted that on Warrender's reading also the power of the sovereign is severely curtailed by the requirements of natural law.

undermines this authority relationship, turns the commonwealth into an (explicit?) enterprise association, and potentially endangers his right to rule. For this reason in the revised introduction Oakeshott ends the section "the rights and 'faculties of the Sovereign" with the observation that "the office of the Sovereign has no rights of 'lordship'; its *dominium* is solely *regale*" (RP 263). Oakeshott, therefore, comes to reject the sort of criticism that T.H. Green levelled against Hobbes that "where there is no recognition of a common good, there can be no right in any other sense than power."[54] It is precisely because authority relationships are *not* tied to a conception of the common good, stand on no extrinsic end, that they circumscribe the use of power and protect individual freedom. The related distinctions procedure/purpose and authority/power are central to Oakeshott's account of civil association to which we now turn.

VI
Authority in Civil Association

Having outlined the way that Oakeshott treats the themes of authority and freedom in Hobbes I will now look at the way these issues are dealt with in *On Human Conduct*. This will be done by first examining Oakeshott's account of authority relationships in terms of his general understanding of practice-based association, before considering in more detail the connection between civil association and freedom. As will be seen many of the important features of Oakeshott's reading of Hobbes are only fully worked out in his later works on authority.

According to Oakeshott, among free agents (self-interpreting beings) there are two general types or modes of association. The first of these is a transactional association where each person enters the association for an anticipated benefit. This can be either an individual or a corporate benefit. The relationship between buyer and seller in the market place is an example of the former, whereas an association for a common cause — such as a fire brigade or a forest protection society — is an example of the second. Transactional relationship since it is concerned with attaining some preordained end or goal requires the organisation of resources. It is essentially a relationship in terms of power.[55] Rules or policies may be formulated in such an organisation, but the organisation is by nature managerial and all the available resources, including its rules and policies, are

---

[54] *Lectures on the Principles of Political Obligation*, par.47.
[55] For Oakeshott's discussion of the nature of agreements *inter homines* in Hobbes see RP 304–5.

directed to attaining the chosen end. In this type of association there exist only instrumental rules whose authority depends upon their perceived effectiveness in attaining the end in question. The rules that are applied here — the regulations governing the fire brigade or the forest protection society — are instances of an instrumental practice.

In contrast to this a moral practice "is not instrumental to the achievement of any substantive purpose or to the satisfaction of any substantive want" (OHC 60). There is no extrinsic purpose which can be furthered by strict adherence to the rules of a moral practice. There are however internal purposes but these cannot be separated, except analytically, from participation in the practice itself. For instance, in these terms it is meaningless to "make a practice" of being punctual. One can be punctual only while pursuing concrete activities, such as, attending a meeting or arriving at a party. To quote Oakeshott again:

> Purely regularian conduct (that is, conduct whose imagined and wished for outcome is solely that a procedure shall have been observed) is impossible: to make a grammatically faultless utterance is always to say *something*, to use an implement 'properly' is always to make *something*, to follow a routine is always to do *something*, and to act 'dutifully' is always to perform some substantive action whose 'meaning' for the agent lies not in the conditional duty, but in its imagined and wished for response (OHC 58).[56]

Oakeshott repeatedly refers to a vernacular language as the archetypal instance of a moral or non-instrumental practice. A language never specifies the content of what is said, it merely imposes formal, grammatical rules to be adhered to. Moreover, these rules are not external to the practice of using the language. Their authenticity is implicitly acknowledged whenever the language is used. Further, even when these rules are abrogated, say, for literary purposes, the validity of these rules, as authentic rules, is not denied.

So, briefly, there are two types of association, or two types of practice, identified here: one prudential or instrumental, that is, one with an extrinsic purpose, and the other moral, or non-instrumental. The rules attached to a moral practice are adverbial rules, which never determine what actions shall be performed, but they impose conditional obligations on the agent in the pursuit of his chosen actions. In other words, they condition or qualify action, but never determine it.

---

[56]   Cf. Bradley here; "To act you must will something, and something definite. To will in general is impossible, and to will in particular is never to will nothing but a form. ... The bare form cannot move. Will, when one wills nothing in particular, is a pure fiction; and (to put the same thing differently) so is will without desire, conscious or unconscious, special or habitual. It is simply a psychological monster' (*Ethical Studies*, p. 153).

For Oakeshott law is an example of the second type of practice; it is a moral practice. However, what he talks about as the rule of law, *lex*, is an ideal character or logical construct. Terms such as law, ruling, politics, in ordinary political discourse have all acquired equivocal and ambiguous meanings. Consequently, his ideal character — the rule of law — is an analytical attempt to determine what authority in the modern state must be given the account of human conduct understood as the expression of free agency. Every modern state is actually an ambiguous mixture of civil association and enterprise association. Oakeshott's primary concern is with elucidating the postulates of civil association: association in terms of *lex*, or the rule of law. Enterprise association is another ideal character that he identifies; it is that understanding of the state consistent with an instrumental practice and is association in terms of a substantive extrinsic goal or end. Though it is probably fair to say that enterprise association is the dominant understanding of the state in contemporary political discourse, neither civil nor enterprise association, taken by themselves, offer an adequate account of the modern state. He even says of civil association or the rule of law that "too much has been claimed for it; when properly understood the rule of law *cannot*, without qualification, characterise a modern European state" (OH 155).

Civil association differs from other moral practices in being composed entirely of rules which are deliberately made explicit.[57] Civil association is a self-contained body of rules. It is a coherent system of rules, not a mere collection of rules. Unlike the rules of an instrumental practice which exist only so long as they further the purpose or purposes agreed upon by all associates, the system of rules contained in civil association is authoritative by virtue of the fact that *cives*, that is, those subject to its rule, recognise it as authoritative.

One of the implications of the distinction between transactional and practice-based association is to divorce authority from power. He rejects the view (common to post Weberian sociologists) that authority is simply legitimised power. For Oakeshott authority and power are distinct. Rules are not considered legitimate and therefore subscribed to because to do otherwise results in punishment, rather, they oblige solely by virtue of their acknowledged authenticity. Power on the other hand is the coercive apparatus employed by the

---

[57] In other moral practices "(r)ules, duties, and their like (moral principles and dogmas) are . . . passages of stringency . . . They may help to keep a practice in shape, but they do not give it its shape. They are abstractions which derive their authority from the practice itself as a spoken language in which they appear as passages of somewhat exaggerated emphasis" (OHC 67–8).

authoritative office to ensure compliance. Power backs up authority but in no way is it identical to it.

There is a certain affinity here with the legal philosopher Herbert Hart who argued that a legal system exists whenever enough people take the "legal point of view" and recognise as authoritative particular laws as well as the more basic rules by which the legal system itself is recognized as authoritative. And Oakeshott suggests that the rule of law ideal "hovers over the reflections of many so-called 'positivist' modern jurists" (OH 162), one of the most significant of recent positivists being Hart. Hart, however, criticised the view of John Austin, who maintained that the sovereign is simply he who has ultimate coercive power in the state.[58] Hart termed this position the gunman writ large. Here, both Hart and Oakeshott share the Wittgensteinian view that rules stand on their own.[59]

For Oakeshott, the authority of a rule rests on nothing external to itself. In other words, to claim that a rule does not carry authority is to misunderstand the nature of a rule. A rule is not, for instance, "a piece of advice, a request, a plea, or a warning" (OHC 124). All these arise in particular situations, whereas rules are general and prospective; they are not used up on the performance of any particular action. More importantly, (as with Hobbes's Natural Laws), the utterances identified in the above list are designed to persuade. Unlike rules, they are not in themselves authoritative. They are hypothetical rather than categorical imperatives; to be adhered to if the agent recognises as authoritative the conditions to which they refer. In contrast, "a rule is an authoritative assertion, not a theorem" (OHC 125). Though they may be approved or disapproved of, their authenticity is immune from such considerations.

Oakeshott however, does not espouse the positivist claim "that morally iniquitous rules may still be law."[60] To the extent that law embodies non-instrumentality it is moral. In one sense he is closer to the legal theorist Lon Fuller who argued that legal systems, when functioning according to the requirements of the rule of law ideal, possess an inherent or inner morality.

According to Fuller a legal system approaches this ideal when it possesses the following criteria — when rules are promulgated, general, prospective, clear, non-contradictory, stable, possible of com-

[58] Both Austin and Hart read Hobbes in this positivist way.

[59] For Oakeshott's discussion of Austin see OHC 171n. Though Oakeshott argued that Austin understood a state to be an enterprise association he praises him for making "a determined attempt to distinguish legality from all other considerations".

[60] H.L.A. Hart, *The Concept of Law* (Oxford: Clarendon Press, 1961), p. 207.

pliance and when there is fidelity to law — that is, when official action corresponds to the pronounced rule.[61] Whenever these conditions apply, relations between subject and ruler exhibit a basic reciprocity and the moral autonomy of agency is preserved.[62] This is precisely the claim that Oakeshott makes for his theory of civil association. Only civil association preserves the link between belief and conduct since recognising a rule as authentic is not dependent on its being approved of (OHC 158). Formal, positive law privileges the view that human beings are agents. That is, they are capable of recognising the minimal rules necessary for their mutual association with other agents. Their association is not dependent on consensus, on substantive beliefs or fundamental principles.[63]

Oakeshott mentions the following as conditions necessary to establish an association governed entirely by non-instrumental law: "the quality of legal subjects; rules not arbitrary, secret, retroactive or awards to interests; the independence of judicial proceedings (i.e. all claimants or prosecutors, like defendants, are litigants); no so-called 'public' or 'quasi-public' enterprise or corporation exempt from common liability for wrong; no offence without specific prescription; no penalty without specific offence; no disability or refusal of recognition without established inadequacy of subscription; no outlawry, etc., etc.,: in short, all that may be called the 'inner morality' of a legal system" (OHC 153n1). In his essay "The Rule of Law"

[61]   *The Morality of Law* (New Haven and London: Yale University Press, 1969), ch2. See also David Mapel, "Purpose and Politics: Can there be a Non-Instrumental Civil Association", *The Political Science Reviewer*, Vol. XXI, Spring 1992, 63–80, who has explored more fully the connections between Oakeshott, Hart and Fuller.
[62]   *Ibid.*, p. 39.
[63]   It should be remembered that for Fuller law contains an immanent purpose: "that of subjecting human conduct to the guidance and control of general rules" (*Ibid.*, p. 146). The purpose of this is to establish a relationship of reciprocity between subject and ruler. Oakeshott rejects even this claim, suggesting that expressions such as "human excellence", "respect for persons", "ideal fairness" are descriptions of the formal conditions of persons related in particular moral practices — "These are not, properly speaking, purposes at all" (OHC 62). It should also be noted that Fuller also reverts to ideal types to distinguish legal relationships from other kinds of social relationship, one of these being managerial direction. Unlike legal relationships, the latter is not marked by reciprocity. Moreover, managerial directives are more like commands; addressed to particular persons and exhausted upon the completion of particular tasks — "The directives issued in a managerial context are *applied* by the subordinate in order to serve a purpose set by his superior. The law-abiding citizen, on the other hand, does not *apply* legal rules to serve specific ends set by the lawgiver, but rather *follows* them in the conduct of his own affairs, the interests he is presumed to serve in following legal rules being those of society generally." *The Morality of Law*, p. 207. See generally p. 207ff.

he made the claim that "it is only in respect of these considerations and their like that it may perhaps be said that *lex injusta non est lex*" (OH 141). Hence one important feature of the rule of law, adjudication, entails "analogical" reasoning between like cases, and not the application of 'ideals' or 'principles' from external sources such as "a set of absolute 'values', a declaration of inalienable 'rights', a charter of unconditional 'liberties', or a Bill of Rights representing a Basic or Fundamental Law". Such doctrines and beliefs are foreign to the rule of law. Far from easing the problems of adjudication they tend to exacerbate disputes "and when invoked as the conditions of the obligation to observe the conditions prescribed by *lex* they positively pervert the association: they are the recipe for anarchy" (OH 159–60).

Oakeshott's 'nominalist' Hobbes reappears in the course of this discussion. Again it is denied that Hobbes's Laws of Nature are laws in the proper sense. The so called 'fundamental law' against treason is simply the basic condition that must be adhered to if there is to be any association at all. 'Natural law' understood as the 'natural right' of each man to all things in a condition outside civil association carries only a metaphorical sociological or psychological meaning. More importantly, the set of prescriptions embodied in the negative rendering of the golden rule, far from either imposing unconditional obligations (even *in foro interno*) on the conduct of individuals or offering a reliable guide to adjudication of the law are in fact "no more than an analytic break-down of the intrinsic character of law . . . the *jus* inherent in genuine law which distinguishes it from a command addressed to an assignable agent or a managerial instruction concerned with the promotion of interests".

The convergence between Oakeshott's theory of *lex* and his reading of Hobbes is nowhere more apparent than here in his final substantial essay on the nature of law. Interestingly Oakeshott here suggests that something more than Hobbes's formal theory of law is needed to complete the account of the state as a civil association. In particular it needs to be supplemented with "the negative and limited consideration that the prescriptions of the law should not conflict with a prevailing educated moral sensibility capable of distinguishing between the conditions of 'virtue', the conditions of moral association ('good conduct'), and those which are of such a kind that they should be imposed by law ('justice')" (OH 157–160). In other words, where for Hobbes legal relationships encompass all other moral relationships, for Oakeshott *lex* is simply one moral practice among many.

Despite this qualification the authority of *respublica*, the common concern of *cives*, is internally constituted. Its authority is not acknowledged on account of its identification "with a 'will' of any sort, that of a ruler, a majority of *cives*, or a so-called 'general' will. Nor . . . with a current 'social purpose', with approved moral ideals, with a common good or general interest, or a 'justice' other than that which is inherent in *respublica*" (OHC 152–3).

There are two points worth making in connection with this. First, Oakeshott's argument that recognition of the authenticity of *respublica* has nothing to do with the recognition of any sort of will is consistent with his earlier account of agency. There he made the point that the capacity to exercise will is not the defining feature of human conduct: "what is called the 'will' is nothing but intelligence in doing" (OHC 39). For Hobbes on the other hand, for whom, according to Oakeshott, "(t)he human being is first fully an individual, not in respect of self-consciousness, but in the activity of willing" (RP 280), what is recognized as authoritative is "a common object of will". However, what the subject transfers to the sovereign is the right to will on the former's behalf. The unity of the association "lies solely in the singleness of the Representative, in the *substitution* of his one will for the many conflicting wills" (RP 281).

By denying that law is associated with will Oakeshott is able to distinguish further law from command. A command "is an utterance addressed to an assignable agent . . . (it) is itself an action in response to a particular situation and is used up on the occasion . . . (it) is an injunction to perform a substantive action and it calls for obedience . . . (finally, it) is an authoritative utterance designed to procure a substantive condition of things" (OH 129). Law, by contrast, is general, prospective, does not specify action but conditions to be taken into account when acting, and is the authoritative association that command assumes. This is not a distinction that Hobbes ever makes explicit, though it is made by Oakeshott in the altered introduction to *Leviathan*.[64]

The second point to be noticed in Oakeshott's denial that law is associated with will is that by definition this extends to a 'general' will. Likewise with Hobbes, what is established is "not a common will (for there can be no such thing), but a common object of will . . . There is in this association no concord of wills, no common will, no common good . . . It is a collection of individuals united in one Sovereign representative, and in generation and structure it is the only

---

[64] According to Oakeshott, "A law, in Hobbes's reading of it, is a command, the expression of the Will of the Sovereign. Not every command of the sovereign is law, but only those commands which prescribe a rule of conduct to be subscribed to indifferently by all Subjects" (RP 262).

sort of association that does not compromise the individuality of its components" (RP 281). As will be discussed in the next section, *lex* preserves the individuality of agents.

As Oakeshott pointed out in his 1935 essay on Hobbes, there is no inconsistency in his rejection of authority in philosophy and his insistence on the need for establishing common rules of conduct. These two views are in fact complementary. This is also the case with Oakeshott's distinction between civil and enterprise association. *Lex* is authoritative not wise rule. The formulation is based on the distinction between *in* authority and *an* authority relationships.[65] Authority in civil association is simply rule recognition whereas enterprise association recognises rules on anything but *in* authority relationships: wisdom, expertise, experience, priestly knowledge, doctors "orders" etc.[66] In a pure enterprise state authority as such is not acknowledged. As in Plato's *The Statesman*, the leaders of an enterprise state claim the right to direct on account of their privileged knowledge.

The account of *respublica* as an internally authoritative, free-floating system of law, indifferent to the values and purposes of the individuals which it rules represents a significant departure from the theory of authority enunciated in his early essay "The Authority of the State". To recall, the claim was made there that law, as the voice of government, "no matter what its particular character be . . . always draws its power from a source outside itself . . . For no government . . . was ever a strictly sovereign power, or had ever a more than derivative 'authority.'" The authority that "resides solely in the completeness of the satisfaction which the state affords itself to the needs of concrete persons" (RPM 85-7) more closely resembles the derivative authority characteristic of enterprise association. The state as a philosophically understood 'going-on' has clearly receded in the face of the ideal character civil association.

---

[65] On this see Richard Friedman "The Concept of Authority in Political Philosophy", in J.Raz (ed.), *Authority* (Oxford: Basil Blackwell, 1990).

[66] For this reason a writer like Marsilius, though a Christian Aristotelian and ostensibly identifying "a realm as a *universitas*", by separating divine from human law and denying that the former could be enforced in this life (thereby disallowing the coercive power of the priesthood — likening them to spiritual doctors) was, according to Oakeshott, a significant early exponent of civil association. For Oakeshott's discussion of Marsilius see OHC 216-8. See also p. lxvi of the original introduction to *Leviathan* where *Defensor Pacis* is likened to the former. This sentence is, however, removed from the revised version. Cf. an early exponent of enterprise association, Thomas Aquinas: ". . . the ministry of this kingdom has been entrusted not to earthly kings but to priests . . . For those to whom pertains the care of intermediate ends should be subject to him to whom pertains the care of the ultimate end, and be directed by his rule." *On Kingship*, ch. III (I,14), §110.

In his 1946 essay 'The Concept of a Philosophy of Politics' we have an indication of the transition of his thinking in this regard. In a discussion of the way in which philosophical definition proceeds Oakeshott points out that certain ordinary political concepts either entirely disappear from view or merge with other more explanatory satisfying concepts. "Hans Kelsen", Oakeshott suggests, has satisfactorily "shown how the concept of the *state* may be reduced to that of *law*" (RPM 131). In his account of civil association we have no reference to concrete persons whom, he earlier claimed, the state exists to serve, but rather a full characterisation of the persona of the *civis*, who, *qua civis*, has only legal relationships.

Much of the criticism of Oakeshott's theory has focussed on this deliberately austere depiction of the character of the *civis* in his purely formal relationships to others of his kind. Judith Shklar, for instance, claimed that civil association more closely resembles Hegel's 'abstract right', devoid of the 'integrative force' of *Sittlichkeit*.[67] Similarly, Richard Flathman has argued that Oakeshott's civil association ultimately breaks down since all authoritative relationships invariably assume a background set of shared values and beliefs with which they interact and qualify. Responding to Oakeshott's theory of authority Flathman argues that, "[i]n thought and action the several roles that any person plays and the several characterizations of which any formulation allows inevitably coexist and interact in a variety of ways. As important as they are, role conceptions and distinguishing characterizations do not and cannot (if only because they are commonly defined in part by reference one to the other) form hermetically sealed compartments or windowless monads that are or could be altogether isolated from one another."[68] In other words, mere *in* authority relationships are never entirely independent of the judgments that persons subject to them make in respect of their validity.[69]

---

[67]   "Purposes and Procedures", *Times Literary Supplement*, 12 September 1975, 1018. For a response see Franco, *The Political Philosophy of Michael Oakeshott*, p. 225.

[68]   *The Practice of Political Authority: Authority and the Authoritative* (Chicago: University of Chicago Press, 1980), pp. 107-8, cited in Timothy Fuller, "Authority and the Individual in Civil Association: Oakeshott, Flathman, and Yves Simon", in *Authority Revisited* (Nomos, Vol. 29 — New York and London: New York University Press, 1987), J.R. Pennock and J.W. Chapman (eds.) , p. 138.

[69]   For an interesting response to Flathman, defending the Oakeshott-Hobbes conception of authority, see T. Fuller "Authority and the Individual in Civil Association". Here Fuller claims that by rejecting the Hobbesian solution to the problem Flathman duplicates authority. He provides a contemporary, secular version of Locke's 'appeal to heaven' where individuals are never able to leave the state of nature. Fuller terms this the politics of 'resolute irresolution'.

The account of civil authority in *On Human Conduct* emerges from a thoroughly transparent project of abstraction. Like Austin, Oakeshott attempts to pin down the concept of authority by a process of specification. In other words, in order to develop his ideal character civil association Oakeshott deliberately puts aside considerations such as the valuations of concrete persons on which, he previously argued, the authority of the state rests. Of course, there is much in this early account that is consistent with the later theory of authority. Authority and coercion are clearly distinguished in each. He never follows the Austinian line that authority is simply the supreme power in the state that is habitually obeyed. Indeed, fidelity to authority is never a matter of mere obedience. It is above all an act of recognition. The state may compel external action but this is only authoritative to the extent that the agent recognises it to be so. Moreover, rule recognition is independent of any judgment pertaining to the desirability of its content. Agents are therefore left free to criticize any, or all particular laws. Despite his divergence from positivist understandings of authority Oakeshott's effort to specify the precise nature of civil relationships in abstraction from all others leaves him open to the sort of criticism that Idealist philosophers (including himself) earlier levelled at Austinian theories of sovereignty. The limited explanatory value of a theory of authority which separates abstract personae, *cives*, from their concrete relations as agents, whose values and judgments give authority its meaning, is the sort of claim that lies behind criticisms such as Shklar's and Flathman's. Oakeshott would simply respond that talk of purposes and ends, that is, the content of valuations and judgments, is irrelevant to, since categorically distinguished from, authority relationships. It is only because *cives* recognize authority for what it is, independent of judgments concerning its 'rightness', that criticism of its content can take place at all. I will take this up further in the following section.

VII
Freedom and Authority in Civil Association

I will end this chapter with some further discussion of the distinction between moral and instrumental law which lies behind Oakeshott's contrasting ideal characters, civil and enterprise association. As I have documented earlier in the chapter this distinction is also central to the changes in Oakeshott's reading of Hobbes on the question of authority. I will therefore begin with some further remarks on Hobbes before discussing the sort of freedom civil association is said to embody. Most of the criticism that Oakeshott's theory of civil association has attracted has centred on the claim that a purely procedural association is inconceivable. We have already seen that his reading of Hobbes presents an ambiguity on this question. Drawing on the insights of recent commentary on Oakeshott, I will question the validity of the distinction between civil and enterprise association as it appears in *On Human Conduct* and suggest that this contentious feature of his theory is prefigured in the way he reads Hobbes.

Oakeshott suggested that in Hobbes the freedom of the subject in large measure lies in the silence of the laws, since "when the law does not speak the individual is sovereign over himself" (Intro lvii [RP 282], see also xliii [RP 264]).[70] Traditionally Hobbes has been read as the classic exponent of the idea that freedom is defined in negative terms. "In cases where the sovereign has prescribed no rule, then the subject hath the liberty to do or forbear according to his own discretion" (Lev 144). Here liberty means liberty *from* the coercive power of the state. The fewer areas of life affected by law the greater the freedom enjoyed by subjects. This is generally taken to be the cornerstone of the English liberal tradition, given full expression in the nineteenth century by writers such as Mill and Spencer.[71]

On this reading freedom is traded for the order that law provides. We are willing to forgo some of our liberty in order to prevent anarchy. However, what is striking about Oakeshott's reading of Hobbes is that though it is acknowledged that "the liberties of subjects depend on the silence of the law", as suggested in the previous section, most of the discussion of this question is concerned with denying the claim that absolute positive law in any way diminishes the freedom of subjects.

The idea that those areas of life on which law does not impinge remain free is also foreign to Oakeshott's depiction of civil association as non-instrumental law. What counts here is the mode of association not the quantity of the laws contained therein. Since law in civil association is entirely formal there is no inconsistency in the claim that though every aspect of the life of a *civis* is governed by *lex* he retains all the freedom inherent in agency. For this reason the anarchist is mistaken to suppose that by renouncing all law he is closer to that state of unconditional freedom to which he aspires (see OHC 319).

---

[70] The latter changed in the revised version where Oakeshott writes in similar vein that "it is in the enjoyment of all those rights which he has not surrendered that the 'true freedom' of the Subject lies" (RP 265). The subject does not give up the right to protect himself if the Sovereign fails to live up to his side of the contract — though it is difficult to know what this amounts to if one does away with purposes entirely.

[71] See for instance Maurice Cranston, *Freedom* (New York: Basic Books, 1967), pp. 47–57.

Most of Oakeshott's critics have accepted one or more of the inter-related assumptions of what John Liddington has termed the liberal-utilitarian view of law.[72] The liberal utilitarian asserts the following: all laws are instrumental; all compulsory associations restrict men's freedom; the fundamental question about freedom in the state is: How far does government determine men's performances? As noted above, much of the discussion of the relationship between law and liberty in Hobbes has traditionally hinged on (at least) the second and third of these assumptions. For the moment I want to discuss the first of these assumptions in connection with Oakeshott's reading of Hobbes.

We have seen that in the original introduction Oakeshott hinted at the idea that law is instrumental to the achievement of an end (i.e. peace), whereas it is removed entirely from the revised version. The original reading was consistent with Hobbes's claim that the obligation to obey the Sovereign lapses to the extent that his laws fail to promote the end for which the commonwealth was erected. Hobbes says that "the obligation, and liberty of the subject, is to be derived, either from those [covenant instituting] words, or others equivalent; or else from the end of the institution of sovereignty, namely, the peace of the subjects within themselves, and their defence against a common enemy". Further, "the obligation a man may sometimes have, upon the command of the sovereign to execute any dangerous, or dishonourable office, dependeth not on the words of our submission; but on the intention, which is to be understood by the end thereof. When therefore our refusal to obey, frustrates the end for which the sovereignty was ordained; then there is no liberty to refuse: otherwise there is" (Lev. 141–2).

Oakeshott (at least in his later phase) would no doubt claim that here Hobbes's discussion of ends are not ends "properly so-called" (in the way that the theorems of natural reason are not properly called laws). That is, peace is not in fact an end but the minimal condition required to make possible the pursuit of the particular ends that individuals make their own. Though 'peace' and 'order' are the defining features of Hobbes's commonwealth they are not its end. This position is consistent with Oakeshott's argument that freedom does not stand in consequential relationship to civil association, rather, "it is inherent in its character" (OH 161).

Despite this it is difficult to escape the conclusion that in some moments Hobbes goes beyond a strictly formalist conception of law and links authority with desirability. Hobbes was doing more than merely specifying the inherent character of *lex* (to use Oakeshott's

[72] See Liddington, "Freedom in a Modern State", pp. 308–9.

term), he was also addressing the ultimate question as to why the terms of civil association should be adhered to in the first place. As well as describing the nature of law he was also justifying it and attempting to persuade his contemporaries to adhere to its requirements. In so doing he offered a criterion by which the validity of particular laws, as well as the whole body of law could be assessed. In what follows I will question Oakeshott's separation of explanation and justification and suggest that these are in fact two inseparable sides of Oakeshott's theory of civil association.

As was outlined in the previous chapter Oakeshott distinguishes several identifying features of free agency. Firstly human conduct is defined in terms of what it is not: causation. It is the exhibition of intelligence. Closely related to this is the idea that human beings are free because they are self-interpreting. As he says on numerous occasions, "we are what we understand ourselves to be". Hence, adherence to the conditions of a moral practice does not diminish freedom because a practice is an "understood relationship, capable of being engaged in only in virtue of having been learned". A practice is not a biological or psychological relationship. "On the contrary", agents "speak to one another in words or gestures and are understood by one another; their responses to one another are in terms of their understandings" (OHC 55). Further, they are continually interpreting and responding to practices and determining how to act in contingent situations. Like a vernacular language, a practice is never fixed or finished but is continually in the process of being created and interpreted by its users.

According to Oakeshott the conditions of a practice never dictate particular performances required from agents. Rather, they are adverbial considerations which must be taken into account whenever an agent chooses and acts. "A rule (and *a fortiori* something less exacting, like a maxim) can never tell a performer what choice he shall make; it announces only conditions to be subscribed to in making choices" (OHC 58). The general nature of these conditions is one reason why Oakeshott claims that subscription to practices in no way compromises the freedom inherent in agency. Practices never specify the content of performances, and performances are always contingent or particular. There are no non-optional ends.

It is this final sense of freedom that is compromised by enterprise association. Enterprise associates are joined in the recognition of substantive performances. According to Oakeshott enterprise association particularises purposes. At one level, purposes, like rules are general. By themselves they do not determine particular acts ("I cannot *want* 'happiness'; what I want is to idle in Avignon or to hear Caruso sing" — OHC 53). For instance, a state that is guided by the overriding purpose of increasing, say, productivity or national income may do so by leaving intact the freedom of the associates to choose their own course of action in pursuit of this end. There is, therefore, no necessary, but only a contingent connection between general purposes (of the state) and particular acts (of individuals). However, the office required by enterprise association is one which makes possible "the engagement to make substantive choices of actions or utterances which are not entailed in the common purpose but which contingently constitute its pursuit" (OHC 115). The mode of government in enterprise association is inherently managerial, and individuals are required by the former to perform specific tasks. In other words, law in enterprise association is recognized only as command.

As discussed earlier, the authority of law in civil association bears no connection to the desirability of its content (OHC 148). *Lex* merely offers authoritative rulings. It does not provide reasons as to why it should be adhered to, nor does it require the approval of *cives*. Since *lex* is only concerned with external compliance, *cives* are left free to criticize any particular law. Moreover, because authority here is purpose-independent, Oakeshott claims there is "nothing in civil association to threaten the link between belief and conduct which constitutes 'free' agency . . ." (OHC 158). This argument seems to be based on the idea specified in the first essay of *On Human Conduct* that agents are free because all human conduct is contingent. Since there are no non-optional ends, "any association that insists that certain purposes or conditions must be *necessarily* approved as rational, beneficial, or morally desirable cannot, therefore, be based on this understanding of the self as an agent."[73] Where civil association respects the contingency of human conduct — treating agents as agents leaving them free to formulate their own purposes — enterprise association makes particular purposes compulsory. That is, the latter disregards the contingency of human conduct, which civil association respects because it is based on the idea that no purposes are necessary and therefore none are made compulsory. The freedom an enterprise associate enjoys is the freedom to join or leave the association. The associates only join the association if they subscribe to its purpose or purposes. If they cease to share the said purpose they are free to leave at any time. This is why Oakeshott claims

[73] David Mapel, "Civil Association and the Idea of Contingency", p. 401. My discussion here owes much to the insights of this essay.

there is some contradiction in the idea that an enterprise association can be both a compulsory association (such as a state) and free.[74]

Since agency is inherently free (it is intelligent movement), no enterprise state, however closely it conforms to the ideal, can dispense entirely with freedom. However, by demanding particular performances from agents, not merely the observance of general rules, the enterprise state diminishes the self-recognition amongst those subject to it that they are in fact free, self-determining beings.

Oakeshott is by no means hostile to the idea of enterprise association *per se*. In fact he would argue that the existence of a variety of such associations is vital to the existence of a pluralistic society. This is precisely the sort of argument he mounted in "The Political Economy of Freedom" (in RP). His argument is rather that by making any actual state conform to the ideal character 'enterprise association', contingent purposes become compulsory, thereby breaking the link between belief and conduct.

Despite this, when the distinction between civil and enterprise association is read in the light of his theory of agency he appears to have loaded the deck in favour of the former. The cogency of the distinction depends on the account of agency developed in the first essay of *On Human Conduct*. It is only in civil association that agents (who have become *cives*) are related to one another in terms of authority. Their freedom is protected because authority in no way diminishes the capacity for choosing contingent ends, the hallmark of free agency. Agents are free because the capacity to choose *this* rather than *that* is a reflective decision, not an unintelligent, or organic, response. Because agents could have chosen an alternative course of action, to make compulsory a purpose which by nature is contingent, must conflict with this understanding of agency. Being an ideal character, civil association excludes from itself relationships which contradict it. This means that it excludes the relationship of role performers, which is what compulsory enterprise association turns agents into by denying them the opportunity to choose between contingent ends. It makes their relationship dependent on knowledge or beliefs they could have rejected.

This is not unlike Hobbes's argument for the necessity of the sovereign. There is an unbroken (not necessarily consistent) chain of reasoning in Hobbes from the pre-civil predicament to the generation of authority relationships in the commonwealth. Like Oakeshott, the validity of Hobbes's theory of authority hinges on his depiction of this predicament. The commonwealth brings about an

---

[74] "The Vocabulary of a Modern European State", *Political Studies*, 23 (1975), 319–41, 409–14, at p. 340.

abatement of inevitable chaos of conflicting wills which is a consequence of the limits of reason and the fact that it is always individu-
ally defined. Had Hobbes argued that human beings are more like
ants or bees: ie. without the power of speech or reason (which, for all
its advantages, is the source of the predicament), then the solution to
the predicament would be an altogether different one. Indeed, the
question of a solution would become superfluous because the predicament would cease to exist (in any case Hobbes would not have
been able to compose a work of philosophy).

Hobbes claims that a relationship of authority is one that all agents
must accept to the extent that they can think rationally. To choose the
state of nature is to act self-contradictorily. Similarly, enterprise
association in Oakeshott's theory posits a form of relationship
which, if not in complete contradiction to his account of agency, is
skewed in such a way that the two do not entirely fit. Though
Oakeshott claims to be merely describing, not justifying, the postulates of these two ideal types of association, the implication of his
argument is that enterprise association constitutes a danger because
it conflicts with his conception of the agent as a self-interpreting
being. It breaks the link between belief and conduct which civil association leaves intact. In enterprise association relationships with others are established on the basis of non-necessary knowledge or
beliefs that must contradict the basis for authoritative association.

If, however, Oakeshott's theory of the self is rejected and contingency is not the defining feature of the human condition, then enterprise association offers itself as a more likely solution to the problem
of political obligation (civil obligation becomes redundant in this
scenario). That is, an association of role performers is consistent with
the understanding of human conduct as organic, non-intelligent
activity.

Moreover, if civil association is entirely purposeless, then there
seems to be some justification for the criticism levelled by numerous
commentators[75] that there is no reason to prefer it to enterprise association. However, if one accepts David Mapel's argument that civil association privileges the self-recognition of agents that they are agents, that
they have the capacity to formulate their own purposes, then it is possible to make sense of the idea of civil association. Indeed, this seems to be
the sort of justification that Oakeshott has in mind when he claims that
the postulate of free agency "does not distinguish one agent from
another and it does not entail any particular mode of association; it is
the postulate alike of relationships of master and slave, of commanding

---

[75] See for instance Flathman, *The Practice of Political Authority*, p. 75.

and obeying, of ruling and being ruled...". Accordingly, "(W)hat has to be reckoned with is a historic disposition to transform this unsought 'freedom' of conduct from a postulate into an experience and to make it yield a satisfaction of its own, independent of the chancy and intermittent satisfaction of actions achieving their imagined and wished-for outcomes" (OHC 235–6).

This is the point at which the ambiguous relationship between the different senses of freedom create some difficulties for his theory. Oakeshott clearly sees freedom as more than a mere 'postulate' of human conduct. The response different individuals display towards the inescapable contingency of the human condition is a moral response. Though he talks about civil association as entirely purposeless, it is difficult to avoid the conclusion many commentators have pointed to regarding his preference for this type of association on account of its privileging a contingent, historic disposition to cultivate individuality. Further, I would contend that this preference is not unrelated to the way he develops the distinction between civil and enterprise association on the basis of his theory of agency. Description and justification are two inseparable parts of his theoretical project.

At one level, the promotion of fully self-conscious individuality can be seen as the purpose of civil association. Unlike a compulsory enterprise association, the very nature of civil association precludes any compromise of individual self-enactment. As Mapel has suggested, "[a]ny association that insists that certain purposes or conditions must be *necessarily* approved as rational, beneficial, or morally desirable cannot, therefore, be based on this understanding of the self as an agent."[76] Though civil association may not be devoid of purpose(s), it privileges the idea that none of the purposes it has are necessary. Since all practices and purposes and the laws and policies that follow from them are contingent, all are open to criticism. "We approve of civil association as a whole precisely because it does not require us to approve of *any* of its particular laws, purposes, or policies. And we approve of *not* having to approve of any particular laws or policies because we understand that as contingent beings we can *always* come to disapprove what we previously found desirable"[77]

Of course, this only puts the problem of justification one step further back. If the disposition to transform the unsought freedom of human conduct into a full individualist 'ethic' of self-enactment is simply an historical contingency then there is no reason to prefer it,

[76] "Civil Association and the Idea of Contingency", p. 401.
[77] *Ibid.*

along with the type of rule concomitant to it, to the collectivist morality of the enterprise state. This conclusion is entirely in keeping with
the tenor of Oakeshott's anti-foundationalist epistemology. All
choices are contingent, even that which seeks, Sisyphus like, entirely
to remove contingency from the world of human affairs.

It should also be pointed out here that this reformulation (at least
the making explicit what was previously only implicit) of
Oakeshott's theory of civil association in instrumentalist terms,
though doing away with the distinction between purposive and
non-purposive association, can be achieved while preserving the
idea of authority that it embodies. That is, a minimalist purposive
state, directed towards the promotion of the experience of individuality does not compromise authority because it does not alter, but
rather strengthens, the idea of agency on which it is based. It does
not replace authority with knowledge, belief, expertise, and so on,
because it encourages the understanding that the substance of these
things, while often persuasive for different reasons, is invariably
open ended. As such, these beliefs cannot form the basis of
authoritative relationships.

In chapter 5 I will explore further the tensions between these competing moral experiences in connection with Oakeshott's discussion
of prideful or noble individuality in Hobbes. It is not the purpose of
this chapter to resolve the apparent difficulties in Oakeshott's theory
of authority, though I have made it clear that I think David Mapel's
reconstrual of civil association along minimally instrumentalist
lines is the sort of approach most likely to make the theory intelligible. It is simply worth pointing out that the issue underlying most of
the criticism of Oakeshott's theory, concerning the plausibility of a
legal system devoid of any common purpose, finds an interesting
parallel in Oakeshott's various readings of Hobbes. This says as
much about Oakeshott's theory of civil association as it does about
his reading of Hobbes.[78]

---

[78] Indeed it seems also to extend to his reading of Hegel, see OHC 257–263. Both
Hobbes and Hegel are read in such a way that they elucidate Oakeshott's own
understanding of civil association. Civil association provides an ideal character
around which their respective political philosophies can be understood. It also
supplies the criteria for determining which aspects of their thought make no
contribution to their specifically political philosophy. If, however, one accepts the
reformulation of civil association along purposive lines that I have suggested then
this brings it closer to the conventional reading of Hegel's understanding of the
modern state as that association in which freedom is made actual. Though of course
for Oakeshott modern individuality is a historic (ie. contingent) disposition, not the
necessary end point of world history. Incidently, this reformulation also makes

The reformulation of Oakeshott I have endorsed perhaps brings his theory closer to his earlier readings of Hobbes where instrumentality played a limited, but vital role in elucidating the character of the *Leviathan*. By interpreting and subsequently appropriating Hobbes in the way that he does he is remaining true to the claims he made in his first essay on Hobbes regarding the nature of the philosophical enterprise. To recall, there he claimed that,

> It is the business of philosophy continuously to renew itself. And such new philosophy may arise from the study of what belongs to an earlier time; and the study of what belongs to an earlier time is profitable, in the end, only when it is related to a genuine renaissance. But the study, if it is to result in anything valuable, must be close: it is only by this detailed study of a philosophical text that it can become, not merely an inheritance, but an inspiration for fresh thought (TH 267)

Whatever the merit Hobbes scholars may accord Oakeshott's reading of him, and whatever the ultimate explanatory value civil association has for understanding the experience of authority in the modern state, it is impossible to deny that Oakeshott's engagement with Hobbes was central to the inspiration that gave rise to this central feature of his political philosophy, and, as I have shown, the ambiguities and difficulties it contains are mirrored in Oakeshott's reading of him. We may question the way he reads Hobbes but perhaps in the end this misses the mark when the nature of Oakeshott's project is understood.

---

civil association closer to Lon Fuller's understanding of law, who, not sharing Oakeshott's understanding of Hegel, seeks to distance his purposive theory of law from 'Hegelian excesses', see p. 146, *The Morality of Law*.

Chapter 4

Religion, the World and Human Conduct

We ought not to dispute of God's nature; He is not a fit subject of our philosophy[1]

I

Though Oakeshott is best known for his contribution to political philosophy his estimation of political activity was limited. "Politics", he wrote in his original introduction to *Leviathan*, "is a second rate-rate form of human activity, neither an art nor a science, at once corrupting to the soul and fatiguing to the mind, the activity either of those who cannot live without the illusion of affairs or those so fearful of being ruled by others that they will pay away their lives to prevent it" (Intro lxiv).[2] Though political activity can achieve things of value it is never more than "a highly specialized and abstracted form of communal activity; it is conducted on the surface of the life of society and except on rare occasions makes remarkable small impressions below that surface ... (RPM 93)". Along with Augustine and Hobbes, Oakeshott held that the gift of civil association to the human predicament was a negative one. At its best it can offer no more than a stable set of rules whereby the inherent contingency of the human condition is to some extent abated (OHC 74). Where political activity occupies a necessary, though superficial, place in the actual conduct of life, it is in religious experience that practical life reaches its deepest, most fulfilling level.

[1]   Thomas Hobbes, *Questions Concerning Liberty, Necessity, and Chance* .
[2]   This sentence is removed from the revised version.

This chapter takes a deliberate departure from the approach of the previous two where I have argued that Oakeshott's engagement with Hobbes was central to the development of his theories of agency and authority. Though Oakeshott wrote an early essay on authority his orientation towards questions concerning political philosophy seems to have coincided in the mid 1930s with an interest in Hobbes. The significant shifts in his thinking on these questions are subsequently reflected in his readings of Hobbes. On the question of religion, however, a somewhat different picture emerges. Oakeshott's interest in religion existed prior to his interest in Hobbes. Indeed, most of his early writings are taken up with questions concerning the nature of religion and though the topic does not take up a large proportion of the pages of *Experience and Its Modes* it was far from peripheral to his argument. This interest was intense and lifelong. Though it was not until *On Human Conduct* that Oakeshott explicitly returned to the question of religion, his concern with Rationalism and the corruptions of practical life seem to derive from an attitude to experience which could be termed religious. Indeed, he seems to have taken the story of the Tower of Babel as emblematic of the modern predicament.[3] The Rationalist's attempt to impose uniformity and remove 'dissonances' from experience stands in contrast to true religious sensibility which offers a language of self-enactment facilitating reconciliation to them (OHC 81).

Though he does not discuss Hobbes's understanding of religion in any great depth, in the essay 'Leviathan: a myth' and elsewhere Oakeshott does indicate an understanding of the strong religious character of *Leviathan*. As I will outline shortly, what Oakeshott does say about religion in Hobbes is consistent with much recent Hobbes literature and I have drawn on scholarship which has developed this aspect of Hobbes's thought more extensively. It is likely that Oakeshott would have endorsed the growing recognition of the importance of Hobbes's theology to his overall argument. Moreover, as has already been shown, because there are many fundamental philosophical affinities between these two thinkers it would be surprising if there were no parallels in their respective philosophies of religion. As well as exploring some of these connections this chapter will serve as a preliminary to the next where I will explore Oakeshott's understanding of civilization and its threats. As will be seen in the discussion that follows, in Oakeshott's estimation, religion is not an incidental component in the

---

[3]   The significance of this will be discussed in the next chapter.

constitution of a civilization but vital, not only to its existence, but to its continued well being.

II

Despite the fact that this preoccupation with the claims of religion seems to be independent of Oakeshott's interest in Hobbes a number of interesting points can be made in connection with what he does say about Hobbes on religion. The first and most obvious point is that Oakeshott, together with commentators such as Taylor, Warrender, Hood and Glover, rejected the traditional view that Hobbes was a covert atheist which he disguised by wrapping his arguments in theological dress. According to Oakeshott, religious belief for Hobbes "is something not to be avoided in this world, and is something of the greatest practical importance" (Intro lxii [RP 289]).

The traditional, atheistic view of Hobbes has had a remarkable tenacity. It first gained currency amongst his contemporaries and has never been without its protagonists. However in the last few decades the tide seems to have turned and most commentators, though in different ways, now take Hobbes's theology to be central to his overall argument.[4] When Oakeshott first wrote the introduction to *Leviathan* this view was a departure from the orthodox reading and, if for nothing else, his interpretation is notable for this reason.

Oakeshott's claim is that unless books I and II of *Leviathan* are read in the light of the theological material contained in books III and IV then the overall argument of the book is disfigured by "an element of unreality". The second half of *Leviathan* is central to the integrity of the book because it takes us back to the universal predicament, only it adds to it an extra dimension. According to Oakeshott, what Hobbes was doing in books III and IV was reading the universal predicament, as outlined

---

[4]   See for example, Pocock "Time, History and Eschatology in the thought of Thomas Hobbes", in *Politics, Language, and Time: Essays on Political Thought and History* (London: Methuen and co., 1972), Eldon Eisenach, *Two Worlds of Liberalism: Religion and Politics in Hobbes, Locke, and Mill* (Chicago: University of Chicago Press, 1981), Paul Johnson "Hobbes's Anglican Doctrine of Salvation", in Ross, Schneider and Waldman (eds.), *Thomas Hobbes in His Time* (Minneapolis, 1974) , Richard Sherlock "The Theology of *Leviathan*: Hobbes on Religion", *Interpretation* 10 (1982), 43–60, Shirley Letwin "Hobbes and Christianity", *Daedalus* 105 (1976), 1–21, A.P. Martinich *The Two Gods of Leviathan: Thomas Hobbes on Religion and Politics* (Cambridge: Cambridge University Press, 1992), Arrigo Pacchi "Hobbes and the Problem of God", in *Perspectives on Thomas Hobbes*, G.A.J. Rogers and Alan Ryan (eds.) (Oxford: Clarendon Press, 1988), Patricia Springborg, "Hobbes on Religion", in *The Cambridge Companion to Hobbes*, (ed.) T. Sorrell (Cambridge: Cambridge University Press, 1996) etc, etc.

in general terms in books I and II, through the particular circumstances as they appeared in his time. "The project, then, of the second half of the argument of *Leviathan* is, by correcting an error in principle, to show more clearly the local and transitory mischief in which the universal predicament of mankind appeared in the seventeenth century" (RP 267).

Oakeshott treads a middle course between the traditional view that Hobbes's theology can be explained away as the disingenuous gloss imposed on an essentially atheistic argument by a timid thinker afraid of the reception his book would provoke and the Warrender/Taylor/Hood view in which the theology is utilised to explain a natural law theory of authority. The theology is integral to the argument of *Leviathan*, but it stands distinct from the strictly philosophical components of his theory. In this Oakeshott's position is consistent with recent scholars such as Pacchi and Pocock[5] who argue that the theological and philosophical aspects of Hobbes's position represent two distinct modes of understanding which cannot be collapsed one into the other. Pacchi, in fact, argues that this distinction generates in Hobbes's thought two images of God, one philosophical, the other theological: "the philosophical God is the final, purely supposed term of a chain of material causes, the merely hypothetical conclusion at which natural reason arrives in its conditional proceeding from experience of facts; on the other hand, the God of *Leviathan* is the biblical God, a physically personal and theologically identified being which stimulates and warrants any orderly human society and is the unavoidable reference for any political theory."[6]

In a similar way, Pocock argues that *Leviathan* should be seen as containing two parallel kinds of argument. The first half employs synchronic, or philosophical reasoning, whereas the second, concerned with developing a theological or sacred history, employs diachronic reasoning. Since *Leviathan* has tended to be interpreted by philosophers and political theorists, this distinction helps explain why the second half of the book has traditionally been overlooked. The distinction between experience and philosophy, which we have seen Oakeshott employ in explaining Hobbes's system, is central also to Pocock's reading. Sense experience, because it takes place in time and is subject to its fluctuations, can only generate particular conclusions. What is called prudence is simply the accumulation of these particular experiences enabling the individual to make reasonable judgements, or guesses,

[5]   Pacchi, "Hobbes and the Problem of God" and Pocock, "Time, History and Eschatology".
[6]   "Hobbes and the Problem of God", p. 186.

about what will happen in the future based on his experience of what has happened in the past. According to Hobbes, "though it be called prudence when the event answereth our expectation, yet in its own nature it is but presumption" (Lev 16). All judgments which are subject to the fluctuations of the historical process, both prudence in the individual as well as the accumulation of traditions and customs in society, rest on what Hobbes calls presumption. By separating philosophy and history in this way Hobbes is able to discuss God in the only way that is meaningfully possible: that is, through a history of the way he has acted in the thoughts and lives of individuals. This brings us no closer to an understanding of his nature, because history, as the record of particular acts in the past (in this case God's acts), is manifestly excluded from the only thing we can have certainty of: scientific knowledge.

These commentators reinforce the point that we have seen Oakeshott make central to his reading of Hobbes concerning the essentially modal nature of human knowledge.[7] For both Oakeshott and Hobbes this notion of modality is central to their respective accounts of religious experience. Hobbes's fideistic scepticism finds a clear parallel in Oakeshott's claim that religion is wholly contained in the world of practice. Neither science nor philosophy has any part to play in determining the truths of religion. However, it is the claims of history on the bearing of religious truth, rather than those of philosophy or science, that assumes a preponderant place in Oakeshott's early writings.

Despite the much trumpeted conflict between science and religion it was perhaps historical thought which had a more profound impact on theological thinking in the late nineteenth and early twentieth centuries. The church historian Owen Chadwick made the point that, "(i)n one sense, the great question of the nineteenth century was the question whether historians, by probing the moments of time associated with religion, could affect its meaning."[8] Collingwood also recognised the centrality of historical thinking to the theological thought of the time when he claimed that "(t)he application to religious problems of historical research has been the most conspicuous and brilliant feature in the theology of the last thirty years."[9] In a similar vein Clement Webb wrote in 1935 that "it is a patent fact that,

[7]   For further discussion of Hobbes's modal view of knowledge in relation to his conception of religion see Conal Condren, *Thomas Hobbes* (New York: Twayne Publishers, 2000), ch.4.

[8]   *The Secularization of the European Mind in the Nineteenth Century* (Cambridge: Cambridge University Press, 1975), p. 191.

[9]   *Religion and Philosophy* (London: Macmillan, 1916), p. 37.

within quite recent times — indeed, in the lifetime of the older among ourselves — a revolution has taken place in the attitude of Christian scholars toward the writings which contain the narratives of those events to which Christians attach so high an importance — a revolution which, we may be well assured, cannot be without far-reaching consequences for our estimate of the importance of the historical element in Christianity."[10] Oakeshott himself wrote in *Experience and its Modes* that "(i)t is only in recent times that new and specifically historical interest has arisen in connexion with Christianity. And how great a revolution this has involved is known to those who have followed it in detail" (EM 105).

There is little doubt that Oakeshott's lifelong concern with elucidating the logic of historical enquiry was tied up with his early reflections on the nature of religion and these writings can be seen as a contribution to the debate over the nature of religion, in particular Christianity, in the light of this revolution in historical thought.

Commenting on the structure of *Experience and Its Modes*, Maurice Cowling suggested that Oakeshott's interest in scientific experience consisted primarily in the attempt to demarcate its boundaries to prevent it from encroaching on the modes of history, practice and philosophy. For Cowling, the real interest of the book was to examine the relations between these non-scientific realms of experience.[11] It is worth adding that since philosophy, according to Oakeshott, is simply thought purged of the abstraction permeating the rest of experience, and most of experience is conducted in one or other of the various abstract modes, the relationship between history and practical life is of central importance to the argument of the book. It is important for the conduct of life to clarify the distinction between practical and historical truth since "the errors of practice are those which enslave, which mislead our conduct and endanger our lives". As with Hume, Oakeshott contends that philosophical errors are only ridiculous, whereas those of religion are dangerous (EM 308). To base conduct on a scientific, historical or philosophical conclusion is to corrupt conduct and destroy the unity of practice as a coherent world of ideas.

So, for both Hobbes and Oakeshott, generally speaking, reflection on the nature of religious experience is to be construed in terms of their respective accounts of knowledge in its different forms. Yet, the specific theory each developed was a response to different challenges to religious experience. Hobbes found it necessary to rethink

---

[10]   *The Historical Element in Religion* (London: George Allen and Unwin, 1935), p. 49.
[11]   *Religion and Public Doctrine in Modern England* (Cambridge: Cambridge University Press, 1980), p. 261.

Christianity in light of the limits imposed on understanding by the emergent post-sceptical science that arose in the early seventeenth century.[12]

Oakeshott's attempt to discern the nature of Christianity, on the other hand, centred on questions raised by the late nineteenth and early twentieth century revolution in historical thought. Though he rejected any association with schools or movements, Oakeshott's effort to deal with such questions by implication allied him with the theological modernist movement then current in Anglican circles. Its flagship journal "The Modern Churchman" bore the following quotation from Erasmus: "By identifying the new learning with heresy, you make orthodoxy synonymous with ignorance".[13] The Modernist movement was never more than a somewhat heterodox collection of scholars and theologians united in the effort to reconcile religious faith with modern critical scholarship[14] and though two of Oakeshott's early essays appeared in "The Modern Churchman", and another was published by the "D" Society — a group of modernist theologians[15] — it is perhaps strained to identify Oakeshott's work too closely with any particular movement. Indeed, in a short review of Percy Gardner's, *Modernism in the Church of England* (1926), Oakeshott criticised the author for identifying Modernism with a particular set of tenets rather than as "something which has always existed and must always exist — a striving to make theology give some answer to 'the force and patience of the present time'."[16]

Since Christianity is a tradition and it is in the nature of a tradition to renew itself in keeping with contemporary circumstances, it will always contain elements of modernism. According to this rather loose understanding, Hobbes's effort to strip Christian theology of the accretions of 'Aristotelity' in light of the intellectual developments of the seventeenth century makes him a prime exponent of modernist teaching. Indeed, it is likely that it was Hobbes's thorough rejection of pagan philosophy (which his contemporaries took

---

[12] For Hobbes's connection with the post-sceptical science of Gassendi, Mersenne, Grotius and others, see Richard Tuck's, "Optics and Sceptics: the philosophical foundations of Hobbes's political thought", in Edmund Leites (ed.) *Conscience and Casuistry in Early Modern Europe* (Cambridge: Cambridge University Press, 1987), and *Philosophy and Government, 1572–1651* (Cambridge: Cambridge University Press, 1993).

[13] It also quoted Burke: "A State without the means of change is without the means of its conservation".

[14] See Arthur Ramsey, *From Gore to Temple: The Development of Anglican Theology from Lux Mundi to the Second World War 1889–1939* (Longmans, 1960), ch. 5.

[15] See Timothy Fuller's note RPM p. 4.

[16] *Journal of Theological Studies*, 28 (1927), p. 316.

to be essential to Christianity) that led to charges of atheism. Ironically then, it may well have been his Christian outlook itself that gave rise to his atheistic reputation.[17]

In what sense then did Hobbes, in Oakeshott's view, set about reworking Christianity in light of the recognition that its medieval foundations were no longer valid? One possible response, which Hobbes rejected, was to do away with all positive religions and re-establish religion on new universal, rationalist foundations. This was the way of deism. Significantly, Oakeshott links the origins of Natural Religion, not to Hobbes as many have done, but to Descartes. Writing in a tradition stretching back to writers such as Varro in late Roman times, Hobbes, in Oakeshott's judgment, was not concerned with reformulating the beliefs of Christianity "in the interest of some universal, rational truth about God and the world to come, but to remove from them the power to disrupt society" (RP 291). His was a Civil rather than a Rational theology. This view is supported by a recent commentator who observes that, "(t)he question of religion as a set of human opinions about God and his relationship to man interested Hobbes immensely and was an issue of crucial importance in his mature political philosophy; the question of the truth of theism was not nearly so important."[18] The basic affinity of this view with Oakeshott's understanding of religion will become apparent when it is considered in the context of his account of human conduct.

Having identified in very general terms the nature of Hobbes's 'modernist' theological project I will now proceed to a consideration of the problems that gave rise to Oakeshott's understanding of religion. Where for Hobbes Christianity had to take heed of the profound transformation in the nature of reason that signalled the eclipse of the medieval world view, for Oakeshott and his contemporaries the challenge to Christianity grew out of the growth of historical understanding that emerged in the nineteenth century.[19]

---

[17] On this see Letwin "Hobbes and Christianity", esp. pp. 2–3.

[18] Sherlock, "The Theology of *Leviathan*", p. 44.

[19] Alisdair MacIntyre makes an interesting point on the modern history of arguments for theism which is worth noting here — "The Debate about God: Victorian Relevance and Contemporary Irrelevance" in MacIntyre and Ricour, *The Religious Significance of Atheism* (New York and London: Columbia University Press, 1969). According to MacIntyre there have been two crises faced by theistic arguments in the last three hundred years. The first of these involved confronting, for the first time in Christian history, the serious possibility of atheism. In the ancient and medieval worlds there had, of course, been non-believers, but for writers such as Anselm, who confronted the problem of the 'fool' who in his heart said there was

Earlier I referred to Pocock's observation that Hobbes, contrary to many of his readers' claims, employed a form of historical understanding in order to construct his theology. History for Hobbes is ultimately arbitrary and incapable of generating demonstrative truth. It is unreliable for the same reason that every other form of experiential knowledge is unreliable: it only ever deals with particulars. Oakeshott departs from Hobbes's conclusion here. For Oakeshott, practice and history represent two distinct modes of experience and as such generate their own respective truth claims, and each in turn are distinct from the claims of the world of science. It is on these terms, according to Oakeshott, that the truth of religion needs to be assessed.

III

In order to give an adequate account of Oakeshott's understanding of historical knowledge, and the place of religion in connection with it, we need first to outline briefly the way in which, he claims, the past is variously interpreted in experience.[20]

According to Oakeshott the past as such does not exist. All experience is present experience, in which the past exists in various forms

---

no God, atheism was "a logical possibility which theism had to consider, but not a live moral option which the theist had to fear as a serious rival". By the seventeenth century, however, writers such as Pascal had to face the threat posed to theism by the non-believer who is "so constituted that he cannot believe" (p. 13). One possible solution to this dilemma was deism, the other was represented by Pascal's famous wager. For the first time orthodox Christian belief was presented as something that could be chosen and here lie the roots of modern existentialism. The second crisis, which presupposed the first, occurred in the nineteenth century when "theism in either of its new formulations was subjected to the critical standards of modern culture, which treats refutability as a necessary character of warrantable belief at every point in the study of history, in science, and in ordinary life" (p. 14). As MacIntyre notes, this crisis is well depicted in Mrs Humphrey Ward's novel *Robert Elsemere* in which a young minister loses his conviction in orthodox Christianity (replacing it with the philosophical Idealism of T.H. Green) after conceding that the New Testament could be subjected to the sort of scholarship applicable to all historical manuscripts. For if the historian is to reject divine intervention as an explanation of historical events then this must carry over into the study of sacred texts such as scripture (pp. 3–5). For our purposes it is worth keeping this twofold crisis in mind when considering Oakeshott's and Hobbes's respective philosophies of religion. Each wrote at a time when Christian theology confronted challenges posed by broader intellectual developments. Though to some extent this has always been the case, these two instances do seem to present themselves as significant moments in the development of modern theology.

[20] Here I will move freely between Oakeshott's various writings on the philosophy of history in order to give a complete synoptic picture of his thesis.

as presupposition. The two most significant here are the practical and the historical pasts. The world of practice contains its own idiomatically distinct discourse that issues in persuasive utterances, rather than the explanatory utterances that characterize philosophical and historical experience. In practical experience the past is interpreted in order to affect present conduct. The past invoked is a 'living' past which contains 'a storehouse' of 'lessons', fables, warnings, pieces of advice, each marked by their present usefulness. The relevant question invoked concerning an object — an artefact or utterance — of present existence interpreted in terms of the practical past is not, what did it mean to the makers or users of the object in the context of their time?, but "What use or meaning has it in a current present-future of practical engagement?" (OH 36–7).

The practical past is most commonly found in one of two domains: politics and religion (EM 103). Since religion, for Oakeshott, is practical experience at its highest, most complete level, the past that it invokes is invariably a practical past. According to Oakeshott, "'God in history' is . . . a contradiction, a meaningless phrase. Wherever else God is, he is not in history, for if he were there would no longer be any history. Where in history he is taken to be a cause, nothing has been said and nothing remains to be said. And this, among other reasons, is why we must deny to the ancient Hebrews any proper historical consciousness. 'God in history' indicates an incursion of the practical past into the historical past, an incursion that brings only chaos" (EM 127). The ancient Hebrews' practical orientation to past happenings was of course taken over by the Christian community and Oakeshott observes that "Christianity seems, almost from the beginning, to have provided a new incentive for studying the past, but it provided no incentive whatever for studying the historical past" (EM 105).

The past invariably comes to us in the form of practical experience and it cannot become the historical past without undergoing transformation. Indeed, the practical implications of the past have no place in the historian's enquiry. He is concerned solely with a 'dead' past, independent of present relevance. "The *differentia* of the historical past lies in its very disparity from what is contemporary" (EM 106). The historian's world is a world viewed *sub specie praeteritorum*. He has an interest in the past for its own sake and every past event is potentially of relevance to him. "In short, the past *for* history is 'what really happened'" (EM 106).

However, the historian's attempt to follow Ranke's dictum and discover the past *wie es eigentlich gewesen*, though a necessary presupposition of historical thinking, misconstrues the character of experience by postulating the existence of two worlds where, in fact, there is only one. The past is never independent of present experience. On the contrary, there is only presently existing evidence which survives from a now 'dead' past. The historian's interpretation of the past is constructed out of this raw material. By Oakeshott's own admission 'history' "is the product of a severe and sophisticated manner of thinking" (RP 182) and it is perhaps not surprising that it has arrived on the scene in relatively recent times.[21]

In his 1928 essay "The Importance of the Historical Element in Christianity" Oakeshott explored the relations between historical thought and the Christian religion. In its concern with "the radical temporality of the human condition"[22] this essay, perhaps more than any of the other early essays, prefigures the argument of *Experience and Its Modes*. The essay originally appeared in a Symposium on Christianity and History conducted by the journal "The Modern Churchman" and the questions it addresses are characteristic of the concerns of the theologians and church historians of the period. The bearing upon Christianity of modern historical criticism of the New Testament Oakeshott referred to as "the most pressing feature of our theological thought"[23] and in this essay he directly addresses the issues at stake.

The historical element in Christianity cannot, for Oakeshott, remain unchanged in the light of modern historical scholarship. Traditionally the importance of the historical element in Christianity lay in "a *belief* in the necessity of that which is *prima facie* historical, or the historical as such" (RPM 64). The question whether or not this element is necessarily as important as it has traditionally been held to be is a complex one. Oakeshott's final answer is that it is not, and on the way he examines the presuppositions underlying the affirmative responses to the question which generally come in one of two forms. They all fail because they rest on a mistaken idea of historical identity. The first claim is that Christianity "is the whole original Christianity" and anything differing from this primitive thing is not Christian (RPM 64). "Its principle is simply that 'everything is equal to itself'; it says nothing more than that *A* is *A*, and that any change whatever in *A* causes it to become other than *A*. Indeed, we may not speak at all of a 'change in *A*'" (RPM 65). This belief issues in claims such as: "The historic Jesus is

[21]   For this reason Hobbes's turn to history in order to affect present conduct was not a return to history *per se*, but a turn to the practical past, see ch. 1 n11.
[22]   Fuller, introduction to RPM, p. 14.
[23]   Review J. Needham, *Science, Religion and Reality*, in *Journal of Theological Studies*, 27 (1926), 317–19, at p. 319. Oakeshott gave editorial advice on this book.

the source which, through changing form and circumstance, have (*sic*) kept it [the Christian mind] Christian."[24] Whether this original Christian experience is identified with the 'historic Jesus', or extended to include the religion of the early church the difficulties remain intrinsic to the position. It is misleading, Oakeshott argues, to make the identity of Christianity synonymous with one period of the historical process since this invariably entails making an arbitrary, that is, unhistorical, choice. For the historian, there is no moment of the historical process of greater importance than any other. Certain events, such as the origins of Christianity, are undoubtedly subject to a disproportionate amount of historical scrutiny but this is to be explained in terms of its practical, not historical interest. In other words, in choosing to study a particular period the historian makes a practical not an historical choice. As he was to subsequently claim, to define historical enquiry in terms of the search for origins assimilates the present to the past by imposing on it an unwarranted teleological structure (see RP 176).

Apart from the fact that drawing such a line in history is arbitrary and therefore unhistorical, the equation of Christianity with either an historical period or series of events is also foreign to the character of experience. According to Oakeshott, "Christianity cannot be simply 'Jesus religion' because, at present, it involves ideas or beliefs *about* him and about His death."[25] Since experience is always present experience there is no way of escaping its constraints. Understanding is never unmediated but is conducted in a modally circumscribed hermeneutical circle.[26] We cannot return to the past because there is none to return to, so there is no question, *a la* Collingwood, of re-enacting the past. All that can be done is to impose on present 'evidences'

---

[24] G.G. Atkins, *The Making of the Christian Mind* (London: William Heinemann, 1929), 22n, cited in Oakeshott's review in *Journal of Theological Studies*, 31 (1930), 203–8, at p. 205.

[25] *Ibid.*, p. 205.

[26] Hermeneutics is a term most often associated with philosophers like Heidegger and Gadamer, and theologians like Bultmann, and Oakeshott's insistence on the 'presentness' of experience is not dissimilar to their existential positions. Oakeshott was fond of F.J.A. Hort's claim that "no line is possible between what has come to men and their interpretation of what has come to them" (*The Way, The Truth and the Life*), which he quoted in the course of elucidating Hobbes's position on the need for assimilating civil and ecclesiastical authority. However, where Oakeshott departs from a philosopher like Heidegger is in his rejection of the claim that there is one level of experience which is radically immediate. For Oakeshott the world of practice and everything contained therein, including religion, is an abstract world of experience and as such it makes no contribution to philosophy. From the perspective of the totality of experience, i.e. philosophy, practice is inconsequential.

various discourses or idioms (as he was later to call that which he originally termed modes) which make the past intelligible to us.

The second response is a modification of the first. Rather than
drawing a line in the historical process it recognizes that Christianity
has a history. However, so it is argued, each of the historical expressions of Christianity are united by a common core or essence which
is impervious to change. The theologian Adolf von Harnack
expressed this position as follows: "(h)istorical understanding is
achieved only as one makes the effort to separate the distinctive
essence of an important phenomenon from the temporary historical
forms in which it is clothed."[27] Oakeshott's major objection to this theory is that when all the merely contingent features of Christianity are
stripped away we are left with a core which is "a bare and bloodless
abstraction, a wretched fraction of any of our experiences . . . 'an invul-
nerable nothing'", which, "(l)ike pure water, it has no taste" (RPM 66).

The identity of Christianity is to be found in the facts of history.
However, it is neither a fixed and original datum[28] which provides
subsequent developments with an external standard, nor is it a common core or essence which remains changeless throughout time.
Rather, it consists, as anything exhibiting an historical identity must, of
"a kind of qualitative sameness" (RPM 67). "Identity, so far from
excluding differences, is meaningless in their absence, just as difference
or change depend upon something whose identity is not destroyed by
that change" (RPM 67). In a review of G.G. Atkins *The Making of the
Christian Mind*, Oakeshott succinctly outlined his position in a series of
points:

> i. The notion that there has been no development or change is indefensible
> both historically and logically. ii. The identity of a historical phenomenon
> cannot be preserved by mere adherence to a fixed original datum, because
> (a) there can be no identity without a real change of some sort, and (b) there
> is no fixed original datum for us to adhere to. iii. If there has been change
> and development there must also be an identity, for without an identity
> there can be no change. Christianity is neither a bottle filled once and for all
> time, nor one into which anything may be poured so long as the label is
> retained. iv . . . What we must keep hold of is the fact that we are discussing
> the development of a world of ideas, and consequently any 'physical' anal-
> ogy is bound to be misleading. Ideas are not like bricks to be added one
> above another, nor are they like the pieces of a jig-saw puzzle merely to be
> replaced by one another. The first idea we have is in no sense the 'founda-
> tion' of all that grows from it; nor may a later stage be tested by comparing it

[27] *Wesen des Christentums*, cited in D.G. Peerman and M.E. Marty, *A Handbook of
      Christian Theologians* (The World Publishing Co., 1965), p. 100.
[28] Review Atkins, "Making of the Christian Mind", p. 207.

with a former. In the development of a world of ideas a former stage, as such, is always lost in a later, and there can be no returning. (v) We must give up speaking of the 'essence of Christianity' if that means merely 'the most important part of Christianity'. Whatever Christianity is it is not its 'essence' unless that be taken to mean the whole of it.[29]

What then is the whole Christianity to which he refers? Here Oakeshott betrays an ecumenical spirit:

> On this view of identity . . . the characteristic of being Christian may properly be claimed by any doctrine, idea or practice which, no matter whence it came, has been or can be drawn into the general body of the Christian tradition without altogether disturbing its unity or breaking down its consistency. This means that an idea or practice may properly be Christian which, in part at least, runs counter to much that had previously been regarded as Christian (RPM 67).

He is ecumenical rather than eclectic because it is contrary to the nature of a tradition to include beliefs or practices at odds with its internal continuity. Christianity is a tradition and as such it possesses an identity, not because it is not susceptible to change but because change is the *sine qua non* of any tradition. In a tradition "every thing is temporary, but nothing is arbitrary" (RP 61). Even ostensibly radical departures from a tradition (such as the Reformation), are, when seen from the perspective of the whole, entirely dependent on it. Indeed, such changes are only made intelligible by relating them to the whole tradition. Here, of course, there are clear echoes of Hooker's claim that the institution of the Church of England represented, not a radical break with the Church in England as his enthusiastic Puritan contemporaries urged, but a continuation of the *ecclesia Anglicana*.

   Christianity is but one tradition of an entire civilization which itself is constantly undergoing modification and alteration. A religion continually renews itself alongside the civilization of which it is a part. "Every religion, each with its own image of deity and of self, has its own idiom of faith which reflects the civilization of the believer" (OHC 86). That is not to say that a religion merely surrenders to the *Zeitgeist*. According to Oakeshott, a religion both conforms to and leads the civilization of its adherents (RPM 67). I will discuss this further below. What needs to be examined here are the implications for the historical element in religion that follow from the idea that religion and civilization are mutually reinforcing. In accordance with his understanding of identity, Oakeshott is able to assert that the *prima facie* historical is not a necessary part of the Christian religion. The late nineteenth-century preoccupation with the historical Jesus is a reflection of

---

[29] *Ibid.*, pp. 207–8.

the general intellectual concern with history as such. Christianity can free itself from a concern with the *prima facie* historical, presumably along with belief in the supernatural, without losing its identity. Indeed to hold to these beliefs once they have been discarded by the prevailing civilization is to rob Christianity of its contemporary "power to give life and to give it abundantly" (RPM 68). John Oman made a similar point in 1925 when he wrote that "the Rationalist view of religion, as concerned with proofs about God as the maker of the world, providence as the direction of it, and immortality as compensation for its injustices and imperfections, and as mainly a matter of "evidences," was due to preoccupation with scientific discussions which had determined the interests and temper of the age for the religious as well as the non-religious people."[30] Presumably Paley's arguments from design suffered a similar fate to the elusive quest to discover the historical Jesus — immensely useful to believers in a pre-Darwinian age preoccupied with evidences and proofs but now with little, if any, power to compel belief.

The value of belief in the *prima facie* historical in Christianity is, then, to be judged in terms of its practical appeal. Since religion is essentially practical it remains unaffected by the claims of historical or scientific, and indeed philosophical truth. "Religion demands not that the necessity for the existence of what it believes in should be proved, for that is an academic interest, but to be made intensely aware of the actual existence of the object of belief . . . We cannot love or live upon the knowledge of a mere necessity; love and life demand an immediate awareness, if not of the senses, at least of memory and mind" (RPM 71). To the extent that the *prima facie* historical facilitates this awareness it is not to be despised.

At this time (1928) Oakeshott detected a general waning of the tendency, expressed perhaps most forcefully in Croce's thought, to assimilate all knowledge to historical knowledge, and a resurgence of "the power to stand on the point of the present" (RPM 69). The challenge to Christianity was to remain relevant by refusing to be overwhelmed by historical thought. Religion is necessarily contemporary and should not be hindered from its ever present tendency to follow the contours of the life of a civilization. Otherwise, all that is left is an abstract set of doctrines with no contact with ordinary life. As in *Experience and Its Modes*, here Oakeshott sought to vindicate religious experience and preserve it from the unhelpful encroachments of other claims to knowledge, and Christianity, he suggests, "has perhaps

[30] In *Science, Religion and Reality*, p. 265.

suffered more and has more to fear from the incursions of history than from those of science" (EM 316). The historical element in religion then has no relation to history *per se*. Along with the religious element in history — God in history — the strictly historical in religion has no place. It is an example of *ignoratio elenchi*.

Oakeshott only devoted a few pages to religion in *Experience and Its Modes* and there it was discussed in terms of the notion of modality, the pre-eminent concern of the book. Consistent with all other aspects of non-philosophic experience, Oakeshott's account of religion is explicable in these terms. Religious truth is conditional, not absolute. The claims of philosophy are irrelevant to religion since they exist in modally distinct regions of experience. The distinction between philosophy and religion/theology is consistently maintained in Oakeshott's writings. In *On Human Conduct*, for instance, he argued that a theoretical understanding of faith cannot replace faith itself. Religious faith, along with other aspects of human conduct, is conducted on one of many conditional 'platforms of understanding' which take the place of what he had termed presuppositions in *Experience and Its Modes*. The postulates of the platform of understanding on which religion operates may be subjected to scrutiny, but this is a theoretical, not a religious, engagement. Needless to say these postulates are not the philosophical 'foundations' of religion since philosophy is marked solely by its determination to supersede conditionality. To the non-philosophical religious believer the idea that religion is an abstract, or conditional feature of experience may seem an impious, subversive claim. Indeed, as has been discussed in chapter 1, Oakeshott even suggests that it is the nature of philosophy to subvert ordinary understandings. However, it is no part of Oakeshott's intention to replace the meaning that religion offers with the unconditional 'truth' that philosophy seeks. Religion and philosophy can happily coexist in their respect modes or platforms of experience as long as it is recognized that the claims of each are categorically independent of one another. In the following section I will explore in greater detail Oakeshott's account of the relationship between moral and religious experience.

IV

We have seen that in Oakeshott's reading of Hobbes religion is a matter of the utmost practical importance and it arises from Hobbes's depiction of the human predicament. The predicament of man is one of unremitting solipsism which artificial contrivances such as the commonwealth can never finally remove. The seeds of religion arise from this predicament; that is, "from fear arising out of the unavoidable limits of human experience and reasoning" (Intro lxii [RP 289–90]). At the conclusion of his brief essay "Leviathan: *a myth*", Oakeshott notices the similarity between Hobbes's account of experience and modern existentialism. Hobbes, for Oakeshott, is a great reteller of the myth of our civilization, itself nothing but a collective dream. Civilization is created by artists, poets and philosophers, who, when they reach a certain level of imaginative insight, have the capacity to reformulate the former by reworking the substance of the myth that defines it. Hobbes's *Leviathan* is a work of this order. He transformed the Pauline/Augustinian, essentially proud, myth of the fall of man by recalling "man to his littleness, his imperfection, his mortality, while at the same time recognizing his importance to himself" (HCA 154). In Hobbes's vision "(t)he destiny of man is ruled by no Providence, and there is no place in it for perfection or even for lasting satisfaction" (HCA 153). Man is a creature of solipsism, whose life is governed by "the permanent and unassuaged" fear of death, which no knowledge can remove (HCA 153). Because man for Hobbes, along with Montaigne, has no communication with Being, he has no hope of a release from this predicament. For solipsistic beings fear is inescapable. It is this emphasis that aligns Hobbes with what proceeded him.

The fundamental modernity of Hobbes's account of religion has been noted by recent commentators. W.B. Glover, for instance, made the following observation in regard to Hobbes: "In the mid-twentieth century, when so much of Christian thought finds deep affinities with existentialism, it should not be hard to understand how religion, and especially Christian faith, may be grounded in a sense of the predicament of man surrounded in his weakness by a world that threatens him in ways beyond his knowing."[31] Likewise, Richard Sherlock, in a passage wholly congruent with Oakeshott's reading suggests that, "(w)ith Hobbes the study of religion has become the study of human speech about the divine and the study of the continuing human effort to find a language and a myth that can shape a viable human community and give meaning to individual human lives."[32]

Underlying Oakeshott's writings on religion is a rejection of all nature/supernature distinctions. This feature of his work also helps explain why he would have found Hobbes's theology conducive to his own philosophy. In his 1929 essay "Religion and the World" Oakeshott sets out what he takes to be the proper distinction

---

[31] "God and Thomas Hobbes", in Keith Brown (ed.), *Hobbes Studies*, p. 162.
[32] "The Theology of Leviathan", p. 59.

between religious and worldly sensibilities. Religion, he maintains, does not involve the escape from this world into another transcendent order.[33] Rather it consists of a transformation of our understanding of this one in line with a different scale of values. The dichotomy between the natural and the supernatural, by which the Christianity of the middle ages interpreted the relationship between religion and the world, was not recognized by the early Christian community. The early Christians were united by their belief that the Day of the Lord was immanent. This day would usher in a new age in which the evils of the present age would vanish. "Religion, to them, defined as keeping oneself unspotted from the world, was easily understood and naturally agreeable. It implied not the quasi-philosophical dualism of material and spiritual interests, but the more simple, more Hebrew notion of a dualism of historical periods" (RPM 28). The Gospels and St Paul's theology were an attempt to reconcile this experience with the disappointment encountered when the end failed to materialize. Thus arose a new understanding of the distinction between religion and the world, based not on a difference in time but place: "the material world was contrasted with a so-called spiritual world. To be unspotted from the world meant to live, without pleasure, a life so divided between this world and the other world that it required the invention of a whole psychology to persuade men of its possibility" (RPM 29). It is this view that Hobbes's materialist ontology and his idea of a corporeal God did much to undermine.

In place of this medieval distinction Oakeshott proposes a new dichotomy between religion and the world that has some affinity with the early Christian view. One based on a competing scale of values. The confidence of the early Christian believer "in the coming dissolution of the world was as much the expression of a certain scale of values as it was a crude expectation of an historical event. Fundamentally he believed that history and the natural world must be held subservient to him, his life and his purposes; and, that the years should pass and nothing happen, need not shatter the force of his belief for him whose imagination it excites" (RPM 30).

According to Oakeshott, the religion that the world preaches places emphasis on external results and achievement. The worldly man's distinguishing feature is "his belief in the reality and permanence of the present order of things" (RPM 30). He is prepared to exchange his self for this order. The self, for the worldly, looks pale

[33] At one point he described Barthes' neo-orthodoxy as a return to Kant — review of Heim, *The New Divine Order*, Sheen, *Religion Without God*, Holmes, *Philosophy without Metaphysics*, in *Journal of Theological Studies*, 32 (1931), 434–5.

in comparison to the things of the world — success, reputation, career, achievement. It is this attitude above all that constitutes the greatest threat to religion. A properly religious attitude involves spurning these criteria in favour of a view of achievement in which self-understanding is the central goal. "Ambition and the world's greed for visible results, in which each stage is a mere approach to the goal, would be superseded by a life which carried in each of its moments its whole meaning and value" (RPM 32). To be religious is to make the most of present experience:

> *Momento vivere* is the sole precept of religion; and the religious man knows how easy it is to forget to live. But he has the courage to know what belongs to his life, and, with it, steps outside the tedious round of imitation by which the world covers up its ignorance of what it is alive for. He loves life too much to pay too highly for mere existence — to pay with his self (RPM 37).

Salvation is not to be found either in another world or in a radical alteration of this one. The possibility of salvation always exists in the present. Religion offers a means by which the identity of the self can be preserved amidst the invariable transience and mutability of the world. It is only the worldly who tie salvation to the future: "The future is the Moloch to which the present is sacrificed, and the life which leaves behind it actual accomplishments is valued more highly than that which strove to be its own achievement" (RPM 31). A truly religious response to existence involves a radical transformation of this understanding. This is what it means to enact oneself religiously. An alteration, not so much of conduct, but of understanding.[34]

For those whose life is primarily concerned with achievement and the alteration of the state of affairs, that is, with the determinations of self-disclosure, religious sensibility will be at a minimum. For Oakeshott, excessive concern with external accomplishment is the antithesis of a religious attitude to existence. "'Achievement' is the 'diabolical' element in human life; and the symbol of our vulgarization of human life is our near exclusive concern with achievement... Whereas the only human value lies in the adventure and the excitement of discovery ... It is our non-recognition of this, or our rejection of it, which makes our civilization a non-religious civilization. At

---

[34] In the last year of his life Oakeshott reiterated the theme of the temporal nature of salvation in a letter he wrote to Patrick Riley in which he expressed his unfulfilled wish to write "a post-Montaigne, post-Pascal, post-Blake version of Anselm's *Cur deus homo* — in which (amongst very much else) 'salvation', being 'saved', is recognized as [having] nothing whatever to do with the *future*". Riley, "Michael Oakeshott, Political Philosopher", in *Cambridge Review*, October 1991, 110–113, at p. 113.

least, non-Christian; Christianity is the religion of 'non-achieve-ment.'"[35]

Again the convergence with Hobbes is manifest. For Hobbes felicity describes a process, not an achievement. Achievement is ultimately illusory as each desire invariably dissolves in the face of another. "Felicity is a continual progress of the desire, from one object to another; the attaining of the former, being still but the way to the latter. The cause whereof is, that the object of man's desire, is not to enjoy once only, and for an instant of time; but to assure for ever, the way of his future desire" (Lev. 63). As Timothy Fuller has pointed out, in Hobbes's reading of the situation, 'the repose of a mind satisfied' can come only at the general resurrection which the Second Coming ushers in. Faith may guarantee this event in the future but there is nothing that can be done to bring this state into the present. All that can be done is to live the life of faith now. "In rejecting the *summum bonum* one disposes the issue of coordinating the natural and supernatural ends... For Oakeshott (as for Hobbes), to reject the *summum bonum* is to begin to appreciate fully what the life of faith really is" (RPM 20–21). Hobbes and Oakeshott therefore share a determination to return to the spirit (though not the *thing* itself) of early Christianity.[36] Moreover, the attempt to establish the 'rational foundations' for

---

[35] From an unpublished notebook — quoted by Charles Moore in *The Spectator*, 15 June 1991, cited in B. Parekh, "Living as an Immortal", in *Cambridge Review*, Oct. 1991, p. 104

[36] Oakeshott's analysis of the various phases in the history of Christian understandings of the distinction between religion and the world, and his suggestion that the early Christian experience has much to teach us about a true religious sensibility was without much doubt a reflection of the influence of Albert Schweitzer's *Quest of the Historical Jesus* on theological circles in Britain at the time. Timothy Fuller has recalled Oakeshott's high estimation of this work ("An introduction: Michael Oakeshott's achievement", in *The Political Science Reviewer* symposium, 21 (1992), p. 2). According to Ramsey, *From Gore to Temple* (p. 171), this book "made Schweitzer's name a theological household word in England", and F.C. Burkitt, one of Oakeshott's teachers at Cambridge, wrote a Preface to it. In commenting on Burkitt's debt to Schweitzer, Ramsey quotes from the former as follows: "The explanation [for the survival of the Christian, rather than the Jewish, hope] is at least partly to be found in the way that Christianity had been organized for a time of catastrophe rather than for a time of peace — in other words, in immediate expectation of the Kingdom of God and of the calamities which proceeded the coming of the Kingdom". "The Gospel is the great protest against the modern view that the really important thing is to be comfortable". "As long as we believe in our hearts that our property, our arts, our institutions, our buildings, our trust-deeds are the most permanent things in the world, so long we are not in sympathy with the Gospel message" [Burkitt, "The Eschatological Idea in the Gospel", *Cambridge Biblical Essays* (1909), cited in Ramsey, p. 172]. All of this finds a clear parallel in Oakeshott's 1929 essay "Religion and the World".

faith or for a proper human life is to mis-describe the nature of faith and subvert a properly religious understanding of existence. Religious faith is prompted by a recognition of the limits of knowledge, not by subscribing to the belief that faith is in some way dependent on it.

For Oakeshott any account of human conduct which fails to account for the religious element is less than adequate. This is not because the validity of religious experience is universally recognized. Indeed, for those whose life is caught up in 'the illusion of affairs' or those either unwilling or unable to acknowledge the evanescence of the human condition it will appear as an irrelevant distraction (OHC 85). However its necessity is felt by many and for Oakeshott practical life is incomplete in its absence. Moral conduct finds its consummation in religion and the practice of neither can be replaced by, nor enhanced by a theoretical understanding of their presuppositions. A similar position is expressed by Matthew Arnold:

> Ethical means *practical*, it relates to practice or conduct passing into habit or disposition. Religious also means *practical*, but practical in a still higher degree; and the right antithesis to both ethical and religious, is the same as the right antithesis to practical: namely, *theoretical*.[37]

However, it is Bradley's, rather than Arnold's work, that Oakeshott's early writings on religion most resembled. Both Oakeshott and Bradley criticised Arnold's idea that religion is sim-

---

[37] *Literature and Dogma*, p. 15, cited in Bearnard Reardon, *Religious Thought in the Victorian Age. A Survey from Coleridge to Gore* (Longmans, 1960), p. 388. In an early essay on Lord Acton ["Lord Acton", *Caian*, 31: I (Michaelmus 1922), 14–23] Oakeshott suggests that Arnold "is the best example of the English temperament affected by", what he calls, "the *nostalgia of the infinite*". Others Oakeshott identifies as possessing this temperament include Pascal, Joubert, Amiel and Acton. What he attempts to explain in this essay is the great gulf between Lord Acton's vast intellect and erudition — "perhaps, the most learned man in the Europe of his day" — and the dearth of his output (p. 14). Oakeshott explains this seeming paradox in terms of Acton's character. Because he possessed a prevision of the perfect, the ideal, the eternal, like others with a similar character, Acton had a "constitutional incapacity to deal with the incomplete and the imperfect: and as we are made, essentially, for imperfection, as the human mind is constructed for strife and not for victory, it was an incapacity to deal with life in its more ordinary forms". He possessed "(a) mind which is ever striving to create, to organize, to understand to the very depth the meaning of things in their universal aspect — not as they seem as they pass, but as they *are*". Such a mind "cannot continue long before it becomes conscious of that over-mastering desire to know all" (p. 17). This overwhelming *nostalgia of the infinite* invariably invokes a paralysis of action when confronted by the imperfect. It is one profound instance of what Oakeshott would go on to describe as self-enactment.

ply morality touched by emotion (RPM 40).[38] Religion is distinct from, yet required by, morality. In his essay "Religion and the Moral Life" (1927), Oakeshott rejected two accounts of the relationship between religion and morality — religion as the sanction of morality and religion as morality itself — in favour of a third view — religion as the completion of morality.

In the first of these, morality arises from the inadequacies of naturalism. For the merely natural individual there is no foundation for morality. What is needed is an external authority which will supply what is lacking in naturalism. This is found in a revealed religion. The moral law, revealed as the will of God, supervenes mechanically on individuals who are moral to the extent that they obey its dictates. The law is completely external to the will of moral persons. Oakeshott suggests that, despite appearances, this view is "both immoral and unchristian" since "the characteristic of moral personality is its autonomy". If the will is a constitutive component of morality and religion involves absolute dependence on God then this position is self-contradictory. We cannot be both moral and religious if we subscribe to the belief that the moral law is entirely independent of our will: "we can keep the law only by *knowing* what we do, not simply by blindly obeying" (RPM 40–43).

According to Oakeshott this position finds is best refutation in John Oman's book *Grace and Personality*. Oman also supersedes this position with what Oakeshott calls 'Morality as the condition of religious belief', which is a modification of 'Religion as morality itself'. According to Oakeshott, Oman's position is correct as far as it goes, however, morality requires more than the mere formal exercise of autonomy. "Free action is not moral action unless it is also wise". Here Oakeshott's early Hegelianism is evident. Morality entails the fusion of content and form. "A concrete moral action is the autonomous, free, *and adequate* reaction of a personality to a situation" (RPM 44).

The most adequate account of the relationship between religion and morality is to be found, in what Oakeshott terms, 'Religion as the completion of morality'. On this view morality taken by itself is a

[38]   For Bradley, see *Ethical Studies*, p. 315. Despite Bradley's criticism of Arnold, T.S. Eliot made the claim that the two were in fact stylistically very similar and the targets of their polemical and philosophical salvos shared a common insularity and crudeness of mind. According to Eliot, "the *Ethical Studies* are not merely a demolition of the Utilitarian theory of conduct but an attack upon the whole Utilitarian mind. For Utilitarianism was, as every reader of Arnold knows, a great temple in Philistia". Like Arnold, Bradley "replaced a philosophy which was crude and raw and provincial by one which was, in comparison, catholic, civilized, and universal". "Francis Herbert Bradley", in *For Lancelot Andrews,* pp. 58-9.

contradiction. Every ought, once obeyed, gives way to a new one. Morality is an endless series of imperatives which never finally comes to a rest.

At the end of this essay Oakeshott acknowledges his debt to Bradley. It is worthwhile recounting Bradley's argument here as it is clearly uppermost in Oakeshott's mind.

According to Bradley morality requires an ideal self that is never finally attained: "For morals the ideal self was an 'ought', an 'is to be' that is not."[39] Without religion the ideal self is forever unrealizable. It is only in religion that morality finds its satisfaction. For Bradley "the object of religion is that same ideal self, but here it no longer only ought to be, but also is."[40] Oakeshott's position is similar: "What in morality was a mere 'should be' in religion becomes an 'is'" (RPM 42). According to Bradley, reconciliation with the divine will by faith is the only way we can attain unity with what is real, our ideal self. Because it is an endless process moral experience ultimately lacks coherence. The distinction between 'is' and 'ought' is never finally overcome even in Bradley's theory of ideal morality. Since, for Bradley, "the moral is what it is only by asserting itself against its opposite", immorality and the non-moral must exist as necessary conditions of morality. Morality continually seeks to overcome the immoral self and "to realize that which can never be realized, and which, if realized, does efface itself as such". To attempt to overcome this contradiction would be to remove the ground which makes morality possible at all. To be perfectly moral involves the realization of the good self by destroying the bad self. This is impossible since the good self only exists in relation to the bad self. Therefore, "No one ever was or could be perfectly moral; and, if he were, he would be moral no longer."[41]

The only way to resolve this contradiction is to supersede the moral point of view and accept the religious viewpoint as superior and as supplying the complete whole that morality cannot ultimately provide. "Reflection on morality leads us beyond it. It leads us, in short, to see the necessity of the religious point of view."[42] Similarly, Oakeshott claimed that though morality is continually "changing, growing", and "purifying itself", it ultimately has "no hope of a final end wherein it can rest". Morality finds its completion in religion where

---

[39] Bradley, *Ethical Studies*, p. 319.
[40] *Ibid.*
[41] *Ibid.*, 155, 233–4.
[42] *Ibid.*, 314.

we achieve goodness, not by becoming better, but by losing ourselves in God. For goodness is never achieved by becoming better: that is the self-contradiction of morality. Religion, then, is the completion of morality, not in the sense of a final end to an historical series, but as the concrete whole is the completion of all the abstractions analysis may discover in it. Religion is not the sanction of morality, but the whole of which morality is an aspect, and in which mere morality perishes, that is, is discovered as an abstraction (RPM 42).

In *Experience and its Modes* a similar argument was sustained. Religion, Oakeshott argued, is the consummation of practical life. The world of practice is the world viewed *sub specie voluntatis*. In it exist a world of optative agents (as he later described it in *On Human Conduct*) seeking to procure from the world and from others the satisfaction of their wants. This unending instrumental engagement is of course qualified by moral considerations: the world viewed *sub specie moris* (RP 501). Practical life is governed by desire and aversion as well as approval and disapproval. In *Experience and Its Modes* he described the world of practice as the attempt to alter the world of 'what is' to agree with 'what ought to be', the world of value. This unending process is what characterizes practical experience. Wherever this process reaches its most fully integrated and coherent stage, wherever it "is least reserved, least hindered by extraneous interests, least confused by what it does not need" it can be said to be religious (EM 292). Religion is not merely inseparable from the conduct of life, it is itself the conduct of life whenever it reaches a certain intensity. It is a way of living, not a separable aspect of experience which can be picked up or put aside at will (EM 292). "There is no exact point in the conduct of life at which religion can be said to begin. Religion differs from other forms of practical activity, not in kind, but in degree; it is characterized everywhere by intensity and strength of devotion and by singleness of purpose" (EM 295).[43]

Religion is not a denial of life, as some, such as Nietzsche, have supposed.[44] Indeed, the world of practice, where existence is altered through human will, is, in the absence of religion, incapable of reaching its highest degree of coherence. Despite the conditional coherence that

---

[43]   Cf. Collingwood "(w)hatever is a life at all, is already for that very reason religious in its degree; and that no one type of life has any right to claim for itself the title of religious at the expense of any other . . . As every life includes, and indeed is, both thought and action, so every life is essentially religious; and the secular life, if that means a life negatively defined by the mere absence of religion, does not exist at all", *Religion and Philosophy*, p. 35.

[44]   Though, of course, what Nietzsche rejected was the nature/supernature distinction that he identified with Christianity — the same distinction that Oakeshott deemed inappropriate

religion can bring to experience it nevertheless resides in a world of ideas that falls short of concrete experience.

If religion consists in losing oneself in God then it needs to be asked what Oakeshott means by God. In *Experience and Its Modes* Oakeshott hints at an answer. Ideas such as God, immortality and salvation are inherently practical ideas, with no bearing on ultimate or concrete truth. Religious ideas are to be assessed pragmatically, in relation to the conduct of life. Since the vast majority of life is conducted in the realm of practice (even for philosophers), religious ideas, such as God, can conceivably become the primary or guiding ideas of our existence. However, they will invariably fall short of ultimate truth because the world of practice itself fails to offer what is ultimately satisfactory in experience. If Oakeshott had argued, along with pragmatists and Heideggerians, for the primacy of practical experience then he might have had some justification for insisting on the ultimate veracity of religious truth. However, religious truth is conditional, not because of the empirical observation that there exist a variety of religious beliefs and practices, but because it belongs to the world of practice and as such it is shot through with abstraction. As soon as practical ideas are subjected to philosophical analysis they cease to be practical.

If we return briefly to Bradley we find there similar arguments. Theoretical consistency, Bradley suggested, is not to be expected in theological discussions. This is not only because religion is inherently practical and has to do with faith and feeling, but because God, though greater, i.e. more real, than any of the other abstractions that present themselves to the understanding, nevertheless falls short of the Absolute on which he is dependent for his existence. In the face of the Absolute, God and religion appear as contradictions since they can only exist in relation to something not themselves. In the endeavour to discover that which is finally absolute, individual, and real, God appears at a high level yet is ultimately superseded: "If you identify the Absolute with God, that is not the God of religion . . . short of the Absolute, God cannot rest, and, having reached that goal, he is lost and religion with him".[45] Like Bradley, Oakeshott suggests that God, the object of religious understanding, falls short of the concrete totality of experience.

As Timothy Fuller suggests, the idea of transcendence in Oakeshott is never expressed in terms of the 'wholly other' as found, for instance, in Rudolph Otto's work (RPM 6). Nor does Arnold's

---

[45] *Appearance and Reality*, 395–6. Cited in Richard Wollheim, *F.H. Bradley* (Peregrine Books, 1969), p. 266. See generally pp. 265–71.

"the eternal not ourselves that makes for righteousness" that Bradley so scathingly mocked form a part of Oakeshott's understanding of religious experience. Like Hobbes, Oakeshott is primarily interested in man as a creature with the capacity for religious understanding. Indeed, for Oakeshott it is meaningless to talk of reality apart from experience. Reality is created and maintained by thought. It is characteristic of Oakeshott to start his enquiry into any particular phenomenon by first laying the theoretical ground for understanding in general. Before 'theorising' human conduct he discusses the meaning of theoretical understanding. Rather than asking 'what is history?' he enquires into the activity of being an historian. Likewise with religious understanding it is impossible, because it is outside the character of experience, to enquire into the postulates of a world wholly apart from our understanding.

Of course, Augustine (who, along with Montaigne, Oakeshott described as one of the most remarkable men who ever lived)[46] recognized that knowledge of God was possible only by turning into the self: "To mount to God is to enter into one's self. For he who inwardly entereth and intimately penetrateth into himself, gets above and beyond himself and truly mounts up to God". "Let it be plainly understood that we cannot return to God unless we enter first into ourselves. God is everywhere, but not everywhere to us. There is but one point in the Universe where God communicates with us, and that is the centre of our own soul. There he waits for us; there He meets us; there He

---

[46] See Riley, "Michael Oakeshott: Political Philosopher", p. 113. It is also worth pointing out that in Charles Taylor's magisterial work on the emergence of the modern identity (*Sources of the Self*) Augustine and Montaigne occupy pivotal positions in what Taylor refers to as the turn inward (see esp pp. 127–143 and 177–185). This inward turn is very much like what Oakeshott understands by the term self-enactment and in his estimation it received its most profound formulation in Augustine and Montaigne. In *On Human Conduct* an explicit link is made between the two. The flowering of the disposition to cultivate individual self-enactment in the early modern period is said to receive its classic expression in the *Essais* of Montaigne: "Here there was no promise of salvation for the race or prevision that it would late or soon be gathered into one fold, no anticipation of a near or distant reassemblage of a 'truth' fragmented at the creation of the world or expectation that if the human race were to go on researching long enough it will discover 'the truth', and no prospect of a redemption in a technological break-through providing a more complete satisfaction of contingent wants; there was only a prompting that 'it is something almost divine for a man to know how to belong to himself' and to live by that understanding. Augustine come again to confound Gnostics and Pelagians" (OHC 240-1).

speaks to us. To seek Him, therefore, we must enter into our own interior".[47]

Oakeshott's God, however, is radically temporalized, inseparable from our understanding. The turn inward does not result in the discovery of an unchanging, eternal being who is 'wholly other' than ourselves. What is found is an image of deity "which reflects the civilization of the believer" (OHC 86). Since man has a history, not a nature, his religion likewise is contingent upon the historical process (OHC 81).

Oakeshott maintained consistently that religion and the moral life are not separable parts of experience, but central to human conduct itself. In *On Human Conduct* he identifies a religion as a practice. It therefore possesses all the characteristics of a practice. It is an historical contingency. There is no one true or natural religion from which particular positive religions derive. Further, in keeping with its character as a moral practice, the conditions prescribed by religion are adverbial, not instrumental, by nature. Excluded from Oakeshott's account of human conduct are all traces of teleology: "there is no ultimate or perfect man hidden in the womb of time or prefigured in the characters who now walk the earth" (OHC 41). It is up to each individual to forge his own character out of the languages of self-enactment available to him.

What religion offers is not a set of timeless truths, the knowledge of which leads to salvation, but a language of self-enactment through which salvation is worked out in the present. Human conduct, or conduct *inter homines*, is a transactional engagement. Agents undertake various actions in the attempt to alter their currently existing unsatisfactory circumstance. The successful abatement of dissatisfaction is often a precarious achievement conditional upon the responses of other agents themselves engaged in the diurnal attempt to alter existence in the pursuit of substantive outcomes. The process of choosing particular responses to circumstances, themselves partly determined by the anticipated responses of others, he refers to as "self-disclosure". It is conduct "concerned with procuring imagined and wished-for satisfaction" sought in the responses of other optative agents. In self-disclosure action is directed toward the achievement of some imagined state of affairs. The moral quality correlative with it is intention. Utilitarian philosophers have tended to place most, if not exclusive, emphasis on this side of the moral life. As Bernard Williams remarks, "the basic bearer of value for Utilitarianism is the *state of affairs*" and "as a

---

[47] *De Adhaerando*, cited in J.G. Davies, *The Theology of William Blake* (Oxford: Clarendon Press, 1948), p. 68.

Utilitarian agent, I am just the representative of the satisfaction system who happens to be near certain causal levers at a certain time"[48]

An equally important feature of any moral action is the motive in which it is performed. The aspect of conduct concerned with the motives or sentiments of agents Oakeshott terms self-enactment. Any action comprises a measure of self-enactment and self-disclosure, and moral judgment takes both into consideration.

Oakeshott suggests that the "'intention' of an action is the action itself understood in terms of the imagined and wished-for outcome the agent means to procure in choosing and performing it". By contrast, "the sentiment has no direct relation to the action as an intention to procure a satisfaction" (OHC 71–72). Since there is a more easily discernible connection between action and intention we tend to judge fellow agents more strictly with regard to self-disclosure than self-enactment. Moreover, self-disclosure is liable to frustration or compromise since it exists in a contingent, mutable world inhabited by other agents similarly seeking to alter the world in the process of disclosing themselves. The success of self-enactment, on the other hand, is not tied to the successful transformation of external circumstances.

Where self-disclosure involves choosing actions to relieve dissatisfactions in accordance with the recognition of the agency of others, self-enactment concerns "an agent's exercise of his powers of agency in respect of himself." (OHC 75) Importantly, self-enactment, as with self-disclosure, is itself a language of moral understanding. The 'authenticity' with which it deals is never merely private, the possession of a self separate from a language which gives the particular expression of virtue its meaning. According to Oakeshott, "(t)here is nothing 'merely' subjective in motives." (OHC 75) Moreover, since it is a language, it is composed of adverbial compunctions not substantive prescriptions. A language of self-enactment, according to Oakeshott, does not "give system to conduct by revealing it as a teleological process in which each action is 'good' in respect of its being

[48] Williams, "Persons, character and morality" in *Moral Luck* (Cambridge: Cambridge University Press, 1981), p. 4. Cf. J.S. Mill: "The morality of the action depends entirely upon the intention — that is, upon what the agent *wills to do*. But the motive — that is, the feeling which makes him will so to do — when it makes no difference in the act, makes none in the morality; though it makes a great difference in our moral estimation of the agent, especially if it indicates a good or a bad habitual *disposition* — a bent of character from which useful, or from which hurtful, actions are likely to arise", *Utilitarianism*, in *Utilitarianism, On Liberty, and Considerations on Representative Government* (London and Melbourne: Everyman, 1972), p. 19. See also OHC 71.

related to a predetermined end, and consequently a morality here does nothing to modify the interminability of doing." (OHC 74) Just as moral practices are devoid of purposes so too there is no virtue or set of virtues which is primary. To become virtuous is to learn to speak with intelligence and sensitivity the particular language through which our understanding of virtue is expressed, and "it is of no consequence that we cannot answer the question, Why is magnanimity a virtue and envy a vice? or even that we do not know how to answer it." (OHC 77) The theorist of human conduct cannot specify the content of either "'virtuous' self-enactment" or "moral self-disclosure." Rather, he can only spell out the formal postulates of conduct. In this respect, conduct which fails to adhere to the conditions of self-disclosure can be termed guilty, whereas the agent who fails to observe the requirements of self-enactment, "of thinking about himself as he should while doing what he ought" is acting shamefully. (OHC 76,7) [49]

Religious faith, according to Oakeshott, is the supreme instance of a language of self-enactment. With it we are able to transcend the otherwise unremitting contingency of the human condition:

> A religion is what I have called a practice; it is a consideration in self-enactment. A man may enact himself religiously, but there are no religious actions. Every religion, each with its own image of deity and of self, has its own idiom of faith which reflects the civilization of the believer. It may be terrible, it may sink to the prose of a merely anticipated release casting its light back upon a malignant present condition, or it may rise to a serene acquiescence in mortality and a graceful acceptance of the *rerum mortalia*, joys and sorrows alike transformed. But the dignity of a religion lies in the intrepidity of its acknowledgement of this human condition, in the cogency of the reconciliation it intimates, and in the poetic quality, humble or magnificent, of the images, the rites, the observances, and the offerings (the wisp of wheat on the wayside calvary) in which it recalls to us that 'eternity is in love with the productions of time' and invites us to live 'so far as is possible as an immortal' (OHC 85–6).

V

Oakeshott's writing on religion contains some of his most poetic, elegant prose. Indeed, the few pages he devotes to it in *On Human Conduct* for this reason stand out in an otherwise dense and precisely argued treatise. I think that reversion to a poetic mode says something important about his estimation of the elusiveness of describing the depth of

---

[49] For further discussion of the terms 'self-disclosure' and 'self-enactment' in the context of Oakeshott's religious thought see Glenn Worthington, 'Michael Oakeshott and the City of God', *Political Theory*, Vol.28 No.3, June 2000, 377–398.

experience that a religious faith could provide. An experience which, if not entirely of the sort that 'passeth all understanding', nevertheless defies the sort of analytical definition that he applied to his account of the rest of human conduct in general and authority in particular. As Fuller observes, "(h)e knew well the difficulties of saying anything of value on the most important questions."[50] For all the reconciliation it offers — whether to sin, to mortality, or to nothingness — religion, no less than any other form of human understanding, cannot remove the mysteries that clothe the human predicament.

Once again the affinity with Hobbes is obvious. Apart from conceding the fact that God's existence is a logical necessity, Hobbes excluded from his metaphysics all discussion of God's nature and his relationship to the world. God is utterly incomprehensible to the understanding and to think otherwise and impose on him our categories of rationality is to court absurdity. According to Pacchi,

> Hobbes aims at demonstrating that all endeavours to apply philosophical ways of thinking to the problem of God's existence, or of God's relation to the world, are destined to arouse inextricable contradictions and paralogisms, mainly where there is an undue conflation between physics and metaphysics, with the worst consequences for metaphysics itself, and even for Christian faith.[51]

Oakeshott however has radically temporalized Hobbes's fideistic conception of God by making the Nietzschean point that he is continually recreated through our languages of self-enactment.

Oakeshott's reticence to concern himself with abstract doctrinal or theological questions is of course a reflection of his estimation of the relative unimportance of doctrine to the actual conduct of life. Religious doctrines, the counterpart of secular doctrines such as 'the rights of man', are abridgments of a lived tradition and when raised to the level of an ideology potentially undermine a living religious or moral sensibility. According to Oakeshott this is precisely what occurred when the ordinary habits of moral conduct practised by the early Christian communities were converted into a set of abstract ideals for the benefit of those with no immediate experience of this way of life (see RP 484–5). Theologians are the grammarians not the perpetuators of religious practices. It is the ordinary believers who, by speaking this language of self-enactment, keep it alive.

The relative indifference of doctrine to the life of faith is also a feature of Hobbes's work for whom the only thing necessary for salva-

---

[50] Introduction to RPM, p. 4.
[51] "Hobbes and the Problem of God", p. 175–6.

tion was belief in the proposition 'Jesus is the Christ'. Various beliefs are, of course, implied by this single article such as "that God is omnipotent; Creator of the World; that Jesus Christ is risen; and that all men else shall rise again from the dead at the last day" (Lev. 392). However, so long as the Sovereign commands nothing forcing the subject to contravene this essential proposition, all questions of doctrine and religious practice are a matter for his discretion. The outward forms of religious observation are entirely mutable. By reducing Christianity to its barest minimum Hobbes sought to minimise the opportunity for sectarian dispute: "All that is NECESSARY *to salvation*, is contained in two virtues, *faith in Christ*, and *obedience to laws*" (Lev. 385). These two virtues are closely related. When properly practised religion strengthens societies by reinforcing the bonds of peaceful coexistence. It is therefore a potential source of strength for a community. However, when it is based on misguided beliefs it has the capacity to threaten civilization itself. Any attempt to reorient Christian practice beyond this bare minimum is to sow the seeds of antinomianism.

Though Oakeshott denies the claim that Christianity can be reduced to a core belief or essence, even if minimally defined, like Hobbes he recognized that substantive disputes over doctrinal issues are not only irresolvable, they merely create the opportunity to undermine the claims of properly instituted authority. The failure to appreciate the transience of religious belief and practice and claim a foundation for it outside the civilization it constitutes is itself a potential source of danger to the authority of civil association. In the following chapter I will consider those forces which Oakeshott takes to constitute a threat to civil association and the image of civilization that it presupposes. In particular, I will examine the close connection Oakeshott discerns between pelagianism and antinomianism and the relevance that the Biblical story of the tower of Babel (which Hobbes also took to be central to the human condition) has for understanding the predicament of modern man.

Chapter 5

Science, Myth, and Civilization

It is perhaps just dawning on five or six minds that physics too is only an interpretation and arrangement of the world (according to our own requirements, if I may say so!) and not an explanation of the world: but in so far as it is founded on belief in the senses it passes for more than that and must continue to do so for a long time to come. It has the eyes and the hands on its side, it has ocular evidence and palpability on its side: and this has the effect of fascinating, persuading, convincing an age with fundamentally plebeian tastes — for it instinctively follows the canon of eternal, popular sensualism. What is obvious, what has to be 'explained'? Only that which can be seen and felt — thus far has every problem to be scrutinised . . . 'Where man has nothing more to see or grasp he has nothing more to do' — that is certainly a different imperative from the Platonic, but for an uncouth industrious race of machinists and bridge-builders of the future, which has nothing but coarse work to get through, it may well be the right one.[1]

I

In the previous chapter it was seen that Oakeshott stressed the basic continuity of religion and civilization. Along with specifying more fully his understanding of civilization, this chapter will explore those beliefs that, in Oakeshott's estimation, constitute a threat to it. I will begin by exploring the relationship Oakeshott discerns between civilization and myth. According to Oakeshott, Hobbes's *Leviathan* offers — what all pieces of great literature offer to a civilization — a profound reinterpretation of the myth that underlies it. *Leviathan* qualifies as such because it displays an awareness that civilization is above all a work of imagination — something that goes unrecog-

---

[1]   Nietzsche — section 14, *Beyond Good and Evil*

nized by the scientist. Part of this chapter will examine Oakeshott's account of scientific knowledge. Along with all other modes of non-philosophic knowledge, science, according to Oakeshott, offers conditional knowledge. A civilization that only recognizes the validity of scientific knowledge fails to appreciate this and its imaginative interpretation of itself is thereby diminished. The remainder of the chapter will outline Oakeshott's account of the myth that Hobbes inherited and retold and tie this in with Oakeshott's own interpretation of an old myth — The Tower of Babel — and the significance this has for modern civilization.

II

As we saw in the discussion on religion, Oakeshott takes the characteristic feature of the worldly man to be "his belief in the reality and permanence of the present order of things" and is apt to believe that this order has a reality independent of "those unstable things we call *selves*" (RPM 30-1). In 1947, at the moment when he launched his attack on the follies of rationalism, Oakeshott wrote a short but suggestive piece on the meaning of Hobbes's *Leviathan* that developed some related ideas. Originally published under the title 'The Collective Dream of Civilization' this essay was renamed on appearance in the 1975 collection of Hobbes essays as '*Leviathan*: a myth'.[2] Here, as in his introduction to *Leviathan*, Oakeshott distances Hobbes's conception of reason from rationalism in Oakeshott's understanding of the phenomenon. In a radical departure from the received wisdom on Hobbes, Oakeshott makes the startling claim that *Leviathan* is a work of myth not science. It represents a profound retelling of the myth of European civilization. The substance of civilization itself is mythical.

> We are apt to think of a civilization as something solid and external, but at bottom it is a collective dream. 'In so far as the soul is in the body', says Plotinus, 'it lies in deep sleep.' What a people dreams in this earthly sleep is its civilization. And the substance of this dream is a myth, an imaginative interpretation of human existence, the perception (not the solution) of the mystery of human life (HCA 150). [3]

---

[2]   The original version appeared in *Listener*, 37 (1947), 966–7. The revised version appeared in HCA

[3]   Two passages that Oakeshott might be drawing on come from Burckhardt and Montaigne. Burckhardt: "In the Middle Ages both sides of human consciousness — that which was turned within as that which was turned without — lay dreaming or half awake beneath a common veil. The veil was woven of faith, illusion and childish prepossession, through which the world

Leviathan, on Oakeshott's reading, is much more than a book of political philosophy of interest only to specialists. It is also a work of literature in the deepest sense of the term. Where most of us live our lives in passive acceptance of the dream that constitutes our civilization, occasionally a work of gigantic imaginative achievement comes along which penetrates to the heart of this dream and retells it giving it a new vitality. *Leviathan*, according to Oakeshott, is a work of this scope. It is a work of myth, not science, principally because it displays an awareness of the fact that civilization is above all a work of imagination. This understanding eludes the scientist who believes he is dealing with something more substantial than imagination. Where the true artist is aware of his dreaming powers — "his genius is to dream that he is dreaming" — the "perverse genius" of the scientist "is to dream that he is awake".

> The project of science . . . is to solve the mystery, to wake us from our dream, to destroy the myth; and were this project fully achieved, not only would we find ourselves awake in a profound darkness, but a dreadful insomnia would settle upon mankind, not less intolerable for being a nightmare (HCA 151).[4]

It should be stressed that Oakeshott wants to criticize not science itself, but the belief that science offers a privileged insight into the human condition. Science is, after all, one of the many participants in the "conversation of mankind". But when any one of the various voices (such as, philosophy, poetry, science, history, practice) in this conversation exaggerates its own importance by identifying itself with the whole of the conversation then "barbarism may be

---

and history were seen clad in strange hues", *The Civilization of the Renaissance in Italy*, (Penguin, 1990), trans. S.G.C. Middlemore, p. 98.

The passage from Montaigne comes from *An Apology for Raymond Sebond*, and is worth quoting at length: "Those who have compared our lives to a dream are right — perhaps more right than they realized. When we are dreaming our soul lives, acts and exercises all her faculties neither more nor less than when she is awake, but she does it much more slackly and darkly; the difference is definitely not so great as between night and the living day: more like that between night and twilight. In one case the soul is sleeping, in the other more or less slumbering; but there is always darkness, perpetual Cimmerian darkness.

We wake asleep: we sleep awake. When I am asleep I do see things less clearly but I never find my waking pure or cloudless. Deep sleep can sometimes even put dreams to sleep; but our waking is never so wide awake that it can cure and purge those raving lunacies, those waking dreams that are worse than the real ones." Michel de Montaigne, *The Complete Essays* (Penguin Books, 1987), trans. M.A. Screech, p. 674.

[4]   Here is how one contemporary scientific 'believer' begins a recent best-seller: "This book is written in the conviction that our own existence once presented the greatest of all mysteries, but that it is a mystery no longer because it is solved". Richard Dawkins, *The Blind Watchmaker* (Penguin, 1986), xiii.

observed to have supervened" (RP 492). In recent times, according to Oakeshott, the conversation of mankind "has become boring" because it has been fixated by the claims to precedence of two voices in particular: practice and science. The danger inherent in the domination of the conversation by these two voices is that they are apt (particularly the latter) to believe that they are involved in something more serious than conversation. The voice of science, though "more severely symbolic" than that of practice, "is not essentially didactic" (RP 508). Though it possesses its own idiomatically distinct manner of enquiry, science, no less than practice and poetry, is concerned with constructing a world of images. Moreover, by paying near exclusive attention to practice and science, the peculiar characteristics of other voices are forced to conform to the character of the dominant voices in order to break into the conversation. In an overtly utilitarian and scientific age, philosophy, history, and poetry, when speaking in their own characteristic idioms, are convicted of irrelevance.

As long as its limitations are recognised, scientific activity is a legitimate mode of human enquiry. It is only when science claims more for itself than is warranted by its nature that it is to be rejected. Like any other mode of experience science views the whole world, not merely a portion of it, from its peculiar perspective. Oakeshott, therefore does not deny that a science of man, or a science of politics is possible. However, when it comes to accounting for human conduct, that is, the actions of interpretative beings, its explanatory capacity is severely limited. What Oakeshott rejects is scientism, the belief that all human understanding can be reduced to scientific criteria. Scientism represents a counterfeit myth and is illusory because it does not acknowledge its conditional nature. Its close ally, Rationalism, a corruption of a proper understanding of reason, is similarly mistaken. According to Oakeshott, "there is as much difference between rational enquiry and 'rationalism' as there is between scientific enquiry and 'scientism', and it is a difference of the same kind" (RPM 99).

Science, in Oakeshott's view, is governed by an impulse "to construct a rational world of consequentially related conceptual images", by excluding all that "is private, esoteric, or ambiguous" (RP 508). Like the historian and the man of practice, the scientist takes his subject matter to be independent of himself. Though this may be a presupposition necessary to carry out scientific enquiry, from the philosophical perspective this position is convicted of abstraction. Nature itself "is a world of ideas" which is "the product, not the datum, of scientific thought" (EM 190).[5]

The scientist views the world *sub specie quantitatis*. His world is amenable to quantitative measurement. Science does not begin with the "collection of data" or observation, "but with a world of scientific ideas". It is "a world of quantitative concepts" which moves from hypothesis to observation and experiment. In seeking to elucidate an "absolutely stable and communicable" body of knowledge the whole of experience is reduced to statistical generalisations (EM 214). In *Experience and Its Modes* Oakeshott argued that science falls short of the concrete whole of experience because of its hypothetical nature. It is an abstract form of experience because it entails generalised knowledge and a generalisation can never be categorically asserted. Scientific propositions merely assert "a relation or a consequence and never the existence of what is related" (EM 211).

Moreover, scientific activity is not prompted by the pursuit of an end antecedent to the scientific enterprise itself. Science advances by exploring the possibilities and contradictions contained in an already existing tradition of enquiry. Like Michael Polanyi, Oakeshott rejects the claim that the scientist is a "truth-finding machine."[6] On the contrary, the scientist is one who has accepted the authority of a particular tradition of enquiry and learned to master its rules and procedures. By imbibing its precepts the scientist is able to make advances by making intelligent guesses. But he must know the rules before he can break or supersede them. The coherence with which scientists tend to express their beliefs is not accounted for by the presumption that they have each independently assented to a fundamental truth or set of truths, rather, "(t)hey are speaking with one voice because they are informed by the same tradition"[7]

In his essay "Towards a Rational Theory of Tradition" Karl Popper offers an account of the development of the Western scientific tradition largely consistent with Oakeshott and Polanyi's anti-empiricist philosophy of science. According to Popper, the ancient Greeks developed a scientific tradition of enquiry by adopting a crit-

[5]   Cf. Bradley: "there is no part of Nature, which we can say is not directly organic to a soul or souls" (*Appearance and Reality*, 339). Also, Collingwood argues "that the scientist's world, so far as it exists, really is material, in the sense that, so far as he succeeds in being a scientist, is right so to believe". But to think of it as an object is to engage in an abstraction. The world thus contemplated is "like all illusions . . . a figment of the mind which tries to conceive it" (*Speculum Mentis*, 267).

[6]   *Science, Faith and Society* (Chicago: University of Chicago Press, 1964), p. 15.

[7]   *Ibid.*, p. 52. Oakeshott praises Polanyi's account of the logic of scientific discovery in RP p. 13n.

ical attitude towards the myths that had been previously accepted on authority. They began discussing and exploring the explanatory value of the traditional myths and offered what they believed to be better explanations of the natural world in their place. Popper suggests that "what we call 'science' is differentiated from the older myths not by being something distinct from a myth, but by being accompanied by a second-order tradition — that of critically discussing the myth."[8] This new, critical posture towards authoritatively received myths opens new explanatory possibilities. Like Oakeshott, Popper rejects the idea that science involves the mere accumulation of observations of the external world. Rather, new theories provide new means of observation which Popper refers to as '*the searchlight theory of science*', whereby some problems are solved and many more created by seeing them in a new light which leads to new enquiries and so on. This is how a scientific tradition is created and continued.

In their reflections on the scientific enterprise Oakeshott, Polanyi and Popper all point to the way in which science emerges from other kinds of human explanation.[9] A scientific tradition never starts from mere observation because observation is never free from interpretation. As with historical enquiry, which only arises by transforming the practical past into the historical past, Oakeshott suggests that scientific thought emerges by emancipating itself, not from dogma, but from the authority of practical thought (RP 507). The likely explanation for the authority with which science speaks in our civilization is, as Polanyi suggests, that our language is permeated by naturalistic terms which are unconsciously absorbed from the moment we learn to speak. We learn to speak the language, not of magic and mythology, but of naturalism.[10]

Since cause and effect are constitutive of our interpretative frame of reference it takes rare powers of imagination to comprehend, in Oakeshott's terms, the invariably 'perspectival' nature of civilization. It is generally acknowledged that Nietzsche possessed such powers of insight. However, this is an honour generally not bestowed on Hobbes. He has traditionally been read as paving the way for the celebration of science and reason that was to characterize

---

[8]   "Towards a Rational Theory of Tradition", in *Conjectures and Refutations: The Growth of Scientific Knowledge* (London: Routledge and Kegan Paul, 1963), p. 127.

[9]   It is worth noting that Popper tended towards what Oakeshott would term scientism. He tended to break the world into science and non-science. In other words, he does not draw the modal distinctions that Oakeshott does — history, for instance, could be understood as either scientific or non-scientific and is not itself a separate mode of understanding.

[10] *Science, Faith and Society*, pp. 42-3.

the eighteenth and nineteenth centuries, the world view that Nietzsche so brilliantly ruptured. That is, Hobbes is most commonly associated with the type of intellectual system that Oakeshott terms scientism.

Though the connection between Hobbes's politics and his scientific system has been taken in different directions by various commentators, the conclusion that Hobbes was a forerunner of subsequent positivism follows from accepting this connection as central to his project. The claim is that Hobbes offered a unified theory of scientific knowledge from which his civil science was deduced. Alan Ryan, for instance, has suggested that Hobbes's effort to base his political science on physics is an anticipation of modern social-scientific positivism.[11] Both Watkins and Goldsmith present Hobbes's political theory as the outcome of the attempt to apply scientific methods — the method of resolution and composition — to all areas of enquiry.[12] More radically, C.B. Macpherson has argued that Hobbes conceived human beings, to be not merely analogous to machines, but to be machines.[13] Needless to say this is not Oakeshott's view.

If we turn to Oakeshott's account of Hobbes's understanding of science we find some illuminating parallels with the former's own position. According to Oakeshott, Hobbes's age was conducive to reconstructing the myth he inherited: "he lived at the moment in our history when this potentiality of the traditional myth was ready to declare itself, but before the tide of science, with its project of destroying all myth, had begun to sweep over our civilization" (HCA 154).[14]

It will be recalled that Oakeshott is careful to distinguish Hobbes's understanding of philosophy from his understanding of science. Though the distinction was not generally made by seventeenth century writers, owing to the then less than systematic understanding of the scientific enterprise, it was discerned by Hobbes. No doubt the

---

[11] *The Philosophy of the Social Sciences* (London: Macmillan, 1970), p. 15.

[12] Watkins, *Hobbes's System of Ideas*, Goldsmith, *Hobbes's Science of Politics* (New York: Columbia University Press, 1966).

[13] See for instance *The Political Theory of Possessive Individualism: Hobbes to Locke* (London: Clarendon Press, 1962), p. 77, where MacPherson describes the derivation of rights from "the need of each human mechanism to maintain its motion".

[14] Cf. Strauss — 'Hobbes philosophized in the fertile moment when the classical and theological tradition was already shaken, and a tradition of modern science not yet formed and established' (Strauss, *The Political Philosophy of Hobbes*, 5)

language he borrowed from the new scientific method[15] tended to
obscure this distinction, and colour the interpretation of generations of
interpreters who failed to appreciate the palimpsistic nature of his writings. Most likely this was central to Hobbes's rhetorical strategy. However, the distinction which Oakeshott claims was discerned by Hobbes
"is that between knowledge of things as they appear and enquiry into
the fact of their appearing, between a knowledge (with all the necessary
assumptions) of the phenomenal world and a theory of knowledge
itself" (RP 239). This distinction between epistemology and ontology
(as it was subsequently understood) was one that Locke and Kant
developed, but it was missed by Bacon and Descartes.[16]

Hobbes, according to Oakeshott, had little time for the methods of
empirical science. Enquiry into the cause of sensations should proceed by way of reasoning, not observation. The former is a philosophical engagement, the latter was employed by the scientists of
Hobbes's day. The so-called 'truths' of science (read philosophy —
i.e. cause and effect) are not absolute, but conditional. They are
established by convention and agreement on definitions. They have
no objective ground in the external world. To recall, Hobbes says,
"(n)o man can know by Discourse, that this, or that, is, has been, or
will be; which is to know absolutely: but only, that if This be, That is;
if This has been, That has been; if This shall be: which is to know conditionally; and that not the consequence of one thing to another; but
of one name of a thing, to another name of the same thing" (Lev. 40).
Since all that can be discerned by observation is a collection of dis-
crete, particular phenomena it requires what Hobbes terms 'ratioci-
nation' to generate the conclusion that the universe is governed by
predictable, regular laws.

As discussed in chapter 1, there are important differences here
between Oakeshott and Oakeshott's Hobbes. Where Oakeshott
argues that philosophy is the only mode of enquiry which refuses to
settle for conditionality, Oakeshott reads Hobbes as saying that philosophy itself is conditional. If, as Oakeshott suggests, Hobbes considered philosophical knowledge to be hypothetical, and therefore
conditional, then Hobbes's understanding of philosophy is closer to
Oakeshott's account of scientific knowledge. In Oakeshott's Hobbes,
"philosophical knowledge . . . (because it is reasoned) is general and
not particular, [is] a knowledge of consequences and not of facts, and

[15]   According to Oakeshott "Hobbes normally uses the word science as a synonym for
       philosophy; rational knowledge is scientific knowledge" (RP 238).
[16]   I will subsequently examine the "counterfeit myth" of Bacon which is related to a
       failure to grasp this truth.

conditional and not absolute" (RP 241). Further, Oakeshott suggests that with Hobbes it is only experience, "a particular knowledge of particulars", that can be characterized as knowledge which is absolute. The only thing of which we can be certain is the fact that we have sensation. In "The Voice of Poetry in the Conversation of Mankind" where Oakeshott elucidates his understanding of the human world as a world of imaginings, he claims that "these images are not made out of some other, less-defined material (impressions of *sensa*), for no such material is available". Among other things, the activity of imagining is not "the 'original fancy' of Hobbes . . . It is not a condition of thought; in one of its modes it is thought (RP 496-7)".

However, of greater significance than the modal disjunction found in Oakeshott and his reading of Hobbes is their fundamental agreement that the establishment and maintenance of a communicable and rational world of ideas is a creative act of the mind. There are no truths which are 'self-evident' to all men of reasonable or rational disposition. Truth is wholly conventional. Where for Oakeshott nature has no essence independent of scientific discourse, for Oakeshott's Hobbes, nature, though real, is invariably elusive to human understanding. As with God, who understands nature because he created it, man only has knowledge of that which he consciously creates.[17] And it is reason, not observation, which generates the mechanical model of the universe. According to Oakeshott, Hobbes "does not say that the natural world is a machine; he says only that the rational world is analogous to a machine" (RP 238).

Indeed, as Oakeshott describes it, Hobbes's account of the distinction between experience and philosophy shows how philosophical activity comes into being: he "shows it as a thing generated and relates it to its cause, thereby establishing it as itself a proper subject of rational consideration" (RP 240). Where, for Oakeshott, particular modes of enquiry, such as history, science and poetry, come into existence by transforming the world of practice, for Hobbes philosophy springs from a transformation of what he calls experience.

Where does all this lead in relation to the question of myth and civilization? Principally it seems that Hobbes did not suffer the twin delusion of believing that truth is anything more than what convention establishes and, consequently, that civilized life is only secured

[17] James Tully in *A Discourse on Property: John Locke and his adversaries* (Cambridge: Cambridge University Press, 1980) in his discussion of Locke who also uses this maker image (though for different purposes) makes clear that it was a widely used image in the late medieval and early modern periods. See for instance, pp. 35–8, 116–124.

by something more substantial than an authority commonly recognised as such. Hobbes is no proto-positivist and his civil philosophy bears no relation to a so-called 'science of politics'. *Leviathan*, Oakeshott tells us, is myth not science.

It is not only in "Leviathan: *a myth*" that Oakeshott reads Hobbes in this manner. In the introduction (both versions) Oakeshott suggested that "*Leviathan*, like any masterpiece, is an end and a beginning; it is the flowering of the past and the seed-box of the future. Its importance is that it is the first great achievement in the long-projected attempt of European thought to re-embody in a new myth the Augustinian epic of the Fall and Salvation of mankind" (RP 278).

Such grand claims raise important questions concerning Oakeshott's modal understanding of experience. What, for instance, is the precise relation of myth to the modes of experience? Oakeshott makes the point that works of philosophical eminence, such as *Leviathan*, transcend the immediate interests of specialist philosophers and political theorists. They belong to a whole civilization. Unlike poetry, the gift of a great philosophical work "is not an access of imaginative power, but an increase of knowledge; *it will prompt and it will instruct*. In it we shall be reminded of the common dream that binds the generations together, and the myth will be made more intelligible to us. And consequently, we must seek the meaning of such a book in its vision of the myth" (HCA 151. emphasis added).

Here Oakeshott is clearly broadening the scope in which *Leviathan* can be read beyond the strictly philosophical. In contrast to the claim made in the preface to *On Human Conduct* that although a philosophical essay "may enlighten it does not instruct", here he is indicating that *Leviathan*, though a work of philosophy, transcends this particular form of understanding. Though it may not offer itself as a detailed guide, *Leviathan*, on this reading, is clearly orientated towards practice. Indeed, Oakeshott suggests that Hobbes's version of the myth is not something created out of nothing. It is rather a recreation of the Christian story, made fresh and given renewed vigour by transforming it in the light of the intellectual preoccupations of his time. The purpose of retelling an old myth in new form is to bring it to life again, to give it a new vitality and with it contemporary relevance. *Leviathan* is an interpretation of experience fused with, not only philosophical truth, but existential meaning.

One recent commentator has suggested that like science and philosophy, myth offers an explanation of experience.[18] However,

[18]   Henry Tudor, *Political Myth* (London: Pall Mall Press, 1972).

where philosophy and science aspire to an unconditional understanding — the disinterested search for truth and objectivity, or knowledge for its own sake — mythical interpretation is principally in the service of practice.

> Myth, then, is neither history, philosophy nor science; and there is no proper sense in which a mythical account can be translated into a philosophical, scientific or historical statement . . . However, the fact that (for instance) a scientific statement is scientific does not mean to say that it cannot be used in a practical argument. Its scientific character depends, not on its logical structure, but on the way it is understood and on the context in which it is used. And the same goes for historical and philosophical statements. There is, therefore, nothing to prevent the myth-maker from converting scientific, philosophical and historical statements into practical arguments and thus integrating them into the framework of an ideology.[19]

Much of the recent historical work on Hobbes has pointed out in minute detail the close connection *Leviathan* bears to the practical exigencies of his time. However, Oakeshott's point in regard to the practical orientation of *Leviathan* represents the opposite end of the historical spectrum. The meaning of *Leviathan* cannot be reduced to the particular historical occasion that gave rise to it. It carries enduring, if not universal, significance because it offers an interpretation of the predicament of mankind. It is the continuation of the myth that has shaped Western civilization and is the common possession of all who belong to it.

III

If the substance of civilization is mythical what must be examined is the specific character of the myth that Hobbes retold.

Oakeshott claims that the predominant feature of the myth that Hobbes inherited from medieval Christian civilization was pride. From the moment man was created he was without blemish. However, like Lucifer before him he overstepped his station and tried to become like God. Once corrupted "man pursued his blind desires, an enemy of himself and of his kind" (HCA 152). His relationship severed him from his creator, and lacking the power of redemption in himself, his only hope of salvation was the acceptance of a gratuity. St. Paul and St. Augustine understood this, but not Pelagius and his heirs.

"Pride and sensuality, the too much and the too little — these are the poles between which, according to our dream, human life springs" (HCA 153). While the emphasis in the old version of the

---

[19] *Ibid.*, p. 125.

myth was on the former, Hobbes stresses the latter. The myth as related in *Leviathan* "recalls man to his littleness, his imperfection, his mortality, while at the same time recognizing his importance to himself" (HCA 154). Of course, this is not to suggest that Hobbes was a mere hedonist who sought to justify unremitting concupiscence. To describe man's life as the quest for unceasing felicity which ends only with death (itself an arbitrary arrest in the process) is simply an acknowledgment of the fact that, *contra* Aristotle, the natural state of the universe is not one of rest but of motion. No sooner is one desire satisfied than another takes its place. Death is to be feared because it puts an end to the only satisfaction man can enjoy — the continuous pursuit of felicity.

Though the emphasis in *Leviathan* may be on the 'littleness' of man, elsewhere Oakeshott pointed out the importance of the passion of pride in Hobbes's writings. In 1935 he wrote that the new bout of research had corrected the conventional wisdom by showing "that Pride, and not Fear, is the master conception of his political philosophy" (TH 272). In "The Moral Life" Oakeshott suggested that, according to Hobbes, man's "supreme and characteristic passion is Pride; he wishes above all else to be convinced of his own superiority" (RP 301).

If Hobbes recognised the centrality of pride to man's makeup, why is it down played in favour of the countervailing passion of fear? Primarily it seems that pride is a volatile and dangerous passion. When it lapses into vain-glory, which happens all too easily, it has the power to convince man of his superiority over others. Since all men are roughly equivalent in strength, the belief in one's own superior strength is generally illusory. Oakeshott describes Hobbes's account of this predicament in the following way: " . . . if pride, the excessive estimate of his own powers, hinders a man in choosing the best course when he is alone, it will be the most crippling of all handicaps when played upon by a competitor in the race. And in a company of enemies, death, the *summum malum*, will be closer than felicity. When a man is among men, pride is more dangerous and death more likely" (RP 255). Moreover, according to Oakeshott, it is not death itself, the mere cessation of life, that is man's greatest fear, it is above all shameful or dishonourable death; violent or sudden death at the hands of a competitor in the race (RP 254n, 302) .[20]

---

[20] There are obvious affinities here with Hegel's account of the struggle for self-consciousness in the master/slave dialectic. In a brief essay from 1963 Oakeshott explored this theme. Here Oakeshott claimed that "[d]eath itself is not the significant thing in Hobbes' argument . . . The point is being killed: or at any rate that's where we begin. But it is not being killed in any manner (eg., struck by

Before reason can demonstrate the means by which man can establish a condition which will partially abate his predicament he must be convinced that his prideful actions increase his chances of suffering a violent death. "The purging emotion (for it is to emotion that we go to find the beginning of deliverance) is fear of death. This fear illuminates prudence; man is a creature civilized by fear of death" (RP 256). Having thus been chastened man is in a position whereby the dictates of 'natural reason' can speak to him.

Though Oakeshott followed Hobbes's argument that pride is a dangerous emotion that must be tamed before civil society can be effectively established, it is significant that he did not follow Strauss's contention that Hobbes simply replaced pride (according to Strauss, the source of Aristocratic honour in the so-called classical tradition) with a new 'bourgeois morality' springing from fear of death. To recognize only this line of argument in Hobbes would entail the judgment that Hobbes only acknowledged "the morality of the tame man, the man who has settled for safety and has no need of nobility, generosity, magnanimity or an endeavour for glory in order to move him to behave justly". This conclusion, as Oakeshott acknowledges, appears to undermine the assertion that Hobbes is above all a philosopher of individuality. That is, it reflects "an idiom of the moral life which, in spite of Hobbes's individualistic reading of human nature, seems to intimate and point towards the notion of a 'common good'. It seems to suggest a single approved condition of human circumstance for all conditions of men, and morality as the art in which this condition is achieved and maintained" (RP 343).

---

lightening or buried in an earthquake); it is only being killed by another man . . . What does being killed by another man signify? It signifies failure in the 'race' for precedence which constitutes human life — failure, not in competition with the natural world, but in competition with other human beings . . . In other words, desire is directed, not towards survival, but towards being *first* (and thus being 'honoured' and meriting 'honour'); and aversion is directed towards being dishonoured. This is what it is to be a man and not an animal . . . What a man wishes to avoid is not merely being killed by another man, or being in some lesser way dishonoured or shamed in human intercourse, but the *fear* of this condition. What he wishes to reach is a condition in which he no longer has even to *fear* being dishonoured. And this is a very large demand; it is the demand for a settled condition of life in which dishonour is unlikely . . . The *civitas* is this condition." (*Political Theory*, vol.29, No.6, December 2001, 834–836). In order that the civil association can be established there must be a recognition of intersubjectivity. Competitors must be recognised as fellow agents, as ends not means. See also Strauss, *The Political Philosophy of Hobbes*, pp. 57–8. Here Strauss claims that Hegel, in the master/slave dialectic, implicitly acknowledged "that Hobbes's philosophy was the first to deal with the most elementary form of self-consciousness".

The principal reason Oakeshott identifies as grounds for rejecting, or at least severely qualifying this conclusion is that pride, *contra* Strauss, is not necessarily the passion which must be countered at all costs, but that it can be constructively directed or moralized. In a few illuminating pages Oakeshott develops this idea.

Following the Augustinian tradition, Hobbes, according to Oakeshott, "recognised the twofold meaning which the word [pride] has always carried". The first issues in the hubristic and delusory attempt to take the place of God. It is both a delusion and sinful and issues in conduct which seeks to control "the world of men and of things". When Hobbes talks about pride in negative terms (which he generally does) it is this understanding that he has in mind. The second meaning of pride does not result in the attempt to usurp God's place but merely to imitate him. Here, according to Oakeshott, "self-love appears as self-knowledge and self-respect, the delusion of power over others is replaced by the reality of self-control, and the glory of the invulnerability which comes from courage generates magnanimity and magnanimity, peace" (RP 341). This character is one

> who would find greater shame in the meanness of settling for mere survival than in suffering the dishonour of being recognised a failure; a man whose disposition is to overcome fear not by reason (that is, by seeking a secure condition of external circumstance) but by his own courage; a man not at all without imperfections and not deceived about himself, but who is proud enough to be spared the sorrow of his imperfections and the illusion of his achievements; not exactly a hero, too negligent for that, but perhaps with a touch of careless heroism about him; a man, in short, who (in Montaigne's phrase) 'knows how to belong to himself' (RP 339).

We may add to this the observation that the man possessed of a healthy pride or nobility is one who, in Oakeshott's terms, has a well developed facility for self-enactment. His self-respect and integrity, in short, his virtue, is not contingent upon successful engagements of self-disclosure (see OHC 70-78).

According to Oakeshott, Hobbes recognised the dual nature of morality when he identified the twofold meaning of the word justice. That is, an action may be termed just regardless of the motive in which it is performed; however "(t)hat which gives to human actions the relish of justice," says Hobbes, "is a certain nobleness or gallantness of courage, rarely found, by which a man scorns to be beholden for the contentment of his life, to fraud, or breach of promise. This justice of the manners, is that which is meant, where justice is called a virtue; and injustice a vice" (Lev. 97, ch 15. see also

OHC 76). Unlike the fearful, rational calculators, who constitute most of mankind, and who obey the law solely out of a fear of the consequences of breaking it, the man of noble disposition obeys the law from "a Glory or Pride in appearing not to need to break it". Since, according to Hobbes, most men act 'justly' from non-virtuous, or self-interested motives, and the powers of the sovereign to enforce the law are limited, it may be that the maintenance of civil authority is more dependent on such men of honour than is generally supposed. Moreover, the establishment of the commonwealth may require this noble character since his endeavour for peace does not arise from a fear that his fellow contractors may fail to fulfil their side of the bargain. Where the latter will only contract where there is a condition assuring mutual compliance, the noble or gallant soul does not fear the consequences of non-subscription on the part of his rivals.[21] Indeed, so firmly established is his self-esteem he is not inclined to look upon others as rivals. For Hobbes, this ideal of aristocratic individuality was reflected in the character of Sidney Godolphin.[22]

Hobbes however, did not base his argument on the existence of such characters because he acknowledged that "(t)his is a generosity too rarely to be found to be presumed on, especially in pursuers of Wealth, Command or sensual pleasure; which are the greatest part of Mankind" (Lev. 92). On Oakeshott's reading, Hobbes down played pride and "recalled man to his littleness" because "he felt constrained to write for those whose chief desire was to 'prosper'" even though he "understood human beings as creatures more properly concerned with honour than with either survival or prosperity" (RP 344). The true Hobbesian ideal of individuality, Oakeshott suggests, is that of the self-reliant, magnanimous, almost heroic character who is contemptuous of injustice and has no need to 'prove' his superiority over others. On this reading Hobbes is no defender of the new 'bourgeois' morality that Strauss discerns, nor of the

---

[21] Oakeshott explores this possibility in the lengthy footnote to "The Moral Life", see RP 344–350.

[22] Hobbes said of Godolphin that, "there is not any virtue that disposeth a man, either to the service of God, or to the service of his country, to civil society, or private friendship, that did not manifestly appear in his conversation, not as acquired by necessity, or affected upon occasion, but inherent, and shining in a generous constitution of his nature" (Lev 2). The best account of Hobbes's estimation of Godolphin and the significance of his death is undoubtedly that of Irene Coltman in *Private Men and Public Causes: Philosophy and Politics in the English Civil War* (London: Faber and Faber, 1962), part II.

'possessive individualism' of nascent capitalism as claimed by Macpherson.[23]

If anything Oakeshott attributes this 'bourgeois' morality to the tradition of Locke. In 1932 Oakeshott wrote that,

> (t)he moderate individualism of Locke has no attraction for those who have embraced a radical, an Epicurean individualism. Locke's 'steady love of liberty' appears worse than slavery to anyone who, like Montaigne, is 'besotted with liberty'. Democracy, parliamentary government, progress, discussion, and 'the plausible ethics of productivity' are notions — all of them inseparable from the Lockian liberalism — which fail now to arouse even opposition; they are not merely absurd and exploded, they are uninteresting. Not a little, indeed, of the revolt against so-called Victorianism is in fact a revolt rather against Locke and his legacy of liberalism.[24]

According to Oakeshott, "Liberalism is Puritanism made respectable, and nobody contributed more than Locke to this piece of 'rescue-work.'"[25] In complete contrast to this, Oakeshott suggested that "(m)an, as Hobbes sees him, is not engaged in an undignified scramble for suburban pleasures; there is the greatness of great passion in his constitution" (RP 293)

The emphasis placed on pride in Hobbes's writings is highly suggestive of some of Oakeshott's own preoccupations. Indeed, it seems that Oakeshott is doing his own piece of 'rescue-work' in order to save Hobbes from the fate that has befallen him. In any case, when seen from the perspective of Oakeshott's concerns it is no surprise that this feature of Hobbes's work assumes the place it does in Oakeshott's reading of him. Oakeshott, as with his account of Hobbes, recognised that the passion of pride is a double-edged sword. On the one hand, it is the preponderant passion of the noble or aristocratic individual concerned above all, not with dominating or controlling others, but with virtuous self-enactment. Though he is self-reliant enough to have no need for the things communal engagements yield, he is not unfriendly or uncooperative, and he may or may not enter public life, though he feels no compulsion to do so. He is simply content to be governed by known rules which do not prevent him from pursuing his own private pleasures alongside others of his kind.

---

[23] For further defence of this position see Alan Ryan "Hobbes and Individualism", in *Perspectives on Thomas Hobbes*, 81–105, esp. 99–105. Also Keith Thomas, "The Social Origins of Hobbes's Political Thought", *Hobbes Studies*, ed. Brown, 185–235, esp. 202–7.

[24] "John Locke", in *The Cambridge Review*, 54 (1932-3). pp. 72-3, at p. 73.

[25] *Ibid.*

The other form of pride, that which Hobbes called 'vain-glory', is invariably illusory. Rather than accept the inherent limitations of the human condition, it seeks to surmount them and take the place of God. Rationalism is undoubtedly one such illusion, driven by the pelagian passion to overcome the imperfections of existence. Like Nietzsche, who discerned that the ostensibly cool, dispassionate investigations of the *Aufklärung* were nothing but the manifestations of another will to power, in Oakeshott's estimation Rationalism springs, not only from epistemological error, but moral error. The morality of the Rationalist "is what other peoples have recognised as 'idolatry'" (RP 41). This passion is most corrupting when it enters the political realm. For the politically inexperienced, who are most susceptible to the lure of Rationalism, the availability of a technique will be too tempting to ignore: "to be told that the necessary knowledge is to be found, complete and self-contained, in a book, and to be told that this knowledge is of a sort that can be learned by heart and applied mechanically, will seem, like salvation, something almost too good to be true" (RP 29).

The obverse of the prideful, self-reliant individual that Oakeshott so much admires is the individual *manqué*. He is the character who was threatened by the individualist idiom of conduct that emerged from the desuetude of communal ties that characterized medieval Europe. Longing for the security that absorption in a group offers, this "'anti-individual' had feelings rather than thoughts, impulses rather than opinions, inabilities rather than passions, and was only dimly aware of his power" (RP 373). The motivating pride of the aristocratic individual is absent in the 'anti-individual'. "He loves himself too little to be able to dispose effectively of the only power he has, his numerical superiority. He lacks passion rather than reason. . . . the heroic future forecast him is discrepant with his character. He is no hero" (RP 382).

Not content with legal equality, this character sought to establish a "single approved condition of human circumstances for all conditions of men" (RP 343), and converted the state from a custodian of formal rules of civility, into a managerial engagement. Moreover, he transformed the character of political activity with his demand for leadership. Not surprisingly, he found such leaders (or at least they found him). Rulership was converted into leadership and he was seduced by his leaders with the false claims of Rationalism and the promise of the unlimited satisfaction of his materialistic desires. He succumbed to both "the too much and the too little" (HCA 153).

IV

In "Leviathan: *a myth*" Oakeshott makes the observation that "from time to time, there have appeared enemies of our civilization, exponents of a counterfeit myth" (HCA 153). It remains to be considered what, in Oakeshott's estimation, those counterfeit myths are and why they constitute a threat to civilization, and to consider the way this is reflected in his reading of Hobbes's diagnosis of the precariousness of civilization.

Earlier in the chapter it was noted in passing that, according to Oakeshott, Bacon and Descartes failed to grasp the distinction that Hobbes observed "between a knowledge . . . of the phenomenal world and a theory of knowledge itself" (RP 239). Oakeshott traces the origins of the modern Rationalist character to Bacon's quest for infallible knowledge of the world. For Bacon, the surest way to overcome the lack of progress towards a stable body of demonstrative knowledge was found in the application of "a consciously formulated technique of research, an art of interpretation, a method whose rules had been written down" (RP 18). Such a technique was to supply 'natural reason' (by itself "capable of only 'petty and probable conjectures', not of certainty") with what had previously prevented it from attaining true understanding. The new technique consisted of a universally valid set of rules that could be learnt by heart and mechanically applied. It led to certain knowledge, complete in itself because it began with a purge of the mind (RP 20). It was contrasted by Bacon with mere opinion because it did not rest on anything external to itself. However subsequent expressions of the Rationalist disposition came to differ from Bacon, they took from him a belief in the sovereignty of technique.

Of course Hobbes, like Bacon, is famous for his methodological individualism and rejection of all established authorities.[26] However, according to Oakeshott, there is a vast gulf between Hobbes and Bacon's epistemological projects. The rationalism that Oakeshott rejects, as typified by Bacon (at least in his hopes, if not his beliefs, in the new method — RP 21) stands in stark contrast to the rationalism that characterizes Hobbes's writings. The rationalism that began to emerge in the seventeenth century understood 'reason' in wholly different terms to scholastic or Platonic rationalism. In the new idiom 'reason' began to be understood as "a faculty of calculation by which men conclude one thing from another and discover fit means of attaining given ends not themselves subject to the criticism of reason, a faculty by

---

[26] See Ryan, "Hobbes and Individualism", pp. 83–90.

which a world believed to be a machine could be disclosed" (RP 22–3). Whereas when Hobbes describes the world in mechanistic terms it is not because he thought it was in fact a machine, but because this is the appropriate level of abstraction for considering the causes of things. The machine analogy is generated not by observation but by reasoning. He is therefore a "scholastic, not a 'scientific' mechanist" (RP 236–8). According to Oakeshott, Hobbes's philosophy lies not in any doctrine about the nature of the world but in his understanding of the nature of philosophical knowledge. He was therefore under no illusion about what can be known about the world and he was not led astray by a mistaken belief in the sovereignty of technique.

In chapter 2 it was observed that Oakeshott's earlier writings on Hobbes stressed the epistemological aspects of Hobbes's individualism while later he gave greater emphasis to individualism as a moral and political ideal. This of course reflects his own changing preoccupations. There is also a similar shift in the case of Bacon. Where in "Rationalism in Politics" Bacon appears as the author of *Novum Organum*, the originator of the modern belief in the sovereignty of technique, later he appears principally as the author of *The New Atlantis*,[27] the archetypal promulgator of the technocratic enterprise association, the greatest threat to the state understood as association in terms of the rule of law (OH 153).

As with Hobbes there are connections between Bacon's epistemological and political projects. Where Hobbes's philosophical scepticism gave rise to the understanding that authority rests on nothing more substantial than the opinions of those who consent to it, Bacon's conviction that nature would yield its secrets if a rigorous technique could be applied to it generated the understanding that the proper activity of government was to further this enterprise. Government was to facilitate the task of exploiting the earth's resources. No longer tied to his conviction that this project had divine sanction, Bacon's successors nevertheless took up his vision with alacrity and, as Oakeshott tells it, the

> enterprise came to be understood as one in which human beings sought the satisfaction of their endlessly proliferating wants and identified themselves merely as participants in a productive undertaking. And it was agreed, also, that success would be qualified (or even frustrated) if the undertaking were not centrally organized both in respect of the wants to be satisfied and

---

[27] Though in the recently published *The Politics of Faith and the Politics of Scepticism* (New Haven and London: Yale University Press, 1996), which, according to Timothy Fuller, was completed by 1952, Bacon's *New Atlantis* gets extensive treatment.

the manners in which satisfactions were sought: each participant must be assigned a determinate function in the undertaking. And the enterprise itself must be under the management of *illuminati* ('scientists') concerned and equipped to unravel the secrets of the natural world and to direct the exploitation of this information. Thus, the way lay open for the emergence of the understanding of a state as a *civitas cupiditatis*: a corporate productive enterprise, centred upon the exploitation of the material and human resources of an estate and managed by a government whose office it was to direct research, to suppress distracting engagements and to make instrumental rules for the conduct of the enterprise, to assign to each of its 'subjects' his role in the undertaking and to deploy their productive energies and talents according to a 'scientifically' deliberated plan (OHC 290-1).

The Baconian vision is a "technologist's dream", where all the efforts of the state are directed towards production. Though the teleocratic understanding of the state has come in various forms, the Baconian is perhaps the most resilient. According to Oakeshott, it resonates in different ways in the writings of writers as diverse as, Fourier, Owen, St. Simon, Comte, Marx, Lenin, Webb. In short:

Wherever it is said that what we need is more technologists, wherever it is said that education should be reformed so as to produce greater numbers of scientists, wherever it is said that industrial effort requires central direction in order to achieve the well-being it promises, the voice that speaks is a voice which was first heard in the writings of Francis Bacon, and has never since been silent (MPME 106-7).

Where Hobbes is the archetypal theorist of civil association, Bacon is the foremost theoretician of enterprise association, at least in one of its dominant modes. If *Leviathan* is a myth, as Oakeshott believes it is, it is worth remembering that *The New Atlantis* also is an imaginative retelling of an old myth. It may be said that we have here two competing myths of civilization, written at a similar moment in history, with two corresponding accounts of the human predicament and the contribution that the political order makes to its resolution. In the Augustinian/Hobbesian account politics offers "something of value relative to his salvation. It offers the removal of some of the circumstances that, if they are not removed, must frustrate the enjoyment of Felicity. It is a negative gift, merely making not impossible that which is sought. Here in civil association, is neither fulfilment, nor wisdom to discern fulfilment, but peace, the only condition of human life that can be permanently established" (RP 293). In the Baconian/teleocratic vision politics is conceived as making a substantive contribution to human perfection. For "a race condemned to seek its perfection in the flying moment and always in the one to come", the temptation to make political action yield a more substantive outcome than a settled condition of civility is a permanent one. It is also generally perilous to the maintenance of this condition. The Rationalist attempts to make politics conform to his image of perfection because, unlike Hobbes, he is blind to the fact that due to its relentless predilection to pursue perfection, mankind's "highest virtue is to cultivate a clear-sighted vision of the consequences of its actions, and . . . [its] greatest need (not supplied by nature) is freedom from the distraction of illusion" (RP 293-4).

However, when the Rationalist attempts to clear up illusion in the name of Reason he simply puts a more insidious illusion in its place. He fails to appreciate what, according to Oakeshott, Hobbes understood, namely, "that there is never anything but a common error, that truth itself is a common error" (TH 276). One commentator has put it thus: "Rationalism is the illusion that philosophical knowledge may produce constructive prescriptions for human action. But the greatest illusion is the notion that it is possible to dispense with illusion altogether."[28] Wisdom, or freedom from illusion, comes not through Reason, but through a recognition of its limitations. Rationalism is contemptuous of the proverb that Hobbes and Augustine (following Job and the Psalmist) took to be central to mankind's predicament: "The fear of the Lord is the beginning of wisdom".

V

In Oakeshott's retelling of the myth of the Tower of Babel (1983, in OH) the consequences of the sins of greed combined with 'the politics of perfection' are examined with a measure of irony that Swift himself would have been proud.[29] In this version of the story, Babel is described as a *civitas cupiditatis*, whose inhabitants are notable for their vulgarity and fickleness. Addicted to affluence, and resentful of authority, the Babelians "are self-absorbed and self-indulgent". Babel "is indeed a City of Freedom: the home of every imaginable lib" (OH 176). In short,

[28] B. Frohnen, "Oakeshott's Hobbesian Myth: Pride, Character and the Limits of Reason", *The Western Political Quarterly*, (December 1990), Vol. 43, No. 4, 789–809, at p. 799. I am indebted to this insightful essay for many of the ideas discussed in this section of the chapter.

[29] Though they are not unrelated, I have concentrated here on the 1983 essay and not the 1948 essay of the same name as it is in the former that Oakeshott deliberately reworks the story of the Tower of Babel. The 1948 essay, in which he is concerned with the way in which the self-conscious pursuit of moral ideals corrupts a tradition of moral affection and behaviour, more readily fits into the immediate post-war essays. Both essays are concerned with the corruptions to practice of "the pursuit of perfection as the crow flies". In both essays the Tower of Babel stands as a symbol of this pursuit, yet it is only in the later version that it assumes the central role in a narrative. In other words, it is only here that he actually retells the myth.

they lack the sort of aristocratic pride that Hobbes detected in men of honour such as Sidney Godolphin.

The character of their ruler Nimrod is typical of the people as a whole. Having been spoilt as a child he never grew out of the expectation that all his wants could be unconditionally satisfied. Though Babel itself was an affluent place, its inhabitants, including Nimrod, had a constant and unassuaged feeling of frustration that God, though the source of all the good things they enjoyed, was of a "stingy disposition", and was reluctant to share with them the full riches of the paradise he enjoyed. Conscious of the Babelians' frustrations Nimrod convinced his subjects that God was directly responsible for their dissatisfaction. "Who is it", he asked them, "who has the means to put an end to your privations, to endow you with limitless profusion of satisfactions, and does not do so? Is it not this miserly God who wantonly withholds what he might give with no loss to himself? Do you not deserve better than you receive? Are we not the innocent victims of a cosmic conspiracy? Or, if not this, then at least of a criminal distributive injustice?" (OH 179).

Having aroused their feelings of resentment at being denied the satisfaction of their desires, Nimrod offered them an ambitious plan by which their circumstances could be radically altered. The solution was to strike at the very source of their predicament: build a tower to the skies and take heaven by force.

The construction of the tower rapidly altered the character of the city. Babel was transformed from a City of Freedom to a city with a new communal identity. However, some objected to the project, even taking their grievances to the High Court; "but their complaints received a dusty answer. In one celebrated judgement a distinguished Justice (named Lord Wensleydale) declared that when great works were afoot designed to increase the prosperity of all, private convenience must yield to public good. And this confirmation of the sovereignty of the *utilitas publica* terminated the civil history of Babel" (OH 181).

All enterprises in the city were transformed in the service of the project. An active program of propaganda was deployed. The university, which still maintained some links to an age where it was understood to be an institution devoted to learning, was made into "an 'educational system' designed to impart . . . 'the skills and versatilities called for by the current engagement of the people of Babel'" (OH 183). A new course called Tower Technology was added to the curriculum, as well as a degree in Tower Studies. The language became impoverished because all conversation revolved around the one topic. All discrepancies between rich and poor were eliminated since "all alike were pauperized". Morality was even transformed so that the terms 'good' and 'evil', 'justice' and 'injustice' were understood relative to the new social enterprise. New theologies were written to accommodate the new understanding of the 'Miser God'. Interest grew surrounding the new set of attitudes that the tower evoked among the Babelians. Nothing went unscrutinized. The Babelians became obsessed with polls and the quantification of opinions concerning the tower. Reflecting their susceptibility to academic fashion and to the exaggerated claims of scientific research the Babelians even begun to evaluate the tower's "scenic quality on a bipolar semantic-differential test" (OH 185). In short, all private interest was sacrificed to the construction of the tower and no feature of society remained unchanged.

In time the raw materials began to run out so the buildings of the city were demolished in order to continue the work and "Babel became a place of tents and caravans, of cave-dwellers and inhabitants of holes in the ground" (OH 187). The Babelians to a man had sacrificed everything for the sake of the new social purpose. Once the tower reached a certain stage many became unemployed. Among these discontent grew and suspicions arose that some of their fellows were conspiring to enter heaven without them; "(o)r worse, there emerged a suspicion that they might all turn out to be dupes of a confidence trick designed for the benefit of others than themselves. Or were they, perhaps, the credulous victims of an illusion? Who was it who had said that all this talk of paradise was no more than a shot of opium to keep the masses quiet?" (OH 189). But what finally precipitated the crisis was the belief that Nimrod himself was planning to enter paradise and leave them behind. When he failed to descend the tower from one of his daily sojourns at the summit these suspicions grew to fever pitch and "at last they could contain their apprehension no longer. A shout and the alarm was raised.

People came running from all quarters of the city in panic fear that they were about to be deprived of what they had spent themselves to get. The slogan 'Take the Waiting out of Wanting' had bitten deep into their consciousness" (OH 191). The whole city scrambled up the tower and "there was none who did not keep moving as if his salvation depended on it" (OH 192). The tower was incapable of supporting the mass of bodies that it now contained and it collapsed killing all the inhabitants of Babel.

Centuries later an archaeologist came upon an inscription written by a Babelian poet in the early years of the project.

It foreboded nothing; it was not a premonition of disaster, but a forlorn comment on the engagement itself. On being deciphered it read:

Those who in fields Elysian would dwell
Do but extend the boundaries of hell (OH 193-4).

The undoing of the Babelians was the absence in their makeup of the sort of prideful self-restraint characterizing the aristocratic individual that Oakeshott detects in Hobbes's writings. Their lack of proper pride made them susceptible to the delusion that they could assure their salvation by changing their circumstances. All that was required was a leader who would articulate (invent?) their grievances and put into effect a radical plan to eliminate the source of their perceived predicament. The typical Babelian was not unlike the character Oakeshott describes elsewhere as the 'anti-individual' who "needed to be told what to think; his impulses had to be transformed into desires, and these desires into projects; he had to be made aware of his power; and these were the task of his leaders" (RP 373). And Nimrod himself seems to fit the character that Oakeshott discerns in the leaders of these 'anti-individuals'. What was required for leadership of the masses

> was a man who could at once appear as the image and the master of his fellows; a man who could more easily make choices for others than for himself; a man disposed to mind other people's business because he lacked the skill to find satisfaction in minding his own. . . . enough of an individual to seek a personal satisfaction in the exercise of individuality, but too little to seek it anywhere but in commanding others. He loved himself too little to be anything but an egoist; and what his followers took to be a genuine concern for their salvation was in fact nothing more than the vanity of the almost selfless (RP 374).

He was ideally suited for leadership,

> for he only had never prompted them to be critical of their impulses. Indeed, the 'anti-individual' and his leader were the counterparts of a single situation; they relieved one another's frustrations and supplied one another's wants (RP 374).

Hobbes also examines the implications that arise from the Babel story. For Hobbes (who sticks to the conventional story) the profusion of languages resulting from this unfortunate episode in man's history is symbolic of his fallen nature. After Adam's fall God gave man a common tongue to enable a degree of mutual understanding with his fellow man. This was a partial compensation for the fact that he no longer enjoyed direct communion with his creator. The confusion of tongues was the punishment meted out to creatures who sought to re-establish this relationship by their own efforts. The present proliferation of tongues represents the artificial nature of all language and therefore all knowledge. Hobbes's interpretation of these stories, as Richard Flathman, succinctly puts it, "tell us how matters now stand with and among us, disabuse us of illusions concerning our resources and possibilities, dramatize the difficulties with which we are confronted and the challenges we have to face. They deny us the security and comfort of a divinely ordained or naturally given world, of a consonance or harmony between us and our world and among ourselves, a consonance that enables knowledge and understanding, cooperation and effective action"[30]

Of the abuses of speech Hobbes lists four: the wrongful registering of thoughts, words used metaphorically ("that is, in other sense than that they are ordained for"), the wrongful declaration of intention, and the use of words to cause grief to another (Lev. 19). According to Hobbes, history is replete with examples of men who have taken advantage of the post-Babelian condition and corrupted language to serve their own ambitious aims. In his own time the chief abusers of language included the Schoolmen who encouraged superstition by the use of 'insignificant speech' (Lev. 51), those who clothe their opinions with the authority of conscience (Lev 41), religious fanatics who mistake belief for knowledge (*ibid*), and those who based their opinions on the authority of books and philosophers and not true reasoning from established definitions (Lev 436). Civilization is not only threatened by men desirous of controlling others but by the ambiguities of language that they are able to exploit. For "as men abound in copiousnesse of language; so they become more wise, or more mad than ordinary . . . . For words are wise mens counters, they do but reckon by them: but they are the mony of fooles, that value them by the authority of an *Aristotle*, a *Cicero*, or a *Thomas*, or any other Doctor whatsoever, if but a man" (Lev. 22).[31]

For both Oakeshott and Hobbes the story of the tower of Babel is symbolic not only of man's imperfect nature but of the impossibility of surmounting the limitations of his condition. And the proper response to this predicament, above all, entails the recognition that this is a true representation of his plight. To extend the claims of reason beyond what is warranted by its nature is to imperil civilization. Hobbes, Oakeshott claims, understood this because he realized that "(m)an above all things else is a creature of passion, and his salvation lies, not in the denial of his character, but in its fulfilment" (RP 293). The solution to his predicament must be commensurate with

---

[30]   *Thomas Hobbes: Skepticism, Individuality and Chastened Politics*, p. 12.
[31]   See further, Ball "Hobbes's Linguistic Turn".

his character. Reason may show him the means to attain peace, but it is his passion that motivates this pursuit.

VI

I now want to return to the point where this chapter began, with Nietzsche's observation that modern democracy provides fertile ground for supporting the illusion that science offers something more stable than a mere interpretation of the world. For Nietzsche, particular interpretations of existence are never the result of a detached process of reasoning. They are generated by the particular moral perspectives we choose for ourselves. Now there is an important distinction to be made here insofar as Oakeshott does not claim along with Nietzsche (and much 'postmodern' thought) that science itself is inherently driven by a 'will to power'. For Oakeshott, science and practice belong to different modes of experience. However, where science assumes an authority in practice that does not belong to it then it takes on a Nietzschean hue. Crucially, both Oakeshott and Nietzsche agree that science is just one perspective on human existence. Moreover, Oakeshott goes along with Nietzsche's estimation that a people given over to trivial, materialistic pursuits are likely to find much security, and not a little practical value, in the belief that science offers unconditional, that is, non-perspectival knowledge.

In Oakeshott's work the individual *manqué*, driven by resentment (*ressentiment?*) at being denied the experience of individuality, and deprecating the proper 'self-love' that is the source of virtuous magnanimity, created for himself a new morality in opposition to the morality of individuality. What he sought above all was uniformity. He could not stand in others anything but a replication of himself. He is therefore susceptible to the false security that the ostensible certainties of Rationalism provides. In short:

> He is specified primarily by a moral, not an intellectual, inadequacy. He wants 'salvation'; and in the end will be satisfied only with release from the burden of having to make choices for himself. He is dangerous, not on account of his opinions or desires, for he has none: but on account of his submissiveness. His disposition is to endow government with power and authority such as it has never before enjoyed: he is utterly unable to distinguish a 'ruler' from a 'leader' (RP 381).

The grandiose dreams of a Nimrod are never far from the surface when the predominant moral disposition of the members of a community is that of the individual *manqué*.

Since Rationalism is concerned principally with problem solving, that is, with finding sufficient means for ends which are not themselves subject to scrutiny, when it enters the political realm it generates, what Oakeshott calls, "the politics of the felt need" (RP 9). The idea that politics should mimic the problem-solving nature of engineering Oakeshott calls the "myth of rationalist politics" (RP 9).[32] Rather than calling into question the ends pursued, the Rationalist attempts to remove the discrepancy between a society and what at any moment it feels to be in need of. What the new leaders lack in character and judgement they seek to make up for in the certainties of technique. But the substitution is misguided. Political activity calls above all for self-restraint and for participants who can resists the temptation to reduce politics to the distribution of substantive goods as if it consisted in simply "waking up each morning and considering, 'What would I like to do?' or 'What would somebody else (whom I desire to please) like to see done?', and doing it" (RP 46).

According to Oakeshott, Rationalism is largely synonymous with the arrival into the political process of previously excluded classes since in the absence of an experience or tradition of political activity they had nowhere else to turn for guidance than to an ideology or a ready made technique. It may also be added here that they are tempted by Rationalism because the preponderant moral character of these classes is that of the 'anti-individual', who was transformed into the 'mass man' by the recognition that his strength lay in his numerical superiority. Oakeshott is careful to resist the claim that the 'mass man' is simply identified with any particular economic class. It is not the 'poor', but "those who by circumstance or by occupation had been denied the experience of individuality" (RP 377). Despite this it is difficult to avoid the conclusion that Oakeshott here is dealing with the sort of problem that was a feature of Hannah Arendt's work. That is, with the introduction of the classes of labour and the expansion of what she calls the realm of the social, politics was transformed from an activity defined in contrast to mere economic management (or household management as it appeared in the Greek *polis*), to one in which such management became its chief function. Of course Oakeshott does not endorse Arendt's conclusion that the political realm itself has vanished with the rise of the social, but he does suggest that political activity has been corrupted by the Ratio-

[32]   Needless to say this use of myth is pejorative — Rationalism is a counterfeit myth.

nalism of those classes whose concerns have traditionally centred on the mere necessities of life.[33]

VII

In a recent essay Tom Sorell has explored the relationship between Hobbes's politics and his broader scientific enterprise.[34] Sorell rejects what he takes to be the standard view that Hobbes sought to deduce his civil philosophy from the more basic sciences, notably physics, mechanics and psychology. Hobbes's civil philosophy, as contained in *De Cive* and *Leviathan*, stand independent of the rest of his scientific work and is to be assessed on its own terms. Notably Hobbes based his civil philosophy on geometry, not physics, because the latter is not demonstrative whereas the former is. Unlike the laws of geometry which we create, we can only guess at physics because it is not us but God who makes its laws. Moreover, Sorell suggests that the method of resolution and composition, while applicable to understanding mechanisms such as watches or engines is not utilized by Hobbes in his analysis of civil society. He refrains from using it because civil society cannot be taken apart and put back together in the way watches can. Unlike a watch which can be broken down into its component parts, the rights and duties of civil society are not susceptible to this sort of analysis. Hobbes sought to determine the nature of rights and duties by imagining a state where they did not exist. He therefore employs what Sorell calls the method of *dissolution and innovation* in order to determine how we can come to have rights and duties and to show how a lasting commonwealth can be created. The laws of nature are therefore not deducible from the laws of physics because they are derived from a totally different source: from a consideration of what human behaviour would be like in the absence of civil society.

---

[33]   But Arendt's Hobbes reads much more like Oakeshott's individual *manqué*. See especially Arendt's *The Origins of Totalitarianism* (New York and London, 1951), ch. 5, "The Political Emancipation of the Bourgeoisie". For a discussion of some of the connections (and disagreements) between Oakeshott and Arendt (and Strauss) see Horst Mewes "Modern Individualism: Reflections on Oakeshott, Arendt and Strauss", *The Political Science Reviewer*, Vol. XXI, Spring 1992, 116–147. See also Hanna Pitkin, "The roots of Conservatism: Michael Oakeshott and the denial of politics", *Dissent*, 20 (1973), 496–525. For further comparison of Oakeshott and Arendt, see Margaret Canovan "Hannah Arendt as a Conservative Thinker" in *Hannah Arendt. Twenty Years Later*, (Cambridge and London: MIT Press, 1996)

[34]   "The Science in Hobbes's Politics", in *Perspectives on Thomas Hobbes*, G.A.J. Rogers and Alan Ryan (eds.).

What is interesting about this argument is that by rejecting the standard interpretation that Hobbes's civil philosophy is the product of a unified scientific project Sorell resists the identification of Hobbes's thought with subsequent positivists such as J.S.Mill (in his social scientific moments), Comte, Saint-Simon, Carnap and Hempel. According to Sorell, Hobbes's civil philosophy actually has more in common with "a certain strain of modern moral rhetoric."[35] That is, with writers such as Collingwood, Schmitt, Mill (in his non-positivist moments), Friedman, von Hayek and others. Interestingly Sorell does not include Oakeshott in this list. However, I would argue that Oakeshott's reading of the history of modern European moral and political experience shows clear affinities with writers such as these, and this is reflected in the way he reads Hobbes.

Some of the most interesting recent material on Hobbes points out that the rhetorical nature of *Leviathan* (in contrast to some of his earlier, more unequivocally demonstrative or 'scientific' texts, such as *De Cive* and *The Elements of Law*) was largely a product of Hobbes's growing recognition that for his thought to be effective it had to appeal to the growing numbers of political significant classes.[36] The full meaning and significance of *Leviathan* accordingly can be understood on more than one level of analysis. The much vaunted 'scientific' dimension of *Leviathan*, which appealed at the level of reason and was directed at those who had the time and the learning to understand demonstrative argument, went hand in hand with symbolic and 'mythical' elements designed to appeal to the majority of Hobbes's countrymen, who, along with the bulk of mankind, were principally "pursuers of wealth, command and sensual pleasure" (Lev. 92) and for whom reason had limited motivational purchase.

---

[35] *Ibid.*, p. 68. Cf. Ball, "Hobbes's Linguistic Turn," *Polity*, 17 (1985), 739–60, who argues that Hobbes's "explicit epistemology and methodological presuppositions matter less than his own covertly rhetorical strategy. The pervasiveness of Hobbes's science relies a good deal less upon his definitions and deductions than upon his metaphors. What after all is his state of nature if not an extended metaphor in which men are beasts, life is war, war is hell, and so on? And who is the sovereign if not a secular saviour, a 'mortall god' sent not from heaven but sprung, Athena-like, from the head of the civil philosopher himself? Hobbes was always more adept at detecting the mote of metaphor in another's eye than the beam in his own" (756).

[36] See especially David Johnston, *The Rhetoric of Leviathan: Thomas Hobbes and the Politics of Cultural Transformation* (Princeton: Princeton University Press, 1986), Quentin Skinner, *Reason and Rhetoric in the Philosophy of Hobbes* (Cambridge, 1996), James R. Jacob and Timothy Raylor, 'Opera and Obedience: Thomas Hobbes and *A Proposition for Advancement of Morality* by Sir William Davenant', *The Seventeenth Century*, 6, 2 (1991), 205–50.

As in Hobbes's day, the crisis of European society between, say, the first and second world wars was in large measure a crisis of authority, occasioned by the entry onto the political stage of whole classes of people who had until this time been excluded from political life, and who, upon becoming politically influential fundamentally transformed the relationship between government and the governed. This phenomenon, one of the consequences of the industrialization of European society during the nineteenth century, and analyzed with piercing insight and a sense of impending doom by writers such as Kierkegaard, Burckhardt and Nietzsche, had reached its zenith after the First World War.[37] In 1930, Ortega y Gasset, for instance, could claim that "(t)here is one fact which, whether for good or ill, is of utmost importance in the public life of Europe at the present moment. This fact is the accession of the masses to complete social power".[38] Moreover, the political battles that emerged from this development — between, say, liberalism and fascism (in their various guises) — were often understood by the participants to be a battle between reason and myth.[39]

If we briefly consider Collingwood, for instance, who took Hobbes for his model because he saw the European decline into barbarism as analogous to the situation that confronted Hobbes in the seventeenth century, we see that, like Oakeshott, Collingwood saw the internal threats to civilization arising from the displacement by science of all rival claims to knowledge. For Collingwood utilitarianism fails to acknowledge that the artist, not the scientist, reveals the essence of civilization. Boucher has nicely summed up Collingwood's estimation of the threats posed by a scientistic or utilitarian attitude towards civilization.

> By devaluing and perverting art, divesting religion of its mystical and emotional strength, worshipping the power and force of scientific technology,

[37] To extend the connections with Hobbes's own day it is worth mentioning here James Harrington's perceptive observation (in *Oceana*) made during the period of Cromwell's rule that the political crisis of the English civil war was the product of a fundamental shift in the balance of land ownership in England commenced over a century earlier by the policies of Henry's VII and VIII. This alteration in economic conditions, Harrington thought, had created new classes of politically interested people and had forever shifted the balance of power from the feudal nobility to the then relatively numerous smaller land owners.

[38] *The Revolt of the Masses* (New York: W.W. Norton & Co., 1932)

[39] This tension is particularly pronounced in the work of Carl Schmitt, and especially in his interpretation of Hobbes. See my 'Leviathan as Myth'. See also John McCormick's extensive treatment of these themes in *Carl Schmitt's Critique of Liberalism: Against Politics as Technology* (Cambridge: Cambridge University Press, 1997).

and, misconceiving the character of the historical science of metaphysics, utilitarianism works against civilization.[40]

Though Oakeshott is less explicit than Collingwood in advertising his purpose in utilizing Hobbes, the intention is very similar. Both wanted to bring Hobbes up to date and both saw him as a bulwark against the decline of civilization.

The links between scientism and barbarism are also explored by Ortega in his most famous book *The Revolt of the Masses*. According to Ortega, "(c)civilization is not 'just there,' it is not self-supporting. It is artificial and requires the artist or the artisan."[41] The new barbarism has arisen on the back of an increasingly technological society: "the actual scientific man is the proto-type of the mass man. Not by chance, not through the individual failings of each particular man of science, but because science itself — the root of our civilization — automatically converts him into mass-man, makes of him a primitive, a modern barbarian."[42] It is above all specialization that produces this. Though the scientist can claim absolute knowledge within the confines of his own highly circumscribed discipline he is utterly ignorant of everything outside it. He is, according to Ortega, "a learned ignoramus."[43] Accordingly, what constitutes the real danger to civilization, is that the scientist will bring his certainty into areas of life which he has no knowledge of. Though science is generally taken to be the high point of European civilization your average scientist has no idea what civilization is. He "believes that civilization *is there* in just the same way as the earth's crust and the forest primeval."[44]The somewhat shrill prognostications of Ortega, and to a lesser extent Collingwood, have tended to be explained in terms of the rise of fascism that threatened European civilization in the 1930s. Whatever the motivation of their respective accounts of modern barbarism they both point to those tendencies of modern thought which Oakeshott also identified as constituting a threat to civilization.[45] The crisis of civilization is both a moral and an

---

[40] Boucher, *The Social and Political Thought of R.G.Collingwood*, p. 241
[41] *Revolt of the Masses*, 88.
[42] *Ibid.*, p. 109.
[43] *Ibid.*, p. 112.
[44] *Ibid.*, p. 114.
[45] Cf. also Hayek on the threat to civilization that positivism poses. Like Oakeshott and Ortega, Hayek detects a close connection between scientism or rationalism and collectivism; " . . . in practice it is regularly the theoretical collectivist who extols individual reason and demands that all forces of society be made subject to the direction of a single mastermind, while it is the individualist who recognizes the limitations of the powers of individual reason and consequently advocates freedom as a means for the fullest development of the powers of the interindividual

intellectual crisis. We have seen that, for Oakeshott, Rationalism contains elements of both and when it enters the political sphere it undermines authority by threatening the individualist disposition that civil association presupposes.

It is difficult to read essays such as "The Masses in Representative Democracy", "The Tower of Babel", and certain sections of the final essay of *On Human Conduct* without picking up the strong moral tone in which they are written, indicating that Oakeshott was concerned with something broader than philosophical explanation on the one hand and historical description on the other. Leaving aside for a moment the historical plausibility of his two-fold account of the modern state and the moral dispositions that gave rise to it, I would argue that Oakeshott deployed this grand narrative to extend the myth that he inherited from Hobbes. In other words, Oakeshott's practice as a philosophical historian does not neatly cohere with the modal strictures he lays down elsewhere in his guise as philosophical map-maker. This is not to take issue with his philosophical account of civil association, which, in any case, can be assessed independently of his account of its particular historical manifestations. Nor is it to deny that his account of the modern European moral and political experience in terms of the ideal characters he deploys contains much that is of *historical* value. Indeed, the learning displayed in essays such as the final chapter of *On Human Conduct* shows historical insight and imagination of a very high order. Rather, it is to apply to our understanding of Oakeshott a mild version of Nietzsche's point that all philosophy is the expression of a particular moral orientation and that Oakeshott was not only a philosopher and an historian of sorts but, above and beyond this, a defender of Western civilization as it comes to us through the imagination of Augustine and Hobbes. And as he sought to extend our

---

process", *The Counter-Revolution of Science: Studies on the Abuse of Reason* (Indianapolis: Liberty Press, 1979 — first published 1952), p. 152). According to Hayek, civilization is built on principles which are invariably submitted to despite the fact that they cannot be fully grasped by the individual mind: "Historically this has been achieved by the influence of the various religious creeds and by traditions and superstitions which made men submit to those forces by an appeal to his emotions rather than his reason. The most dangerous stage in the growth of civilization may well be that in which man has come to regard all these beliefs as superstitions and refuses to accept or to submit to anything which he does not rationally understand. The rationalist whose reason is not sufficient to teach him those limitations of the powers of the conscious reason, and who despises all the institutions and customs which have not been consciously designed, would thus become the destroyer of the civilization built upon them. This may well prove a hurdle which man will repeatedly reach, only to be thrown back into barbarism" (*Ibid.*, pp. 162-3).

understanding of Hobbes beyond the strictly philosophical, so too the vision that Oakeshott presents transcends the boundaries of each of the particular modes of experience. Finally, to notice the deeply rhetorical nature of much of Oakeshott's writing is not for a moment to deny his significant contribution to contemporary philosophy. After all, the combination of acute philosophy and powerful rhetoric is a quality that Oakeshott shares with (amongst others) Plato, Hobbes and Nietzsche.

Conclusion

In the introduction I pointed to the different ways in which Oakeshott contextualises Hobbes and indicated that understanding the relationship between the two involves taking into consideration the different explanatory frameworks deployed. By way of bringing together the various threads that run through this work I will explore the status of Oakeshott's account of modality once his many-sided reading of Hobbes is taken into consideration. As well as continuing the argument that the modes exhibit more permeability than Oakeshott explicitly acknowledges, I will use this conclusion as an opportunity to locate Oakeshott's place in a broader methodological debate, which, though he did not contribute to it in any direct sense, is nevertheless reflected in his reading of Hobbes. I need, therefore, to return to Oakeshott's account of the way in which the meaning of a text is elucidated.

I

According to Oakeshott, all interpretation involves reconciling text to context. The question that arises however, is which is the appropriate context that the text assumes. As with all understanding, the meaning of a 'text' is never simply a something given. It does not stand outside experience merely awaiting discovery. It is the task of the interpreter to determine the appropriate context in which the text finds its meaning. In the course of describing the process of philosophical enquiry Oakeshott makes the following points concerning the way in which a text finds its meaning in a context.

> Given a 'text', something partially disconnected, obscure, imperfectly conceived, explanation is the attempt to find the 'context' and to relate text and context so that they become a single whole. But each context which presents itself as *prima facie* appropriate is seen itself to require explanation, to belong to a setting and to lack significance so long as it is not seen in that setting. Consequently, the process becomes the search for a context which

does not require a further setting in order to be understood, a universal, self-complete context. And the task in philosophical enquiry is, precisely, to find and elucidate such a context and the special subject of its enquiry in that context; it has a fresh meaning for each context to which it is related; and it has its full and comprehensive meaning only in a universal, self-complete context (CPJ 350). [1]

In the case of a work like *Leviathan*, for instance, it would seem that a number of contexts are possible. There is first the immediate historical and intellectual context in which Hobbes wrote. Here the interpreter seeks to discover the immediate practical purpose(s) that *Leviathan* was written to address. In recent years our understanding of Hobbes has benefited from a wealth of material of this sort. The second sort of context is also historical though it exhibits a broader compass. Oakeshott's account of the modern experience of individuality and the mode of government understood as the ideal character civil association which this experience gave rise to is an example of this type of historical explanation. No doubt other ideal characters may be elicited from a reading of the course of events but this is Oakeshott's chosen abridgment for reading not only Hobbes, but other accounts of the political theory of individuality. This ideal character is deployed in the final essay of *On Human Conduct*, "The Masses in Representative Democracy", *Morality and Politics in Modern Europe*, *The Politics of Faith and the Politics of Scepticism*, and is invoked at the outset of the "The Moral Life in the Writings of Thomas Hobbes".

The third context also has a historical dimension but it is essentially a form of philosophical explanation. Here *Leviathan* is reconciled with a particular intellectual tradition. For Oakeshott the appropriate sub-tradition that *Leviathan* belongs to is the tradition of Will and Artifice (RP 276-8). However this sub-tradition presupposes an entire world of philosophical ideas reflecting an entire civilization, which, when seen from the philosophical standpoint is reconciled into a coherent whole. Political philosophy achieves this reconciliation of the many into the one from a particular standpoint — in its perception of the human predicament and the role that political activity makes to its resolution. According to Oakeshott, a work like *Leviathan* must therefore "be judged by none but the highest standards and must be considered only in the widest context . . . the context of the masterpiece itself, the setting in which its meaning is revealed, can in the nature of

---

[1]   Though the 'text' that Oakeshott refers to here is actually law the principle is transferable to any phenomenon that we are seeking to explain, including, for instance, *Leviathan* — "All explanation, all interpretation may be seen as a matter of deciding upon and examining the appropriate setting for what is to be explained and of exhibiting it in its place in that setting" (CPJ 350).

things be nothing narrower than the history of political philosophy"
(RP 223).

In the introduction to *Leviathan* Oakeshott offers a brief run down of
the contextual apparatuses the interpreter may bring to bear in order to
elucidate the meaning of this work. It is worth quoting him in full here
as it reveals much about Oakeshott's approach to Hobbes when he
views the latter in a philosophical mood.

> *Leviathan* is a masterpiece, and we must understand it according to our
> means. If our poverty is great, but not ruinous, we may read it not looking
> beyond its two covers, but intent to draw from it nothing that is not there.
> This will be a notable achievement, if somewhat narrow. The reward will
> be the appreciation of a dialectical triumph with all the internal movement
> and liveliness of such a triumph. But *Leviathan* is more than a *tour de force*.
> And something of its larger character will be perceived if we read it with the
> other works of Hobbes open beside it. Or again, at greater expense of learn-
> ing, we may consider it in its tradition, and doing so will find fresh meaning
> in the world of ideas it opens to us. But finally, we may discover in it the true
> character of a masterpiece — the still centre of a whirlpool of ideas which
> has drawn into itself numberless currents of thought, contemporary and
> historic, and by its centripetal force has shaped and compressed them into a
> momentary significance before they are flung off again into the future
> (RP 228).

Oakeshott is only able to make the judgment that the *true* character of
Leviathan is disclosed in the universal context (ie. the entire history of
political philosophy) because he is explicitly invoking a philosophical,
not an historical, interpretation of the past.

In contrast, "The Moral Life in the Writings of Thomas Hobbes"
moves between philosophical and historical interpretation. As in
Morality and Politics in Modern Europe and *The Politics of Faith and the Politics of Scepticism*, here Oakeshott employs the ideal character of moral
individuality to explore the meaning of Hobbes's thought. That is, he
explicitly invokes the second of the contexts noted above. Unlike the
introduction which, because it is explicitly philosophical, invokes the
tradition, not the history, of political philosophy, the 'Moral Life'
employs a form of enquiry which can perhaps be termed philosophical
history. It has a closer connection with the actual course of events.

Though in his explicit pronouncements Oakeshott rules out the
merely historical approach to the work of past political philosophers, his 'philosophical' reading of Hobbes by no means offends
judgments that historians, before or after Oakeshott, have made concerning the former. Indeed, Oakeshott's emphasis on Hobbes's
nominalism in particular, and the connection of his thought with
currents in late medieval philosophy generally have been thor-

oughly explored by subsequent scholars. Though Oakeshott's account of these connections consists of only a few suggestive comments, the nominalist/individualist direction that his reading took certainly broke new ground and has only subsequently been fully explored by historians and philosophers.[2] I have argued that Oakeshott did update Hobbes for his own philosophical purposes, but he managed it with a degree of historical sensitivity which is born out by the subsequent work of Hobbes scholars. Not only can his reading of Hobbes be viewed for the purpose of providing clues to the direction of Oakeshott's own thought as I have maintained throughout this work, it can also be viewed purely in terms of the great twentieth century debate over the meaning of Hobbes. This contrasts with writers such as T.H. Green, Collingwood and, at the other end of the political spectrum, Carl Schmitt, whose discussions of Hobbes are likely to be consulted principally for the purposes of determining the nature of their own political theories rather than for understanding Hobbes himself.

What I want to suggest is that though his approach is primarily philosophical (I am leaving aside for the moment the practical component of his reading) and since philosophy and history represent two independent forms of experience it would not be inconsistent for Oakeshott, given his understanding of the philosophical enterprise as continuously in the process of renewal, to have left aside any pretence to historical respectability and to have lifted Hobbes self-consciously out of his historical context to make him address contemporary philosophical problems in the way, for instance, Collingwood did. This contrast with Collingwood provides a curious paradox given their differing pronouncements on the modal nature of human understanding. That is, Collingwood's attempt to find a *rapprochement* between history and philosophy and the consequent denial of the existence of perennial problems in philosophy, issued in the understanding that present philosophical activity involves the deliberate modification of past thought in the light of con-

---

[2]   I have in mind writers such as W.B. Glover (see, for instance, "God and Thomas Hobbes", in *Hobbes Studies* (Oxford: Blackwell, 1965), ed. K. Brown), J.W.N. Watkins, *Hobbes's System of Ideas* (London: Hutchinson and Co., 1965), Ryan ("Hobbes and Individualism"), Richard Flathman, *Thomas Hobbes: Skepticism, Individuality and Chastened Politics* (Sage Publications, 1993) to name just a few. Richard Tuck's recent work exploring Hobbes's philosophy as a response to the widespread scepticism of late sixteenth and early seventeenth century Europe also develops themes consistent with Oakeshott's reading. See, for instance, *Philosophy and Government 1572–1651* (Cambridge: Cambridge University Press, 1993) and 'Optics and Skeptics: The Philosophical Foundations of Hobbes's Political Thought' in *Conscience and Casuistry in Early Modern Europe* (Cambridge: Cambridge University Press, 1987) ed. E. Leites.

temporary problems. *The New Leviathan* is the product of this under-standing of the philosophical enterprise. The questions that philosophers ask today are different from those asked by Hobbes, which in turn are different from those of other philosophers living in different historical circumstances. What unites Hobbes with Plato, for instance, is not their attempt to answer in their respective ways the same fundamental question, but their participation in the historical process that is constantly in the process of transformation and with it the questions that can be legitimately asked, and answers legitimately given.[3] In contrast, because Oakeshott refuses the assimilation of phi-losophy to history — that is, there is a universal predicament which as a whole remains unchanged (whereas for history, as for practice, there is only change) — he can interpret Hobbes with greater historical sensi-tivity because the substance of Hobbes's perception of the predicament will remain relevant despite the fact that the topical issues that his the-ory addressed have moved on: "What remains relevant, then, is Hobbes's diagnosis of the situation."[4] It is not merely the spirit of Hobbes's philosophy that remains relevant (for instance, his "hard boiled" realism),[5] nor is it the fact that Hobbes started his enquiry into political matters from first principles which need to be redone in the light of contemporary problems.[6] For Oakeshott, Hobbes's substantive doctrine, formulated in response to the immediate and pressing practi-cal circumstances of his time, but addressing concerns of universal sig-nificance, remains relevant.

A further paradox is that historians such as Skinner and Dunn, for instance, though drawing on Collingwood's idea of recovering the purposive actions of agents in order to develop methodologies for recovering the historical explanations of philosophical texts, have developed interpretations of past philosophers (Hobbes especially in the case of Skinner) completely unlike Collingwood's own read-ing of Hobbes. In his reading of Hobbes, Oakeshott seems to stand somewhere between earlier philosophical Idealists such as Green and Collingwood with their philosophical *cum* practical reading of the history of philosophy and historical revisionists such as Skinner, Pocock and Dunn, who, at least explicitly, eschew the contemporary philosophical or practical relevance of the original, and for them, the essential meaning of such texts. The result of much of the recent histori-

---

[3]   Collingwood, *An Autobiography* (London: Oxford University Press, 1970 — first
        published 1939), ch. V.
[4]   "A Reminder from Leviathan".
[5]   See Boucher, *The Social and Political Thought of R.G. Collingwood*, p. 67.
[6]   See Collingwood's preface to *The New Leviathan*.

cal revisionist literature has been to restrict the range of meanings that can with validity be recovered from any particular text. In contrast, Oakeshott's intention is to expand the possibilities of meaningful interpretation. It is ultimately the task of the interpreter to choose his context and determine the meaning of the text within it. This does not imply a mere chaos of conflicting, essentially subjective interpretations. No interpretation is ever merely subjective, but always implicates a whole world of evidence that is brought to bear on the determination of a 'fact' or 'meaning'. Rather, the interpreter must remain faithful to the mode of interpretation, or experience, to which he subscribes.

Oakeshott showed no interest in formulating a methodology or epistemology for determining the meaning of past political theory. He rejected the idea that the meaning of any particular text is solely a function of its author's intention and that this original meaning can be recovered if the appropriate methodology is employed. It is perfectly possible to subject a book like *Leviathan* to strict historical scrutiny, but this does not exhaust the meaning of the text, and is, in any case, not the most profitable approach to take to it.

Moreover, because Oakeshott draws a clear distinction between historical and philosophical contexts he does not offer anything approaching a methodology for subjecting philosophical texts to historical explanation. The traditions of political philosophy that he invokes in the introduction to *Leviathan* are simply heuristic devices that help elucidate the philosophical identity of a particular text. Unlike ideal characters that are deliberate abstractions from historical experience and therefore take on a settled and fixed character, these philosophical traditions are essentially open and fluid and are useful for contemporary philosophers as a means of building on past thought. They form a part of the philosophical enterprise itself. Indeed, the contemporary debate over Hobbes points to the difficulties of interpreting past philosophy in terms of these traditions. For instance, in response to Skinner, Warrender explicitly suggests that Hobbes's meaning is not exhausted by the immediate linguistic and ideological context that recent historiographers have deemed appropriate for interpreting him. This is merely one historical scale that can be invoked. Another is the entire history of natural law which despite its changing expressions constitutes a single tradition because it is the expression of a particular teaching which Warrender defines as, "a body of prescriptive rules concerning human conduct, capable of being discovered by all men of right reason, applicable to all men (regardless of nation, race, religion, historical period, etc.) and superior to the positive laws of individual states". Warrender then suggests that "Hobbes's laws of nature fall under this definition, and it is against such a wide canvas that my state-ment on Hobbes is relevant."[7] As we have seen, Warrender has shown that a natural law doctrine can plausibly be elicited from Hobbes. If Warrender's reading is correct then Hobbes can be assimilated to Oakeshott's 'Reason and Nature' tradition. Conversely, if Oakeshott's reading is truer to the meaning of Hobbes then this clearly casts doubt on Warrender's identification of Hobbes with natural law thinkers "(f)rom the Stoics and Cicero, to Grotius and the jurists, or to Locke; or from the Aristotelian legacy developed (and still continued) by the Roman Church."[8]

None of this greatly affects the validity of Oakeshott's reading of Hobbes, which, as I have maintained, is to be understood in terms of the broader philosophical project that he sets himself. It does, how-ever, point to the considerable practical difficulties entailed in the extension of Oakeshott's concept of philosophical traditions for the purpose of drawing concrete historical explanations of the meaning of philosophical texts as Greenleaf, for instance, has proposed.[9]

Oakeshott's rejection of epistemological or methodological approaches to the interpretation of philosophical texts in favour of a general consideration of the nature of human understanding aligns him with the ontological hermeneutics of Heidegger and Gadamer. On this issue he is perhaps closer to Gadamer than any other modern theorist. According to Gadamer, the interpreter's attempt to over-come the subjectivity of present preconceptions and grasp the origi-nal meaning of the text, ie. the authorial intention, by the application of a method of historical interpretation contradicts the character of human understanding. Like Oakeshott, Gadamer stresses the contemporaneity of all understanding. For the latter we have under-standing because we have language and all language forms are par-ticular. The *mens auctoris* cannot be recaptured because it belongs to another linguistic framework. However, according to Gadamer, this is not a barrier to understanding a text but the very condition of our capacity to understand it. The meaning of the text is therefore disclosed in the 'fusion of horizons' that occurs when our contemporary 'fore-understandings' interact with those of a past author. For Gadamer, the treatment of the text as an object with its own independ-ent meaning which can be discovered if approached with the correct methodology is beside the point once the contemporaneity of all

---

[7]   Warrender, "Political Theory and Historiography", p. 993.
[8]   *Ibid.*
[9]   Greenleaf himself has run into difficulties in classifying thinkers such as Burke and Hume. On this see Boucher "W.H.Greenleaf . . .", esp. pp. 247–249.

human understanding is understood. However, as David Boucher has pointed out, Oakeshott is not in entire agreement with the ontological hermeneutics of writers such as Gadamer because he rejects their postulation of a past that has existed, which, while never accessible on its own terms, can be met "half-way in an encounter between horizons."[10] In his rejection of all experience save present experience, and therefore in his scepticism concerning the recovery of the past, Oakeshott is even more radical than a writer such as Gadamer.

Though Oakeshott refers to "Leviathan: *a myth*" as "a conversation piece, a flight of fancy", this brief essay is highly suggestive of Oakeshott's intention to assimilate Hobbes to contemporary purposes. Whatever Hobbes's intention may have been in composing *Leviathan* (a topic that will no doubt continue to engage historians and philosophers) it is inconceivable that Hobbes himself thought he was involved in rebuilding and perpetuating a myth. Apart from the *philosophes* themselves it is difficult to imagine a thinker in whose mind the oppositions between myth and enlightenment, superstition and knowledge, "insignificant speech" and precise definitions was more clearly distinguished and insistently urged. One recent commentator has suggested that Hobbes sought nothing less than an entire cultural transformation from myth, superstition and false belief toward enlightenment and reason and "that he considered myth a product of egregious ignorance. Such ignorance, he thought, is incompatible with any genuinely rational political society, which must be founded upon an enlightened populace."[11] There is little doubt that Hobbes was fond of metaphor, word pictures, colourful speech, indeed most of the traditional arts of rhetoric, and that he employed them to good effect, yet if, as Oakeshott claims, he was engaged in a piece of myth-making, he was very much a myth-maker *malgré lui*.

II

Throughout this study I have used Oakeshott's reading of Hobbes — which, as we have seen is closely connected to Oakeshott's own substantive political theory — to explore the ambiguities in the modal arrangement of experience that he constructs. I have suggested that there are elements of philosophy, practice and, to some extent, history

---

[10] Boucher, *Texts in Context: Revisionist Methods for Studying the History of Ideas* (Dordrecht: Martinus Nijhoff Publishers, 1985) p65. See chapter 1 generally for a full consideration of Collingwood's and Oakeshott's ideas on the philosophy of history and the history of philosophy.

[11] Johnston, *The Rhetoric of Leviathan*, p. 217, see generally chs. 4–6.

in his reading and that each of these interact in various ways. Perhaps it is not stretching it to far to suggest that these ambiguities can perhaps be seen as, in some sense, a reflection of the broader developments in the discipline of the history of political thought which has in recent years taken on a high degree of explicit methodological sophistication. In both England and America this discipline emerged out of a convergence of historical, philosophical, and practical interests. J.G. Gunnell, for instance, has suggested that most of the standard textbooks on the history of political thought have been, and continue to be, written in the idiom of Oakeshott's practical past.[12] Similarly, Boucher has traced the emergence of this discipline in England and noted that most textbooks on the history of political thought "were intensely practical in their concerns and included the terms 'history' in their titles more as a courtesy, since they often emerged from schools, or departments, of history, than as an indication of the mode of enquiry pursued. 'History' was often a convenient term for the past body of literature designated political thought"[13]

It was not until the 1960s that the methodological implications of this mixture of modes was given a full critique in the work of historical 'revisionists' such as Skinner, Pocock and Dunn, who pointed out that much of what had previously passed as history was in fact the product of enquiries which failed to cohere with the proper methods of historiography. This revisionist material arose from a determination to free historical enquiry from present practical and philosophical interests. It was closer in spirit (if not in method) to Oakeshott's understanding of an historical approach to the past.[14]

The seventeenth century generally and Hobbes particularly has been central to this project of historical revision. Skinner, for instance, through a series of essays has used Hobbes as something of a case study to illustrate his understanding of the proper methods of historical enquiry and to criticise readings of Hobbes, such as those of Strauss, Warrender and Hood, which, in Skinner's estimation,

---

[12] *Political Theory: Tradition and Interpretation* (Cambridge MA: Winthrop, 1979), pp. 25–6.

[13] "Philosophy, History and Practical Life: The emergence of the history of political thought in England", *The Australian Journal of Politics and History*, 35 (1989), 220–37, p. 225.

[14] More recently Skinner has suggested that his method of uncovering past authorial intentions can in fact help elucidate ideas and arguments used in contemporary philosophical discourse — see "The Idea of Negative Liberty: Philosophical and Historical Perspectives", *Philosophy in History: Essays on the historiography of philosophy*, Richard Rorty, J.B. Schneewind, Quentin Skinner eds. (Cambridge: Cambridge University Press, 1984).

produce erroneous interpretations by failing to take into consideration these historical strictures. Skinner's work has in turn provoked a response from political theorists who have pointed to the limitations of his method for fully explaining the philosophical meaning of Hobbes's work (in particular the theory of obligation) and have defended the traditional role demarcation between the philosopher and the historian.[15]

One of the criticisms that has been pressed against the revisionist critique of the traditional studies in the history of political philosophy is that in attacking the latter as unhistorical the revisionists fail to appreciate the purposes which these works were designed to address. As Boucher argues:

> To concentrate upon the logic of enquiry, as recent commentators have done, and to assume that the historical mode of enquiry constitutes the standard by which to assess the products of the discursive formation [the interaction of the modes of history, philosophy and practice], is to filter out of consideration a whole set of values and purposes which contributed to the peculiar character of its manner of enquiry. A more appropriate question would be to ask how successful the practitioners were in their intensely practical concerns of contributing to current debates about perennial problems as they had become manifest in their own times . . . The mode of discourse was recognisably hybrid, and was explicitly meant to be so. The historian of political thought stood at the centre of a complex of systems of interaction, taking on the injunctive role of politics, the critical role of philosophy, and the explanatory role of history thus forming a cultural system which gradually fell under the auspices of departments of politics or political science.[16]

A similar argument is sustained by Gunnell in his discussion of writers such as Strauss, Voegelin, Arendt, and Wolin who perpetuated the idea of what Gunnell calls 'the myth' of the tradition of political philosophy. Each of these writers invoked the idea of the tradition for essentially unhistorical purposes. Therefore, to criticise these authors for failing to adhere to the canons of historical enquiry is to miss the point of their enterprises.[17]

---

[15] See Warrender, "Political Theory and Historiography" and Preston King "The Theory of Context and the Case of Hobbes", in Preston King (ed.), *The History of Ideas: An Introduction to Method* (London and Canberra: Croom Helm, 1983).

[16] "Philosophy, History and Practical Life", p. 230.

[17] J.G. Gunnell, *Political Theory:Tradition and Interpretation* (Cambridge MA: Winthrop, 1979), pp. 22-7. Skinner, for instance, seems to miss the point of Plamenatz's work. In the preface to his *Man and Society: A critical examination of some important social and political theories from Machiavelli to Marx,* 2 vols. (London: Longmas, 1963) Plamenatz explicitly denies that he is concerned with developing a history of political thought. As the subtitle to this work indicates

Gunnell's discussion of Strauss is particularly interesting since he is one of the major twentieth century interpreters of Hobbes. According to Gunnell, Strauss invokes the myth of the tradition of political philosophy for his essentially rhetorical purpose of impugning the intellectual foundations of modernity. We have seen that Hobbes is central to this enterprise. Strauss went on to qualify his early conclusion that Hobbes was the founder of modern political philosophy, suggesting instead that Machiavelli made the substantial break with the 'tradition', and that writers such as Hobbes and Locke softened and made more acceptable the former's fundamentally original teaching.[18] Hobbes is nevertheless a central player in this narrative and Strauss returns to him because he gave a full theoretical elaboration of the 'bourgeois' morality of modernity.

Though Strauss, like Oakeshott, urges the separation of philosophy and history, he suggests (unlike Oakeshott) that historical investigation is a necessary preliminary to philosophy, enabling the contemporary recovery of the intention of past authors. This intention bears no relation to Skinner's claim to be able to recover the intention that is expressed in past authors' 'speech acts'. As Strauss conceives it, what needs to be recovered is the political philosopher's intention to contribute to an ongoing intellectual tradition. Gunnell suggests that the tradition is actually an abstraction from the historical course of events, which is then employed by Strauss *as* an *a priori* concept and little, if any, concession is made to historical method itself. This invocation of the tradition provides the enquiry with a semblance of historical symbolism. What we have is "an approach in which a philosophical argument about politics is entirely dependent upon a

---

he is concerned with exploring the logical coherence of some major political theories, for which task he employed a strictly textualist approach. Were his project to determine the practical intention of these theories then such an approach would undoubtedly be inadequate. Yet because this is not Plamenatz's purpose Skinner's critique of his textualist approach fails to hit its target. As Ken Minogue observes, "Skinner assimilates Plamenatz to Skinner's own question, remarking that 'we can never hope to attain such an understanding simply by reading the text 'over and over again' in the way that some commentators have urged'. Plamenatz, of course, never said you could. Altogether, there is a lot of loose talk about approaches, and not enough concern with *what* it is that is being approached" — "Method in intellectual history: Quentin Skinner's *Foundations*", in *Meaning and Context: Quentin Skinner and his Critics*, James Tully (ed.) (Princeton: Princeton University Press, 1988), 176–193, at p. 181. For Skinner's critique of Plamenatz see "Meaning and understanding in the history of ideas", in *ibid.*, esp. pp 38, 51–2. See also the same volume pp. 95, 105.

[18]   Strauss, *What is Political Philosophy?* (Glencoe, Ill.: Free Press, 1959), pp47–9, cited in Gunnell, *Tradition and Interpretation*, p. 40.

historical account and in which interpretations of past thinkers are absolutely inseparable from his [Strauss's] critique of contemporary politics."[19] According to Gunnell, Strauss succumbs to the very historicism that he condemns in others since most of his work consists in the attempt to recover, as he sees it, the philosophical meaning of past authors through a historical reconstruction of the problems they intended to address, where historical reconstruction involves locating an author in a preconceived tradition of enquiry.[20]

What Gunnell is suggesting is that Strauss's distinction between philosophy and history can be called into question when it is considered in the light of his work as an intellectual historian. So despite Strauss's rejection of a Collingwoodian convergence of history and philosophy,[21] when we consider the way in which he reads writers like Machiavelli, Hobbes and Locke, not only can we treat the distinction between these two forms of enquiry with some degree of scepticism, we also find that they are tied to a moral critique of contemporary political thought and practice. Strauss's reading of these authors needs to be viewed in terms of the way in which he constructs the tradition in order to trace its decline into the nihilism of modernity.

Gunnell also cites Arendt as one of the builders of the 'myth' of the tradition of political philosophy. Along with Strauss, Arendt largely views the past as a reservoir of ideas that enable us to judge the present. For her the story is also one of decline which starts from the Greeks. However, in contrast to Strauss, Plato and Aristotle are criticised for privileging the *vita contemplativa* which, Arendt thinks, undermined the unique political experience of the *polis*. The modern crisis is primarily a political, not an intellectual crisis. Though it is a long and complex story which takes us from the rise and decline of the *polis*, to the medieval separation of the *vita activa* from politics, to Hobbes, Descartes, modern science, Marx and finally totalitarianism, Arendt constructs her history around a set of distinctions which she thinks are basic to politics — the public versus the private sphere, labour and work versus action, the active versus the contemplative life. These distinctions, she thinks, were central to the political experience of the Greeks and have largely been lost to us. The purpose of history for Arendt is to recover these distinctions and hopefully recover something of the genuine experience of politics that the Greeks began. So Arendt's past is also a practical past. As one commentator suggests, for

---

[19] Gunnell, *Tradition and Interpretation*, p. 74.
[20] *Ibid.*, pp. 74–5.
[21] See, for instance, Strauss, "On Collingwood's Philosophy of History" in King (ed.), *The History of Ideas.*

Arendt, "the political theorist who focuses on intellectual history some-how keeps alive those extinct traditions that have rendered past experiences useful as a point of orientation in the present."[22]

I have suggested throughout this work that Oakeshott's engagement with Hobbes provides a similar focal point through which his categorial vision of experience can be questioned. This tendency to conflate the modes is perhaps most fully revealed in his determination to read Hobbes as the perpetuator of a myth. We have seen that the failure to appreciate the mythical substance of civilization gives rise to many beliefs that pose a threat to it. We are told that Hobbes appreciated this because he recognised the limitations of reason and science and saw the need to minimise the opportunity to provoke the anarchical passions of the majority of mankind. Oakeshott's own determination to describe the predicament of modern man by retelling an ancient myth demonstrates the basic affinity of his own project with that which he detects in Hobbes. Where Strauss links Hobbes with the modern bourgeois individualism that the former deplores, the aristocratic individuality that Oakeshott detects in Hobbes's writings is reminiscent of Oakeshott's own celebratory account of virtuous self-enactment. Unlike Strauss and Macpherson, Oakeshott makes a fundamental distinction between the moral ideal that underlies the respective philosophies of Hobbes and Locke. According to Oakeshott, it is the tradition of Locke, not Hobbes, that has given rise to the identification of liberalism with acquisitive individualism. We have seen that this slant on the reading of Hobbes is closely tied to the story of the rise of the individualist disposition and the threats posed to it by those who were not equal to its challenges. This is a narrative that Oakeshott presents in the guise of history, but it clearly shuttles back and forth between an historical and a practical arrangement of the past.

In the first chapter the respective philosophical 'systems' of Oakeshott and Oakeshott's Hobbes were explored. The convergence of their substantive philosophical teachings is only possible because, despite initial appearances, there is a basic metaphysical affinity between them. Oakeshott's insistence that philosophy and science, despite being used synonymously by Hobbes, are nevertheless categorially distinct, opens the way for Oakeshott's assimilation of the latter for his own purposes. This is not to suggest that Oakeshott's reading of Hobbes's system in terms of distinct forms of

[22] Helmut Dubiel, 'Hannah Arendt and the Theory of Democracy' in Kielmansegg, Mewes, Glasser-Schmidt (eds.), *Hannah Arendt and Leo Strauss: German Emigrés and American Political Thought after World War II*, p. 13.

knowledge came at the price of distorting Hobbes. Indeed, it is now something of a commonplace of Hobbes scholarship to stress the existence in his writings of the late medieval distinction between reason, experience and faith. However, where Oakeshott's reading clearly does stand out from others is in his silence over the question of Hobbes's estimation of the utilitarian value of his theory. It may be that Oakeshott thought Hobbes mistaken in this belief and that, despite its creator's intention, *Leviathan* is a profound work of theory, and not the blueprint of the theoretician. But this interpretation must come at the price of overlooking some of Hobbes's explicit intentions.

In chapters 2 and 3 we saw the gradual convergence of Oakeshott's theories of agency and authority with the way these come to be interpreted in his reading of Hobbes. This convergence is perfectly consistent with Oakeshott's understanding that philosophy is forever undergoing renewal. This is not to suggest that Oakeshott simply takes over from Hobbes the concepts he finds there. Hobbes's nominalist theory of volition is clearly reworked in the light of the insights of the Hegelian 'Rational Will' tradition. Further, the theory of authority, while based on the same fundamental distinctions as those which he finds in Hobbes, presupposes Oakeshott's detailed elaboration of the traditional nature of all human activity. This was further clarified in *On Human Conduct* in terms of the idea of practices as the context of all human conduct. The effect of this elaboration of the conventional nature of all human activity is to render obsolete Hobbes's contract as the origin of authority. Oakeshott is able to preserve an essentially Hobbesian theory of authority while endorsing Hume's insight that institutions arise less from conscious construction than from the unintended by-product of the interplay of countless individuals each choosing contingent ends in their never ending effort to affect change in the world of practice. I have argued that despite Oakeshott's early sympathetic reading of Hobbes, his own early accounts of agency and authority were written from the perspective of the tradition of 'Rational Will', which, according to its defenders, had overcome the defects found in writers such as Hobbes. As his work develops Hobbes clearly assumes a more prominent place. This incorporation of Hobbes into his own work indicates that Oakeshott has transformed the Rational Will tradition by purging it of all traces of teleological development. Further, this convergence of the Rational Will and Will and Artifice traditions needs to be read in conjunction with his account of the ideal characters *societas* and *universitas* and the contingent moral dispositions that are concomitant to these rival understandings of the modern state because it is here that

Oakeshott turns from a philosophical reading of the past to something much closer to a type of historical understanding. It is this 'historical element' that shapes Oakeshott's political theory given its most fully developed expression in *On Human Conduct*.

III

In an essay on the work of Hume, Shirley Letwin made the observation that "every great philosopher has been rendered into diverse characters."[23] There is perhaps no better illustration of this insight than the posthumous life (or lives) of Hobbes. The proliferation of ways in which Hobbes is read is not only an indication of the undoubted fact that Hobbes is a rich, complex thinker whose work contains many lines of often conflicting argument, it also reflects the nature of contemporary political theory. Of course, Hobbes as symbol and focal point for wider disputes in political theory is not a new development. He was a central figure in the nineteenth century philosophical disputes between the sovereignty theorists and the Idealists. The Idealists deemed it necessary to criticise Hobbes because it was considered that his ideas in some sense buttressed the utilitarian conception of human nature as well as the Austinian theory of sovereignty.[24]

Though the more or less stable consensus on the meaning of Hobbes has broken down in the twentieth century we still find philosophers returning to him in order to confront contemporary philosophical and political problems. Discussing the various identities that modern interpreters have foisted on Hobbes, M.M. Goldsmith has suggested that modern psychologists would be in their element. On Goldsmith's reading, Strauss's Hobbes had a modernity complex, Macpherson's Hobbes had subconscious Marxist tendencies, and for Warrender, Hobbes had an obligation fixation.[25] Without denying their relative strengths, Goldsmith finds each of these readings ultimately unsatisfactory: "(e)ach identification turned out to be markedly peculiar to the analyst. By emphasising a particular characteristic, each imposed a strange and narrow consistency upon Hobbes."[26] Though it is neither strange nor narrow, I would suggest that there is also a consistency in Oakeshott's reading that is "peculiar to the ana-

---

[23] 'David Hume: Inventor of a New Task for Philosophy', *Political Theory* 3 (1975), 134–58, at 134.
[24] On this see Mark Francis, "The Nineteenth Century Theory of Sovereignty and Thomas Hobbes", *History of Political Thought*, vol.1, no.3, Autumn. December 1980, 517–40.
[25] "A Case of Identity", in Parekh and King (eds.), *Politics and Experience*.
[26] *Ibid.*, p. 91.

lyst". But Oakeshott is more than another Hobbes analyst and his reading needs to be assessed not only for its value as a contribution to our understanding of Hobbes but because it is central to his broader philosophical vision.

D.D. Raphael said of Oakeshott's introduction to *Leviathan* that, "(l)ike all Oakeshott's writings . . . [it] impresses the reader both by its imaginative style and by glimpses of a novel vista. But the vista is seen through a glass, darkly, and it is not easy to say just what Oakeshott's interpretation comes to."[27] In this work I have attempted to unravel precisely what his interpretation does come to and suggested that like Oakeshott's own thought his reading of Hobbes is multi-faceted and that each facet is a reflection of his own changing preoccupations. Though not all Hobbes scholars will agree with Oakeshott's interpretation, few will deny its breadth of vision or its sheer literary achievement. Though I have pointed out where I think Oakeshott's reading is inadequate it is also important to stress that this sort of questioning has its limitations in assessing the worth of Oakeshott's creative engagement with Hobbes. Perhaps it is not going too far to extend Goldsmith's psychological terminology and suggest that Hobbes is, or at least became, Michael Oakeshott's seventeenth century alter-ego.

---

[27] *Hobbes: Morals and Politics* (London: George Allen and Unwin, 1977), p. 84.

Bibliography

In what follows I have only listed those works referred to in the text. For the most complete bibliography of Oakeshott and Oakeshott interpretation up to 1993 see J. Liddington's bibliography in *The Achievement of Michael Oakeshott*, ed. J. Norman. London: Duckworth 1993. Subsequent additions to this can be found on the Michael Oakeshott association web site: www.michael-oakeshott-association.org

I
Works by Oakeshott

1. Books

Experience and Its Modes. Cambridge: CUP. 1933.
Rationalism in Politics and Other Essays. Indianapolis: Liberty Press, 1991. Ed. T. Fuller.
On Human Conduct. Oxford: Clarendon Press, 1975.
Hobbes on Civil Association. Oxford: Basil Blackwell, 1975.
On History and Other Essays. Oxford: Basil Blackwell, 1983.
Religion, Politics and the Moral Life. New Haven and London: Yale University Press, 1993. Ed. T. Fuller.
Morality and Politics in Modern Europe: The Harvard Lectures. New Haven and London: Yale University Press, 1993. Ed. S.R. Letwin.
The Voice of Liberal Learning: Michael Oakeshott on Education. New Haven and London: Yale University Press, 1989. Ed. T. Fuller.

2. Articles and Letters

"Lord Acton", *Caian* (the magazine of Gonville and Caius College), 31: i (Michaelmas 1922), pp.14-23.
"John Locke", *The Cambridge Review*, November 4, 1932, pp.72-3
"Thomas Hobbes", *Scrutiny*, 4 (1935-6), pp.263-77

"The Concept of a Philosophical Jurisprudence", *Politica*, 3 (1938), pp.203-22, 345-60
Introduction to Hobbes's *Leviathan*. Oxford: Basil Blackwell, 1960.
"Contemporary British Politics", *Cambridge Journal*, 1 (1947-8), pp.474-90.
"Science and Society", *Cambridge Journal*, 1 (1947-8), pp.689-97.
"A Reminder from '*Leviathan*'", *The Observer*, (29 July, 1951), p.4.
"The Vocabulary of a Modern European State", *Political Studies*, 23 (1975), pp. 319-41, 409-14.
"On Misunderstanding Human Conduct: A Reply to My Critics". *Political Theory* 4 (1976), pp.353-67.
Letter to J.W.N. Watkins on Hobbes, in *Political Theory*, 29, 2001, pp.834-836.

3. Reviews

Review of J.Needham (ed.), *Science, Religion and Reality*, in *Journal of Theological Studies*, 27 (1926), pp.317-19
Review of A.C.Bouquet, *The Christian Religion and its Competitors Today*, in *Journal of Theological Studies*, 27 (1926), pp.440
Review of P.Gardiner, *Modernism in the Church of England*, in *Journal of Theological Studies*, 28 (1927), pp.316
Review of G.G.Atkins, *The Making of the Christian Mind*, in *Journal of Theological Studies*, 31 (1930), pp.203-8
Review of K.Heim, *The New Divine Order*, F.J.Sheen *Religion without God*, E.Holmes, *Philosophy without Metaphysics*, in *Journal of Theological Studies*, 32 (1931), pp.434-5.
Review of O.Gierke, *Natural Law and the Theory of Society, 1500 to 1800* (tr. Barker), in *Cambridge Review*, 56 (1934-5), pp.11-12
Review of C.C.J. Webb, *The Historical Element in Religion*, in *Journal of Theological Studies*, 37 (1936), pp.96-8
Review of B. Pfannenstill, *Bernard Bosanquet's Philosophy of the State*, in *Philosophy*, 11 (1936), pp.482-3
Review of J.D.Mabbott, *The State and the Citizen*, *Mind*, 58 (1949), pp.378-89
Review of K.Brown (ed.), *Hobbes Studies*, in *English Historical Review*, 82 (1967), pp.123-5
Review of H. Arendt, *Between Past and Future*, in *Political Science Quarterly*, 77 (1962), pp.88-90.
Review of S.Avineri, *Hegel's Theory of the Modern State*, in *European Studies Review*, 5 (1975), pp.217-20

II
Works on Oakeshott

Anderson, P. 1992. "The Intransigent Right at the End of the
Century", *London Review of Books*, 24 September, pp.7-11

Auspitz, J.L. 1976. "Individuality, Civility, and Theory: The
Philosophical Imagination of Michael Oakeshott", *Political Theory*
4, pp.261-94

Boucher, D. 1989. "Overlap and Autonomy: The Different Worlds
of Collingwood and Oakeshott", in *Storia, antropologia e scienze del
linguaggio*, 4, pp.69-89

Boucher, D. 1991. "Politics in a Different Mode: An Appreciation
of Michael Oakeshott", *History of Political Thought*, 12, pp.717-28

Boucher, D. 2001. 'The Idealism of Michael Oakeshott',
Collingwood and British Idealism Studies, vol.8, pp. 73-98.

Brown, J.M. 1953. "A Note on Professor Oakeshott's Introduction
to the *Leviathan*", *Political Studies*, 1, pp.53-64

Collingwood, R.G. 1970. "Oakeshott and the Modes of
Experience". in *The Cambridge Mind*, ed. E.Homberger. Boston:
Little Brown.

Cowling, M. 1980. *Religion and Public Doctrine in Modern England.*
Cambridge: CUP, pp 251-282

Crick, B. 1991. "The Ambiguity of Michael Oakeshott", *The
Cambridge Review*, 112, pp.120-4.

P.Franco. 1990a. *The Political Philosophy of Michael Oakeshott.* New
Haven and London: Yale University Press.

Franco, P. 1990b. "Michael Oakeshott as Liberal Theorist", *Political
Theory*, 18, pp.411-36.

Franco, P. 1992. "Oakeshott's Critique of Rationalism Revisited",
Political Science Reviewer, 21, pp.15-43

Friedman, R.B. 1989. "Oakeshott on the Authority of Law" in *Ratio
Juris*, 2., pp.27-40.

Friedman, R.B. 1992. "What is a Non-Instrumental Law" in
Political Science Reviewer, 21, pp.81-98.

Frohnen, B. 1990. "Oakeshott's Hobbesian Myth: Pride, Character
and the Limits of Reason", *The Western Political Quarterly*, 43,
pp.789-809

Fuller, T. 1987. "Authority and the Individual in Civil Association:
Oakeshott, Flathman, Yves Simon" in *Authority Revisited*
(Nomos. Vol. 29), Ed. J.R.Pennock and J.W.Chapman. New York
and London: New York University Press, 1987.

Fuller, T. 1992. "An Introduction: The Achievement of Michael
Oakeshott", in *The Political Science Reviewer,* 21, pp.1-14.

Fuller, T. 1993. Introduction to Michael Oakeshott's, *Religion, Politics and the Moral Life*. New Haven and London: Yale University Press.

Gerencser, S. 2000. *The Skeptic's Oakeshott*. NY: St.Martin's Press

Greenleaf, W.H. 1966. *Oakeshott's Philosophical Politics*. London: Longmans.

Himmelfarb, G. 1987. 'Does History Talk Sense?', in *The New History and the Old* Cambridge MA and London: Harvard University Press.

Liddington, J. 1984. "Oakeshott: Freedom in a Modern European State" in *Conceptions of Liberty in Political Philosophy*, Ed. J.N.Gray and Z.Pelczynski. London: Athlone Press, pp.289-320.

Mapel, D. 1990. "Civil Association and the Idea of Contingency", *Political Theory*, 18, pp.392-410.

Mapel, D. 1992. "Purpose and Politics: Can There be a Non-Instrumental Civil Association" in *The Political Science Reviewer*, 21, pp.63-80.

Mewes, H. 1992. "Modern Individualism: Reflections on Oakeshott, Arendt, and Strauss", *The Political Science Reviewer*, 21, pp.116-147.

Miller, T.H. 2001. 'Oakeshott's Hobbes and the Fear of Political Rationalism' *Political Theory* 29, pp.806-32.

Minogue, K. 1993. Introduction to Michael Oakeshott's, *Morality and Politics in Modern Europe: The Harvard Lectures*, ed. S.R.Letwin. New Haven and London: Yale University Press.

Nardin, T. 2001. *The Philosophy of Michael Oakeshott*. University Park, PA.: The Pennsylvania State University Press.

Orr, R. 1992. "A Double Agent in the Dream of Michael Oakeshott", *Political Science Reviewer*, 21, pp.44-62

O'Sullivan, L. 2001. "Michael Oakeshott on European Political History". in *History of Political Thought*, 21, pp. 132-151.

O'Sullivan, N. 1987. *The Problem Of Political Obligation in Green, Bosanquet and Oakeshott*. New York and London: Garland Press.

Parekh, B. 1991. "Living as an Immortal", *The Cambridge Review*, October, pp.100-106.

Pitkin, H. 1973. "The roots of Conservatism: Michael Oakeshott and the denial of politics", *Dissent*, 20, pp.496-525.

Rayner, J. 1985. "The legend of Oakeshott's conservatism: sceptical philosophy and limited politics", *Canadian Journal of Political Science*, 18, pp.313-38.

Riley, P. 1991. "Michael Oakeshott, Political Philosopher", *The Cambridge Review*, October, pp.110-113

Shklar, J. 1975. "Purposes and Procedures", Review of *On Human Conduct*, *Times Literary Supplement*, 12 September, p1018.

Tregenza, I. 1997. 'The Life of Hobbes in the Writings of Michael Oakeshott'. *History of Political Thought*. 18, pp. 531-557.

Tregenza, I. 2002. 'Leviathan as Myth: Michael Oakeshott and Carl Schmitt on Hobbes and the Critique of Rationalism'. *Contemporary Political Theory*. 1, pp. 349-369.

Tseng, R. 2003. *The Sceptical Idealist: Michael Oakeshott as a Critic of the Enlightenment*. Thorverton: Imprint Academic.

Worthington, G. 1997. "Oakeshott's Claims of Politics". *Political Studies* 45, pp.727-38.

Worthington, G. 2000. "Michael Oakeshott and the City of God". *Political Theory* 28, pp.377-98.

III
Works by Hobbes

Leviathan. Oxford: Basil Blackwell, 1960. Ed. M. Oakeshott.

The English Works of Thomas Hobbes, ed. Sir W. Molesworth (11 vols, 1839-45)

De Cive, The English version, H. Warrender ed.. Oxford: Clarendon Press, 1983.

De Homine, in *Man and Citizen*, B. Gert ed. New York: Anchor Books, 1972.

IV
Works on Hobbes

Ball, T. 1985. "Hobbes's Linguistic Turn", *Polity*, 17, pp.739-60.

Bell, D. 1969. "What Hobbes Does with Words", *Philosophical Quarterly*, 19, pp.155-8.

Burgess, G. 1990. "Contexts for the Writing and Publication of Hobbes's *Leviathan*", *History of Political Thought*, 11, pp.675-702

Burgess, G. 1994. "On Hobbesian Resistance Theory", *Political Studies* (1994), XLII, pp. 62-83.

Coltman, I. 1962. *Private Men and Public Causes: Philosophy and Politics in the English Civil War*. London: Faber and Faber.

Condren, C. 1990. "On the Rhetorical Foundations of *Leviathan*". *History of Political Thought*, 11, pp.703-20

Condren, C. 2000. *Thomas Hobbes*. New York: Twayne Publishers.

Eisenach, E. 1981. *Two Worlds of Liberalism: Religion and Politics in Hobbes, Locke, and Mill*. Chicago: Chicago University Press.

Flathman, R. E. 1993. *Thomas Hobbes: Skepticism, Individuality and Chastened Politics*, Sage.

Francis, M. 1980. "The Nineteenth Century Theory of Sovereignty and Thomas Hobbes", *History of Political Thought*, 1, pp517-40.

Glover, W.B. 1965. "God and Thomas Hobbes" in K.Brown ed., *Hobbes Studies*. Oxford: Blackwell.

Goldie, M. 1991. "The Reception of Hobbes", *The Cambridge History of Political Thought 1450-1700*. ed. J.H.Burns and M.Goldie. Cambridge: CUP, pp.589-615.

Goldsmith, M. 1966. *Hobbes's Science of Politics*. New York.

Goldsmith, M. 1968. "A Case of Identity" in *Politics and Experience: Essays Presented to Professor Michael Oakeshott on the Occasion of his Retirement*, P. King and B.C.Parekh eds. Cambridge: CUP.

Greenleaf, W.H. 1972. "Hobbes: The Problem of Interpretation", in *Hobbes and Rousseau: A Collection of Critical Essays*. R.Peters and M.Cranston eds.. Garden City, New York: Anchor Books.

Herbert, G. B. 1989. *Thomas Hobbes: The Unity of Scientific and Moral Wisdom*. Vancouver: University of British Columbia Press.

Hood, F.C. 1964. *The Divine Politics of Thomas Hobbes*. Oxford: Clarendon Press.

Jacob, J.R., and Raylor, T. 1991. 'Opera and Obedience: Thomas Hobbes and *A Proposition for Advancement of Morality* by Sir William Davenant'. *The Seventeenth Century*, 6, pp.205-50.

Johnson, P. 1974. "Hobbes's Anglican Doctrine of Salvation", in Ross, Schneider and Waldman, eds., *Thomas Hobbes in his time*. Minneapolis.

Johnston, D. 1986. *The Rhetoric of* Leviathan: *Thomas Hobbes and the Politics of Cultural Transformation*. Princeton: Princeton University Press.

King, P. 1983. "The Theory of Context and the Case of Hobbes" in P. King ed. *The History of Ideas: An Introduction to Method*. London and Canberra: Croom Helm.

Letwin, S.R. 1976. "Hobbes and Christianity", *Daedalus* 105, pp.1-21

Martinich, A.P. 1992. *The Two Gods of Leviathan: Thomas Hobbes on Religion and Politics*. Cambridge: CUP.

Macpherson, C.B. 1962. *The Political Theory of Possessive Individualism: Hobbes to Locke*. London: Clarendon Press.

Minogue, K. 1994. "Hobbes and his Critics", in T. Hobbes, *Leviathan*. London: Everyman, pp.441-453

Pacchi, A. 1988. "Hobbes and the Problem of God", in *Perspectives on Thomas Hobbes*, Eds. G.A.J. Rogers and A. Ryan. Oxford: Clarendon Press.

Parry, G. 1967. "Preformative Utterances and Obligation in Hobbes", *Philosophical Quarterly*, 17, pp.246-52.

Pocock, J. 1972. "Time, History and Eschatology in the Thought of Thomas Hobbes", in *Politics, Language and Time: Essays on Political Thought and History*. London: Metheun.

Prokhovnik, R. 1991. *Rhetoric and Philosophy in Hobbes'* Leviathan. New York and London: Garland.

Raphael, D.D. 1977. *Hobbes: Morals and Politics*. London: George Allen and Unwin.

Riley, P. 1982. *Will and Political Legitimacy: A Critical Exposition of Social Contract Theory in Hobbes, Locke, Rousseau, Kant, and Hegel*. Cambridge, MA: Harvard University Press.

Ryan, A. 1988. "Hobbes and Individualism", in *Perspectives on Thomas Hobbes*, Ed. G.A.J. Rogers and A. Ryan. Oxford: Clarendon Press.

Seifert, G.F. 1979. "The Philosophy of Hobbes: Text and Context and the Problem of Sedimentation", *The Personalist*, 60, pp.177-185

Sherlock, R. 1982. "The Theology of *Leviathan*: Hobbes on Religion" in *Interpretation* 10, pp. 43-60.

Skinner, Q. 1972. "The Context of Hobbes's Theory of Political Obligation", in M. Cranston and R.S. Peters, eds., *Hobbes and Rousseau: a collection of critical essays*. Garden City, New York,: Anchor Books, pp.109-142

Skinner, Q. 1990. "Thomas Hobbes on the Proper Signification of Liberty", *Transactions of the Royal Historical Society* 40, pp.121-151

Skinner, Q. 1996. *Reason and Rhetoric in the Philosophy of Hobbes*. Cambridge: CUP.

Sorell, T. 1988. "The Science in Hobbes's Politics", in *Perspectives on Thomas Hobbes*, Eds. G.A.J. Rogers and A. Ryan. Oxford: Clarendon Press.

Springborg, P. 1996. "Hobbes on Religion". in *The Cambridge Companion to Hobbes*, ed. T. Sorrell. Cambridge: CUP.

Strauss, L. 1952. *The Political Philosophy of Hobbes: Its Basis and Its Genesis*. Chicago: University of Chicago Press.

Taylor, A.E. 1908. *Hobbes*. New York: Dodge.

Taylor, A.E. 1965. "The Ethical Doctrine of Hobbes", in K.C.Brown ed., *Hobbes Studies*. Oxford: Blackwell.

Thomas, K. 1965. "The social origins of Hobbes's political thought", in K.C. Brown, ed. *Hobbes Studies*. Oxford: Blackwell.

Trainor, B. 1988. "Warrender and Skinner on Hobbes", *Political Studies* 36, pp.680-91.

Tuck, R. 1987. "Optics and Skeptics: The Philosophical Foundations of Hobbes's Political Thought". in Edmund Leites, ed., *Conscience and Casuistry in Early Modern Europe*. Cambridge: CUP.

Tuck, R. 1993. *Philosophy and Government, 1572-1651*. Cambridge: CUP.

Warrender, H. 1957. *The Political Philosophy of Hobbes: His Theory of Obligation*. Oxford: Clarendon Press.

Warrender, H. 1960. "The Place of God in Hobbes's Philosophy", *Political Studies*, 8, 48-57.

Warrender, H. 1969. "Hobbes's Conception of Morality", in *Hobbes's* Leviathan: *Interpretation and Criticism*. Bernard H. Baumrin ed.. Belmont CA: Wadsworth.

Warrender, H. 1979. "Political Theory and Historiography: A Reply to Professor Skinner on Hobbes", *The Historical Journal*, 22, pp.931-940

Watkins, J.W.N. 1965. *Hobbes's System of Ideas: A study in the political significance of philosophical theories*. London: Hutchinson and Co.

V
Other Works

Aquinas, T. 1978. *On Kingship, to the King of Cyprus*. Trans. Phelan, G.B. and Eschmann, I.T. Toronto: Pontifical Institute of Medieval Studies.

Arendt, H. 1958. *The Human Condition*. Chicago: University of Chicago.

Arendt, H. 1968. 'What is Authority?' in *Between Past and Future*. New York: Viking Press.

Arendt. H. 1973. *The Origins of Totalitarianism*. New York and London: Harcourt Brace Jovanovich.

Atkins, G.G. 1929. *The Making of the Christian Mind*. London: William Heinemann.

Aubrey, J. 1975. *Brief Lives*. Suffolk: The Boydell Press.

Austin, J. 1965. *The Province of Jurisprudence Determined*. London: Weidenfeld and Nicholson.

Bentham, J. 1975. *The Theory of Legislation*. Bombay: Oceana Publications.

Bosanquet, B. 1923. *The Philosophical Theory of the State*. London: Macmillan and Co.

Boucher, D. 1985. *Texts in Context: Revisionist Methods for Studying the History of Ideas*. Dordrecht: Martinus Nijhoff Publishers.

Boucher, D. 1986. "W.H.Greenleaf, Idealism and the Triadic Conception of the History of Political Thought", *Idealistic Studies*, 16, pp.237-52.

Boucher, D. 1989a. *The Social and Political Thought of R.G.Collingwood*. Cambridge: CUP.

Boucher, D. 1989b. "Philosophy, History and Practical Life: The emergence of the history of political thought in England, *The Australian Journal of Politics and History*, 35, pp.220-37.

Bradley, F.H. 1897. *Appearance and Reality*. Oxford: OUP.

Bradley, F.H. 1927. *Ethical Studies*. Oxford: OUP.

Burckhardt, J. 1990. *The Civilization of the Renaissance in Italy*. Translated by S.G.C. Middlemore. London: Penguin.

Canovan, M. 1996. "Hannah Arendt as a Conservative Thinker". *Hannah Arendt. Twenty Years Later*. Eds. L. May and J. Kohn. Cambridge and London: MIT Press.

Chadwick, O. 1975. *The Secularization of the European Mind in the Nineteenth Century*. Cambridge: CUP.

Child, A.H. 1953. *Making and Knowing in Hobbes, Vico, and Dewey*. Berkeley: University of California Press.

Coleridge, S.T. 1969. *The Collected Works*. Vol.4, no.1 Barbara E. Rooke ed. Routledge and Kegan Paul and Princeton University Press.

Coleridge, S.T. 1978. *The Collected Works*. Vol. 3, no. II, David V. Erdman (ed.), published 1978. Routledge and Kegan Paul and Princeton University Press.

Coleridge, S.T. 1990a. *The Collected Works*. Vol. 7, no. I, Kathleen Coburn and Bart Winer (eds.), published 1983. Routledge and Kegan Paul and Princeton University Press.

Coleridge, S.T. 1990b. *The Collected Works*. Vol. 14, no. II, Carl Woodring (ed.), published 1990. Routledge and Kegan Paul and Princeton University Press.

Coleridge, S.T. 1951. *Selected Poetry and Prose of Coleridge*. Random House. ed. D. Stauffer.

Collingwood, R.G. 1916. *Religion and Philosophy*. London: Macmillan.

Collingwood, R.G. 1924. *Speculum Mentis: Or the Map of Knowledge*. Oxford: Clarendon Press.

Collingwood, R.G. 1970. *An Autobiography*. London: Oxford University Press.

Collingwood, R.G. 1942. *The New Leviathan: Or Man, Society, Civilization and Barbarism*. Oxford: Clarendon Press.

Collingwood, R.G. 1994. *The Idea of History* ed. J van der Dussen. Oxford: Oxford University Press.

Cranston, Maurice. 1967. *Freedom*. New York: Basic Books.

Davies, J.G. 1948. *The Theology of William Blake*. Oxford: Clarendon Press.

Dawkins, R. 1986. *The Blind Watchmaker*. London: Penguin.

Dubiel, H. 1995. 'Hannah Arendt and the Theory of Democracy' in *Hannah Arendt and Leo Strauss: German Emigrés and American Political Thought after World War II*. P. Kielmansegg, H. Mewes, E. Glaser-Schmidt eds. Washington and Cambridge: German Historical Institute and Cambridge University Press.

Eliot, T.S. 1970. *For Lancelot Andrewes: essays on style and order*. London: Faber and Faber..

Flathman, R.E. 1980. *The Practice of Political Authority: Authority and the Authoritative*. Chicago: University of Chicago Press.

Flathman, R.E. 1992. *Willful Liberalism: Voluntarism and Individuality in Political Theory and Practice*. Ithaca and London: Cornell University Press.

Foster, M. 1935. *The Political Philosophies of Plato and Hegel*. Oxford: Clarendon Press.

Friedman, R. 1990. "The Concept of Authority in Political Philosophy" in J.Raz ed. *Authority*. Oxford: Basil Blackwell.

Fuller, L. 1969. *The Morality of Law*. New Haven: Yale University Press.

Green, T.H. 1986. *Lectures on the Principles of Political Obligation and Other Writings*. Eds. P. Harris and J. Morrow. Cambridge: CUP.

Green, T.H. 1885-89. *Works*, 3 vols. ed. R.L.Nettleship. London: Longmans.

Greenleaf, W.H. 1968. "Idealism, modern philosophy and politics" in *Politics and Experience: Essays Presented to Michael Oakeshott on the Occasion of his Retirement*. P. King and B.C.Parekh eds. Cambridge: CUP.

Gunnell, J.G. 1979. *Political Theory: Tradition and Interpretation*. Cambridge MA: Winthrop.

Harrington, J. 1977. *The Political Works of James Harrington*. Ed. J.G.A. Pocock. Cambridge: CUP.

Hart, H.L.A. 1961. *The Concept of Law*. Oxford: Clarendon Press.

Hayek, F.A. 1979. *The Counter Revolution of Science: Studies on the Abuse of Reason*. Indianapolis: Liberty Press.

Hegel, G.W.F. 1896. *Lectures on the History of Philosophy*. Translated by E.S. Haldane and F.H. Simpson. London: Routledge and Kegan Paul.

Hegel, G.W.F. 1952. *The Philosophy of Right*. Translated by T.M. Knox. Oxford: Clarendon Press.

Hegel, G.W.F. 1977. *The Phenomenology of Spirit*. Translated by
   A.V.Millar. Oxford: Clarendon Press.
Hume, David. 1974. *An Enquiry Concerning Human Understanding*, in
   Hume's Enquiries. P.H.Nidditch (ed.). Oxford: Clarendon Press.
Letwin, S.R. 1975. "David Hume: Inventor of a New Task for
   Philosophy', *Political Theory* 3, pp.134-58.
Letwin, S.R. 1976. "Morality and Law" in *Encounter* 35, November,
   pp.35-43.
Mabbott, J.D. 1948. *The State and the Citizen: An Introduction to
   Political Philosophy*. London: Hutchinson's.
MacIntyre, A. 1969. "The Debate about God: Victorian Relevance
   and Contemporary Irrelevance" in A. MacIntyre and P. Ricour
   eds., *The Religious Significance of Atheism*. New York and London:
   Columbia University Press.
MacIntyre, A. 1985. *After Virtue: a study in moral theory*. London:
   Duckworth.
Mackie, J. 1977. *Ethics*. Harmondsworth: Penguin.
McCormick, J. 1994. "Fear, Technology, and The State: Carl
   Schmitt, Leo Strauss, and the Revival of Hobbes in Weimar and
   National Socialist Germany", *Political Theory*, 22, pp.619-652
McCormick, J. 1997. *Carl Schmitt's Critique of Liberalism: Against
   Politics as Technology*. Cambridge: CUP.
Meier, H. 1995. *Carl Schmitt and Leo Strauss: The Hidden Dialogue*.
   Chicago: University of Chicago Press. Trans. J. Harvey.
Mill, J.S. 1972. *Utilitarianism*. in *Utilitarianism, On Liberty, and
   Considerations on Representative Government*. London and
   Melbourne: Everyman.
Minogue, K. 1988. "Method in intellectual history: Quentin Skinner's
   Foundations" in *Meaning and Context: Quentin Skinner and his Critics*.
   James Tully ed. Princeton: Princeton University Press.
Montaigne. 1987. "An Apology for Raymond Sebond". In *The
   Complete Essays*. London: Penguin. trans. M.A.Screech.
Moore, G.E. 1903. 'The Refutation of Idealism'. in *Mind*, 12,
   pp.433-53.
Nietzsche, F. 1990. *Beyond Good and Evil: Prelude to a Philosophy of the
   Future*. Translated by R.J. Hollingdale. London: Penguin.
Ortega y Gasset, J. 1932. *Revolt of the Masses*. New York:
   W.W.Norton.
Peerman, D.G. and Marty, M.E. 1965. *A Handbook of Christian
   Theologians*. The world publishing Co.

Pitkin, H. 1972. *Wittgenstein and Justice: On the Significance of Ludwig Wittgenstein for Social and Political Thought.* Berkeley, Los Angeles, and London: University of California Press.

Plamenatz, J. 1963. *Man and Society: A critical examination of some important social and political theories from Machiavelli to Marx*, 2 vols. London: Longmans.

Polanyi, M. 1964. *Science, Faith and Society.* Chicago: University of Chicago Press.

Popper, K. 1963. "Towards a Rational Theory of Tradition", in *Conjectures and Refutations: The Growth of Scientific Knowledge.* London: Routledge and Kegan Paul.

Quniton, A. 1982 'Absolute Idealism'. in *Thoughts and Thinkers.* London: Duckworth.

Ramsey, A. M. 1960. *From Gore to Temple: The Development of Anglican Theology between Lux Mundi and the Second World War 1889-1939.* Longmans.

Reardon, B.M.G. 1971. *Religious Thought in the Victorian Age. A Survey from Coleridge to Gore.* Longmans.

Robbins, P. 1982. *The British Hegelians 1875-1925.* New York: Garland.

Russell, B. 1903. *The Principles of Mathematics.* London: Unwin

Ryan, A. 1970. *The Philosophy of the Social Sciences.* London: Macmillan.

Ryle, G. 1990. *The Concept of Mind.* London. Penguin.

Shklar, J. 1976. *Freedom and Independence: The Political Ideas of Hegel's Phenomenology of Mind.* Cambridge: CUP.

Skinner, Q. 1984. "The Idea of Negative Liberty: Philosophical and Historical Perspectives", *Philosophy in History: Essays on the historiography of philosophy*, R. Rorty, J.B. Schneewind, Q. Skinner eds. Cambridge: CUP.

Skinner, Q. 1988. "Meaning and Understanding in the History of Ideas" in *Meaning and Context: Quentin Skinner and his Critics*, James Tully ed. Princeton: Princeton University Press.

Strauss, L. 1953. *Natural Right and History.* Chicago: University of Chicago Press.

Strauss, L. 1983 "On Collingwood's Philosophy of History", in *The History of Ideas: An Introduction to Method.* P. King ed. London and Canberra: Croom Helm.

Taylor, C. 1985. "What is Human Agency", in *Human Agency and Language: Philosophical Papers 1.* Cambridge: CUP.

Taylor, C. 1989. *Sources of the Self: The Making of the Modern Identity.* Cambridge: CUP.

Taylor, C. 1992. *The Ethics of Authenticity*. Cambridge and London: Harvard University Press.

Tudor, H. 1972. *Political Myth*. London: Pall Mall Press.

Tully, James. 1980. *A Discourse on Property: John Locke and his adversaries*. Cambridge: CUP.

Vico, G. 1999. *New Science*. London: Penguin.

Vollrath, E. 1995. "Hannah Arendt: A German-American Jewess Views the United States - and Looks Back to Germany". in *Hannah Arendt and Leo Strauss: German Emigrés and American Political Thought after World War II*. eds. P. Kielmansegg, H. Mewes, E. Glaser-Schmidt. Washington and Cambridge: German Historical Institute and Cambridge University Press..

Webb, C.C.J. 1935. *The Historical Element in Religion*. London: George Allen and Unwin.

Williams, B. 1981. "Persons, character and morality" in *Moral Luck*. Cambridge: CUP.

Willis, K. 1988. 'The Introduction and Critical Reception of Hegelian Thought in Britain 1830-1900'. in *Victorian Studies*, Autumn 1988, pp. 85-111.

Winch, P. 1958. *The Idea of a Social Science*. London: Routledge and Kegan Paul.

Wollheim, R. 1959. *F.H.Bradley*. Harmondsworth. Penguin.

Wood, H.G. 1934. *Christianity and the Nature of History*. Cambridge: CUP.

Wood, A.W. 1990. *Hegel's Ethical Thought*. Cambridge: CUP.

Author Index

A

Acton, Lord., 149n

Anderson, P., 103

Arendt, H., 36-8, 48n, 77, 81, 83, 187, 188n, 204, 206-7

Aristotle., 36, 78, 90, 172, 185, 206

Arnold, M., 149, 150n, 153

Atkins, G.G., 140n, 141

Aubrey, J., 21n, 46

Augustine, St., 10, 14, 62n, 129, 154, 171, 181, 192

Auspitz, J.L., 28

Austin, J., 88, 89n, 112, 118, 209

Austin, J.L., 38-9

Avineri, S., 4

B

Bacon, F., 9, 42, 49, 55, 168, 178-80

Ball, T., 39, 49n, 185n, 189n

Barthes, K., 146n

Bell, D.R., 39n

Bentham, J., 42, 62n

Blake, W., 147n

Bodin, J., 44

Bosanquet, B., 2, 9, 13, 55, 57-8, 75, 88-9

Boucher, D., 11-12, 15, 22, 39n, 43, 57n, 190, 191n, 199n, 201n, 202-4

Bradley, F.H., 2, 21-2, 57-8, 110n, 149-51, 153-4, 165n

Brown, J.M., 84n, 91, 93-6, 99

Bultmann, R., 140n

Burckhardt, J., 66, 76, 162n, 190

Burgess, G., 100n, 105n

Burke, E., 8, 9n, 14, 42, 64, 135n, 201n

Burkitt, F.C., 148n

C

Calvin, J., 42

Carnap, R., 189

Carnovan, M., 188n

Chadwick, O., 133n

Child, A.H., 48n

Coleridge, S.T., 2n, 56

Collingwood, R.G., 7n, 12-13, 21, 39n, 41, 46, 56-7, 62n, 133, 140, 152n, 165n, 189-91, 198-9, 202n, 206

Coltman, I., 175n

Comte, A., 180, 189

Condren, C., 133n

Cowling, M., 134

Cranston, M., 119n

Croce, B., 143

D

Dawkins, R., 163n

Descartes, R., 9, 136, 168, 178, 206

Dewey, J., 50

Dubiel, H., 207n

Dunn, J., 199, 203

E

Eisenach, E., 131n
Eliot, T.S., 150n
Erasmus, D., 135
Erastus., 8

F

Flathman, R., 73n, 77-8, 108n,
　117-8, 124, 185, 198n
Foster, M., 106-7, 108n
Francis, M., 53n, 209n
Franco, P., 9n, 13, 75, 85n, 108n,
　117n
Friedman, M, 189.
Friedman, R., 116n
Frohnen, B., 1n, 181
Fuller, L., 112, 113n, 127n
Fuller, T., 117n, 135n, 139n, 148,
　153, 158, 179n

G

Gadamer, H.G., 2, 140n, 201-2
Gardner, P., 135
Gerencser, S., 1n, 19-20, 28, 91n,
　103n
Glover, W.B., 131, 145, 198n
Goldie, M., 73n, 100n
Goldsmith, M.M., 167, 209
Green, T.H., 9, 22, 56-8, 88-9,
　109, 137n, 198-9
Greenleaf, W.H., 11n, 12-13, 38,
　93n, 201
Gunnell, J.G., 203-6

H

Habermas, J., 39
Hare, R.M., 38

Harnack, A., 141
Harrington, J., 190n
Hart, H.L.A., 112, 113n
Hayek, F., 189, 191n
Hegel, G.W.F., 2, 4, 8, 11-14,
　20-3, 28, 31, 37-8, 42, 44, 46-8,
　55-7, 61, 72-3, 75, 79, 82-3, 85,
　88, 101, 117, 126n, 150, 172n,
　208
Heidegger, M., 140n, 153, 201
Hempel, C., 189
Himmelfarb, G., 46n
Hood, F.C., 99n, 131-2, 203
Hort, F.J.A., 140n
Hume, D., 22, 64, 134, 201n,
　208-9

J

Jacob, J., 189n
Johnson, P., 131n
Johnston, D., 189n, 202n

K

Kant, I., 22, 42, 57, 67, 75, 146n,
　168
Kierkegaard, S., 190
King, P., 38n

L

Leibniz, G., 73
Letwin, S.R., 13n, 42n, 131n,
　136n, 209
Liddington, J., 75n, 120
Locke, J., 14, 42, 55, 68n, 87,
　117n, 168-9, 176, 201, 205-7

M

Mabbott, J.D., 31n, 33n, 63
Machiavelli, N., 62n, 205-6

MacIntyre, A., 83, 136n
Mackie, J., 61n
Macpherson, C.B., 77, 167, 176,
    207, 209
Maine, H., 64
Mapel, D., 113n 122n, 124-6
Marsilius., 116n
Marx, K., 42, 180, 206
McCormick, J., 190n
Meier, H.,82n
Mewes, H., 83n, 188n
Mill, J.S., 14, 42, 119, 156n, 189
Miller, T.H., 1n, 27n, 50
Minogue, K., 13n, 16, 205n
Montaigne, M., 76, 145, 147n,
    154, 162n, 163n, 174, 176
Montesquieu., 44
Moore, G.E., 21

N

Nardin, T., 44n, 45n
Needham, J., 139n
Nietzsche, F., 152, 158, 161,
    166-7, 177, 186, 190, 192-3

O

O'Sullivan, L., 41
O'Sullivan, N., 58n
Ockham, W., 28, 62n, 100n
Oman, J., 143, 150
Orr, R., 54, 65n, 69, 75
Ortega y Gasset, J., 190-1
Otto, R., 153
Owen, R. 42, 180

P

Pacchi, A., 131n, 132, 158
Parry, G., 39n
Pascal, B., 137n, 147n, 149n
Paul, St., 146, 171

Pitkin, H., 39n, 188n
Plato., 5, 11, 14, 31-2, 36, 47, 49,
    116, 178, 193, 199, 206
Pocock, J., 131n, 132, 137, 199,
    203
Polanyi, M., 165-6
Popper, K., 165-6

Q

Quinton, A., 21n

R

Ramsey, A., 135n, 148n
Ranke, L., 138
Raphael, D.D., 210
Raylor, T., 189n
Rayner, J., 9n
Reardon, B., 149n
Riley, P., 97n, 147n, 154n
Robbins, P., 21n
Rousseau, J-J., 55, 57, 82
Russell, B., 21
Ryan, A., 167, 176n, 178n, 198n
Ryle, G., 38

S

Schmitt, C., 82, 83n, 189, 190n,
    198
Schweitzer, A., 148n
Seifert, G., 26n, 49-50
Sherlock, R., 131n, 136n, 145
Shklar, J., 55, 117-8
Simon, St. 42, 180, 189
Skinner, Q., 7n, 15, 77, 103-4,
    189n, 199-200, 203
Smith, A., 42
Sorell, T., 49n, 188-9
Spinoza, B., 5, 14, 31, 42, 67
Spragens, T., 6, 71
Springborg, P., 131n

Strauss, L., 6, 27n, 36, 38, 55, 60,
    62n, 77, 82-3, 91, 99n, 167n,
    173-5, 188n, 203-7, 209

T

Taylor, A.E., 93n, 131-2
Taylor, C., 73n, 154n
Thomas, K., 176n
Trainor, B., 105n,
Tseng, R., 9n
Tuck, R., 135n, 198n
Tudor, H., 170n
Tully, J., 169n

V

Vico, G., 47-8
Voegelin, E., 204
Vollrath, E., 81n

W

Ward, H., 137n
Warrender, H., 6, 91, 93-6,
    99-100, 105, 108, 131-2, 200-1,
    203-4, 209
Watkins, J.W.N., 98n, 167, 198n
Webb, B., 180
Webb, C.C.J., 133
Williams, B., 155, 156n
Willis, K., 21n
Winch, P., 70
Wittgenstein, L., 38, 70-1, 73n,
    112
Wolin, R., 204
Wood, A., 72n
Worthington, G., 45n, 157n

Subject Index

A

agency, 2, 8, 13, 54-5, 63, 68-79, 84, 155-7
    and authority, 102, 107, 111, 113, 115, 119, 121-4, 126
authority, 6, 8, 10, 55, 63, 81-2, 91, 150, 159, 170, 175, 190, 192, 208
    of the state, 85-90
    civil association and, 109-118, 120, 122, 126,7
    Hobbes on, 90-109, 123-4, 179-80

C

civil association, 40-1, 44-5, 51, 71, 78, 84, 91, 98, 129, 159, 180, 192, 196
    and authority, 109-118, 120, 122, 126-7
    and freedom, 118-127
    Hobbes on, 90-109, 123-4, 179-80
civilization, 6, 10, 31, 79, 161-3, 166-7, 169, 170-1, 178, 180, 185, 190-2, 196, 207
    religion and, 130-1, 142-3, 145-6, 155, 159, 161
civitas, 98, 173n
    cupiditatis, 180-1
common good, 14, 47, 65, 109, 115, 173
contingency, 72, 122, 124-6, 129, 155, 157

E

egoism, see hedonism,
enterprise association, 14, 43, 105, 107, 109, 111, 112n, 116, 119, 121-5, 179-80
epistemology, 9, 18, 49, 66, 126, 168, 200

F

freedom, 56-8, 69, 72-9, 83
  and civil association, 118-127
  and authority in Hobbes, 102-9

H

hedonism, 53, 55-7, 61, 62n, 172
hermeneutics, 2, 10, 140, 201-2
history, 1-5, 7, 10, 19, 20, 23, 27n, 41, 155, 167, 189, 197-200, 202-7
  as a mode, 24, 29, 163-4, 166n, 169, 198-9
  of political thought/philosophy, 11-16, 41-48
  and Christianity, 132-4, 136-144

I

ignoratio elenchi, 3n, 12n, 23, 43, 51, 58, 144
individual *manqué* (anti-individual), 67-8, 79, 177, 184, 187
individuality, 2n, 14, 20, 41, 47, 53-4, 62-8, 73-4, 76-79, 83-4, 106,
  116, 125-6, 173, 175, 184, 186-7, 196-7, 207

L

law, 32-3, 87-9, 118-127, 150, 159, 179, 188, 196n
  natural, 61, 77, 82, 93-100, 103, 108, 114, 132, 188, 200-1
  civil, 94, 96, 101-2, 104-6, 111-13
  and command, 57, 91-3, 101-2, 105-7, 112n, 114-5, 122
liberalism, 68, 74n, 82, 176, 190, 207
liberty, see freedom,

M

masses (mass man), 67-8, 183-4, 187, 190-2
metaphysics, 45, 158, 191
modes (modality), 3, 6, 8, 9. 15, 19, 22, 24-5, 27-9, 43-4, 132-4, 137,
  140, 144, 162, 164, 166n, 170, 192, 195, 198, 202
morality,
  of individuality, 14, 47, 64-5, 67, 76, 186
  of the common good, 14, 47, 65
  of communal ties, 14, 47, 64-6
  bourgeois, 76, 77n, 173, 175-6, 188n, 205, 207
myth, 3, 82, 130, 145, 160, 162-172, 178, 180-1, 187, 189-90, 192, 202,
  204-7

N

nominalism, 12, 38, 59, 62n, 63-4, 100, 197

O

obligation, 65-6, 77, 79, 84, 88
    Hobbes on, 90-109
    In civil association, 109, 114, 120, 124, 204, 209

P

philosophy,
    and system, 8-9, 17-8, 25-6
    political, 9, 29-38, 40, 129
    history/tradition of, 11-14, 63, 196-208
    and idealism, 20-23
    and other modes, 24-8, 40, 132-4, 144, 202
    and history, 41-48, 196-208
    and practice, 48-50
    and science, 167-9
practice
    as a mode, 2, 12n, 19,23-4, 28n, 29-31, 34-5, 46, 48, 50, 58-61, 133, 137-8, 140n, 152-3, 163-4, 169, 186, 199, 202, 204
    moral, 8, 64-5, 70-3, 76, 109-111, 113n, 114, 121, 125, 155, 157, 208
pride, 39, 71, 76, 78, 100, 126, 171-7, 182, 184

R

rationalism,
    Oakeshott on, 2n, 6, 8-9, 63, 68-9, 82, 130, 162, 164, 177-8, 181, 186-7, 191
    in Hobbes, 6, 9, 26, 37, 178
rational will (tradition of), 11, 13, 43, 54-7, 63, 72, 75, 82, 84, 103, 208
reason, 18, 25-8, 35-7, 39, 56-7, 72-3, 75, 82, 86, 93, 95, 97, 99, 100-1, 105-7, 114, 120, 124, 132, 136, 162, 164, 166, 168-9, 173, 174, 177-9, 181, 185-6, 189-200, 202, 207-8
reasoning, 25-7, 35, 57, 100, 114, 132, 168, 179, 185-6
religion, 10, 23, 95, 129-162
    and history, 132-4, 136-144
    and morality, 150-7
    Hobbes on, 130-3, 135-6, 144-5, 148, 158-9

rule(s), 65, 67, 70-2, 99, 101, 107, 109-116, 118-9, 121, 123, 125-6, 129, 176-80, 200

S

scepticism, 1n, 9, 19, 20, 22-3, 36-8, 60, 72-3, 133, 135, 179, 198n
science, 2, 10, 23, 25-9, 35-7, 39-40, 47-50, 53, 61, 133, 135, 137, 162-171, 186, 188-191, 206-7
self-disclosure, 72, 76n, 147, 155-7
self-enactment, 72, 76, 125, 130, 149n, 154n, 155-8, 174, 176, 207
societas, 14, 42-3, 208
solipsism, 58-9, 62, 64, 144-5
sovereign (sovereignty), 33, 49, 60, 62, 73, 77, 82, 88-90, 92-4, 96, 98, 99n, 101-9, 112, 115, 116, 118-9, 120, 123, 159, 175, 182, 189n, 209
sovereignty of technique, 178-9
state of nature, 39, 55, 62, 92-4, 98-9, 104, 108, 117n, 124, 189n
subjectivity, 48, 53, 55, 61, 106, 173n, 201

T

tower of Babel, 70, 130, 159, 162, 181-6
tradition, 63-4, 69-70, 83, 86, 93n, 107, 133, 135, 173, 181n, 187
    philosophical/intellectual, 11-13, 28, 43, 47, 55, 62n, 63, 68, 75, 83, 100-1, 103, 196-7, 200-1, 204-8
    and Christianity, 142, 158
    and science, 165-6

U

universitas, 14, 42-3, 116n, 208
utilitarianism, 53, 62n, 150n, 155-6, 190-1, 209

V

volition, 13, 54-5, 57-64, 71, 75, 78-9, 89, 97n, 208

W

will and artifice (tradition of), 11, 13, 43, 47, 62n, 63, 100, 196, 208